Kisses from Boys

Mike Willis

ISBN: 9798626380088

Cover design by: Art Painter
Library of Congress Control Number: 2018675309
Printed in the United States of America

Dedication

For Leo's parents, Ace and Joe, whose understanding was far greater than that of the Catholic Church, which was so important in their lives.

They loved Leo for what he was and welcomed me into their family with open arms.

May they rest in peace.

About the Author

Mike was born in London in 1946. After grammar school in Reigate he went on to medical school at Liverpool University. Soon after qualifying he met Leo. Medicine was not been a good choice of career – he really wanted to work in theatre or television. In 1981 he was offered an interview with a top B.B.C. producer. Unfortunately, this was cancelled as the producer had been summoned to Buckingham Palace to take charge of televising Charles and Diana's wedding. After 25 years in General Practice, Mike finally left medicine. The next 10 years were spent working with the R.N.I.B. As part of a team with 6 recording studios and over a hundred volunteers, he helped produce recordings and braille for blind and partially sighted people throughout the North West – anything from a Gas bill to the complete Koran. In 2013 he and Leo fulfilled a long-time ambition and opened a guest house on the Mawddach Estuary in Gwynedd. After 4 years, mainly due to the incredible location and Leo's culinary skills, Coedmor became number one on Trip Advisor. They now live in Shropshire. This is Mike's first (and probably last) book.

Praise for the Author

It's been some time since I've read a manuscript I enjoyed quite as much as yours. The pleasure of reading *Kisses from Boys* comes from a variety of factors: it's a touching and ultimately heartwarming story, there are moments of suspense, it's frequently amusing and you have a great feel for the period. There are also some genuinely likable and sympathetic characters.

Contents

Chapter 1 - In Nomine Patris.

Sister Equinus was an imposing woman. Standing in front of the class, dressed from the top of her head to the tips of her toes in a long black habit, she had an air of authority. Should you catch her from behind bending over, perhaps to retrieve a pencil from the floor, she gave the impression of a large black boulder, dropped by some giant from heaven onto the classroom floor. As she rose and turned to the front, her hands would disappear into the large pocket on the front of her tunic. All that was now visible of her flesh was the face. This was enshrined in a black balaclava-like garment that tucked under her chin and was topped by an enormous white head-dress.

The front of this head-dress protruded some three inches out from her forehead and was held in place, we thought, by some invisible structure under the folds. It looked as though she was peering at us from under an awning. It also made it necessary, if she was to maintain eye-contact with all her charges, to constantly move her head from left to right. What fascinated us five-year-old boys, was, that as she did so, the awning would tilt up and down. As she looked to the left, the right end would rise. As she looked to the right, the left end would rise. Quite involuntarily we would mimic this movement - ever so slightly tilting our heads from left to right in unison with her. Whether or not she was aware of this, I do not know. When she spoke, her head would protrude forward from under the awning and then retract, tortoise-like, into its shell.

Sister Equinus belonged to the order of the Sisters of Charity. She was also head of Our Lady of the Assumption Infant School for Boys and Girls (both taught, of course, in separate classes, in separate buildings. Her holy, God-given mission in life was to prepare us boys for our first Holy Communion. I think she was a kindly woman at heart, but she rarely smiled and her litany was of fire and brimstone – enough to give a five-year-old boy the runs!

My first class teacher was Mrs. Fitzgerald. She was a nice lady. I must have liked her because I took every opportunity to go up to her desk - to show her my work, to ask a question or just to pass the time of day.

'Leo, would you go and sit down.'

'Now dear, will you go back to your desk, we must get on.'

'Holy Mother of Mary, Leo, will you please go back to your place.'

Much of our time in that first year at school was spent with the three 'R's.

'Altogether now children, C is for...'

'Catholic.'

'M is for...'

'Mary.'

'S is for...'

'Sin.'

She also introduced us to speaking and writing our native language. The study of Irish was extremely important. The vast majority of children left school at the age of fifteen and in their final year would sit for their Leaving Certificates – the equivalent of the British 'O' Levels. Five or six subjects would be taken including compulsory Irish. Ridiculous as it seems today, if you failed the Irish Exam you would be failed in all other subjects – even if you received 100% marks - so we all paid attention.

'Is e mo ainm Leo – My name is Leo.'

'Pas a dom mo bainne – Pass me my milk.'

'Na a bheith ina bhuachaill trom – Don't be a bold boy.'

It was in Mrs Fitzgerald's class that I met my life-long friend Thomas Doyle. We discovered we had lots in common. We both had very vivid imaginations. Neither of us liked football but we did like playing with our sisters' dolls.

In the second year at infant school, preparation for our first Holy Communion took on a new more urgent pace. One morning Sister Equinus appeared in front of the class carrying a candle on a small metal plate. She ceremoniously placed this in the centre of Mrs. Fitzgerald's desk.

'Now boys' she said, 'today we are going to talk about purgatory and hell.' This sounded serious.

From the large pocket in the front of her habit she produced a box of Swan Vestas matches, which were placed on the desk next to the candle. Taking a match from the box, she struck it and lit the candle. We all followed this drama in silence and waited with eager anticipation for what was to follow. She spoke slowly and deliberately.

3

'Now class…' she said, 'I have a present for any boy that will come out and help me'. A sea of eager hands shot up, 'Me Sister…', 'Me Sister…', 'Oh me Sister, please!'

Holding up her hand for silence she continued.

'The first boy… who will come out here… and place his finger in the candle flame for three minutes…. I will give him…'

There was a dramatic pause as her hand disappeared back into her habit. It reappeared holding aloft a shiny half-crown coin – a small fortune to every boy present.

In the ensuing silence, one by one, all the hands went down, as it sank in what she was asking us to do.

'Can I not tempt just one of you?… It's only for three minutes? Think of all the sweeties you could by with two shillings and sixpence in your pocket.'

She looked round the room but not a boy stirred from his seat. She had us now and was ready for the big climax of her performance.

'Just remember boys…' She had a smile on her face and was obviously pleased with the effect she had had on us, 'Just remember boys… that in hell… you will burn… not for three minutes… not for three hours… but forever!'

As we gazed into the tiny light of the candle, every boy in the room could feel the heat of the flames engulfing his body. Patrick Manzar, who sat next to me, was physically quaking.

She was not finished yet… 'So boys… It's very important to confess your sins and be sorry for them. If you're not fully sorry… you'll go to Purgatory!'

Silence…

Feilim Lally put his hand up.

'Yes, Feilim?'

'What's Purgatory, Sister?'

'Purgatory…' she replied, fixing him with a glare, 'Purgatory is a place where you do penance… There's no-one else there except you… And you wait there for God to decide when to take you to heaven. You could wait for years… and he might NEVER decide!'

The lesson left our impressionable six-year old minds in no doubt about the dangers of sinning. Catholic guilt was well and truly established into yet another generation of young innocent Irish children.

It wasn't only Sister Equinus. Every adult you came into contact with would emphasize the importance of being good and pure. Your parents, your teachers, the priests and the nuns were all at it. If you did anything slightly naughty, they'd say,

'Now you have to pray for forgiveness.'

This cycle of 'Fall and Redemption' was impressed on us over and over again until we knew it by heart:

> We feel contrition for our sins and want to change our ways.
> We confess our sins to a priest.
> We receive and accept forgiveness and are absolved of our sins.
> We celebrate God's everlasting love for us and commit to live out a Christian life.

It's weird to think back now how vulnerable we all were but, even as a six-year old, something inside of me wanted to rebel against this teaching. There was a defiance in me, which I'm sure I inherited from my father. I wanted to dare God to strike me down if I didn't confess every little sin.

But it was hard to forget Sister Equinus and her candle and it eventually took me thirty-five years to overcome the notion of Catholic Guilt. I suppose I was lucky because, for so many with a similar upbringing, it becomes a chain worn for life.

Some weeks after the Fire and Brimstone lesson, Sister Equinus made another appearance in the classroom.

'Excuse me Mrs. Fitzgerald, I want to show the boys something of great importance.'

This turned out to be the School's one and only Holy Relic – a piece of cloth from the actual robe worn by Saint Martin de Porres. We all knew three things about Saint Martin. One, he was a black man. Two, he could talk to animals. And three, with God's blessing, he was able to levitate.

Standing in front of the class she held up a piece of card in a black frame, about the size of a picture post-card. On the top half we could see a picture of Saint Martin. On the lower half was a picture of a chalice, about two centimetres in height, with rays of light emanating from it. Straining forward, in the centre of the bowl of the chalice, we could just make out a tiny hole – we're talking millimetres now! Behind this hole, so we were led to believe, was a minute piece of cloth. As she spoke, she moved up and down the aisles to make sure everyone had a good view.

'This piece of cloth...' said Sister, in her most reverent voice, 'This piece of cloth has touched the bones of Saint Martin de Porres.'

You could hear a pin drop.

'Now boys,' she went on, 'if you touch this sacred relic...' She paused for dramatic effect.

6

'If you touch this sacred relic... You will be cured!' She didn't actually say what we would be cured of and neither did she say that if you went to the church in Whitefriars Street in Dublin City centre, you could buy these relics by the dozen – Saint Martin must have had a lot of robes!

Every boy in the class was familiar with the service of Mass. From the day we were born we'd attended every Sunday with our parents. Now, however, we had to be word perfect in all parts of the service spoken by the congregation. This was 1961 and the commencement of the Second Vatican Council, inaugurated by Pope John XXIII, was still a year ahead. The entire mass was in Latin – we were now expected to become tri-lingual.

'In nomine Patris et Fillii et Spiritus Sancti.'

'Amen.'

'Dominus vobiscum.'

'Et cum spiritu tuo.'

'Confiteor Deo omnipotenti...'

I confess to almighty God... and on, and on, and on. Most of the meaning went over our heads of course but it all had to be learnt.

My friend, Thomas Doyle, was a bright boy. He was Sister Equinus's favourite – we all knew that. He was always running errands for her. So, it was no surprise when he was chosen to carry the banner of the Immaculate Conception at our first communion service, which was on the following Sunday morning.

On the Friday before, a full rehearsal was held and we all lined up behind Thomas and the banner - girls on the left and boys on the right. Slowly and reverently we made our way out from the school and across the road to the west end of the church. Down the aisle we snaked and after bowing our heads to the altar, took our seats in the front pews – girls on the left and boys on the right. Sister Equinus was already stationed in the sanctuary behind the altar rail, where she would take the role of the priest.

After pausing for absolute silence, she started.

'In nomine Patris et Fillii et Spiritus Sancti.'

The mass began with the now familiar words and 'Amen' we all replied - loudly and clearly as we'd been taught. And then on through confession and absolution and interminable prayers and readings until, at last, we reached the climax. The moment the host transubstantiated into the actual body of Christ. We waited for our cue, stood and made our way out of the pews to form a line in front of the altar rail.

We obviously couldn't rehearse with the actual host, so Sister had taken some ice-cream wafers and cut them into neat little squares. These were placed in a small round tray on some tissue paper. Unlike the Anglican Church, where the Communion bread or wafer is placed in the recipients' hands to be transferred to the mouth, in the Catholic Church, the host is placed directly onto the tongue. We'd practiced this many times in the classroom and were now quite proficient at sticking out our tongues ready to receive.

Starting on the far right, Sister Equinus made her way slowly along the line, placing one of her wafers on each waiting tongue with the words 'Corpus Christi', the body of Christ. To which the recipient replied 'Amen'.

As she approached me, I opened my mouth and stuck my tongue out as far as it would go.

'Corpus Christi.'

'Amen.'

With the sacred cargo safely in place, I slowly retracted my tongue, whereupon the wafer immediately stuck to the roof of my mouth, where it remained for the rest of the mass.

Standing to my left was Miles Brennan, hapless boy. Whether he moved his head a bit or, through nerves, retracted his tongue a little early. Maybe Sister's hand slightly misjudged the distance. But, for whatever reason, the wafer missed its target and fell to the floor. Instinctively, Miles bent to retrieve it and stretched out his hand to return the wafer. From somewhere within her voluminous robes Sister Equinus whipped out her thick, hand stitched leather tawse. She didn't miss her target the second time. God's mercy came crashing down with such velocity that Miles' hand was pinned to the alter rail.

'You do NOT' she shouted, 'You do NOT on any account touch the holy sacrament!'

Presumably this did not include touching it with a leather tawse. The heavenly host, transubstantiated or otherwise, was now back on the floor, completely shattered by the blow.

'DO YOU UNERSTAND?' she bellowed.

'DO YOU UNERSTAND?'

Miles was now quietly crying. I could see the tears running down his cheeks.

'Yes Sister' he whimpered. Oh, he understood alright.

Chapter 2 - Gay Parade.

The Rotunda Maternity Hospital is situated in the centre of Dublin, in Parnell Square. It is reckoned to be the oldest continuously operating maternity hospital in the world and since its establishment in 1745 over 300,000 babies have been born there.

I joined the statistics on June 7, 1955 and in due course of time was received into the bosom of the Holy Catholic Church and baptized Leo Augustine Donaghy. At the time of my confirmation in 1963 I was able to choose for myself a confirmation name. I chose Bartholomew – I rather fancied being called Barty. My mother, however, wasn't so keen and we settled for Peter, thus adding a third pope to the previous two. I thus became L.A.P.D. – Leo Augustine Peter Donaghy.

I was the third of seven children. Joe and Aileen assiduously and skilfully practiced the rhythm method and produced an offspring approximately every two years. Maria was the eldest, then Anthony, me, Martin, Philomena, Gregory and finally, in 1964, the baby, Janette was born.

Council regulations stipulated that families with up to three children should live in two bed-roomed houses. You had to wait for the fourth child to qualify for a third bedroom. So, as soon as Martin arrived in 1957, my parents applied to the housing department and we all moved to Walkinstown.

Walkinstown was a housing estate in the suburbs of Dublin, some four miles south-west of the city centre. Prior to its construction, which began in the 1930's, the area had been a dairy farm. The name Walkinstown being a corruption of Wilkinstown – named after Wilkins, a tenant farmer who lived in the area in the 15th century. And indeed, well into my childhood, the estate was still surrounded by open countryside. Fields and meadows where we played and picnicked. Woods and streams where we splashed about and got wet and muddy. A kid's paradise that stretched all the way to the distant Dublin Mountains that formed a backdrop to all our games.

My maternal grandparents, who lived nearby, owned working horses. They had two main sources of income. The first was transporting sand from the local pits to the many building sites in and around the City. On the return journey they called at the Guinness brewery in St. James's Gate where the carts were loaded up with barrels of the black stout. These were then conveyed out to the country pubs in the surrounding area. They also had a pony and trap and would go trotting up the lanes to visit relatives in nearby Tallaght, which was a tiny village with one pub and a water trough. But that was back in the fifties. A distant memory of the days before the housing estates perniciously crept up to and into the mountains, obscuring all but the highest ridges to the folks of Walkinstown. Nowadays Tallaght has motorways and skyscrapers and a population of seventy-five thousand.

We lived at Number 30, Walkinstown Parade, just off the Long Mile road. Our part of The Parade was a row of twelve terraced houses facing a triangular green where all the kids played. The houses all had the coveted three bedrooms.

Downstairs, off a narrow hallway, were a lounge, a kitchen, a tiny toilet and separate bathroom. At the front was a small garden and, at the back, a slightly larger one. When the family was complete, there were nine of us living there.

To the left of the house, some fifty yards away, was the infant school, with its separate buildings for the boys and the girls. To the right was the church that dominated all our lives - the Catholic Church of the Assumption of the Blessed Virgin Mary. Built, in the 1950's, a massive brick structure of cathedral-like proportions which was topped by a small belfry with a green copper roof. From here the bell would ring out calling the faithful to the daily services. The first, the one which my father attended every day of his adult life, was the 7 a.m. Mass. Then, at 12 noon for the midday Angelus and again at 6 p.m. for the evening Angelus, when everything would stop in the house as the required prayers were recited.

That church must have held some five or six hundred people and in those days, on Sundays, it was full - not once, but five times. As well as the seven o'clock, there were masses at 9:00, 10:00, 11:00 and twelve mid-day. Each service lasted some forty-five minutes and on the quarter to the hour the bell would start tolling for the next one. People flooded in and on special occasions a service would often start with the congregation over-flowing into the porches outside.

Sunday mass was the focal point of the week and everyone attending made an effort. Every man was in a suit and tie and many of the older men wore a waistcoat as well. The women were in their Sunday best frocks and, of course, they all wore a hat. I can see my mother in a little orange pill-box number with a small net that just covered her eyes (Dad muttering, slightly disapprovingly – he didn't like her in that hat.) On alternate Sundays she wore a blue creation that had blue silk flowers on top.

Beyond the church was what we called The Compound. This was an area of waste ground where the builders of the estate had left mounds of earth and rubble which were now overgrown. It was a great place for building camps and dens among the brambles and nettles and we kids spent a lot of our free time there. Despite the ever-present fear of eternal damnation, these were very happy years.

My father, Joe, was down to earth and practical, ahead of his time in many ways. He had a life-long interest in photography that had started in his childhood. He would create scenes by painting on sheets of glass and sticking on coloured sweet papers. Then, using a torch, he'd project them onto the wall to entertain his parents. When, as an adult, his contemporaries were messing around with their box cameras, Joe had moved on to cine film and was winning competitions at the newly formed Dublin Cine Club. When Video arrived on the scene, he was in his element.

Every notable event in the life of the Donaghy's was recorded, edited with music and a copy made for each member of the family.

Aileen, my mother, was known to everyone as Ace. As her family grew, her life centered more and more on the house and in particular the kitchen. Before marrying she had trained and worked as a confectioner. Most days when we kids came in from school, delicious baking smells would be wafting from the kitchen and there was always a spoon to lick or a bowl to run your finger round. She was always baking. There would be homemade pies, cakes, scones and of course, Irish soda bread.

At 5:30 each afternoon, when my father was due in from work at the Drimnagh Paper Mill, she would always put on a fresh dress for him. She had beautiful skin but never wore any make-up, except for lipstick. To me she was a very glamorous woman who took a great interest in what she wore until the day she died. Even now the family talk about the evening dress she wore in the fifties - green silk with a flocked leaf pattern. She would never leave home, even to cross the road to the corner shop, without dressing up.

Dad would often come home on a sunny evening and say,

'Get your togs, kids.' Then to Ace, 'Can we get a flask together, Mother? We'll go out to Sea Point for a dip.'

She was always game for a trip out.

'You know me, Joe. Never miss a beat!'

The oven would be turned off (whatever was cooking was put away to have later or the next day) and in a few minutes, sandwiches, an apple tart and thermos flasks would be ready for a picnic. We'd pile into the old car and off we'd go to the beach at Blackrock.

Joe later acquired an old camper van and we were able to go away for family weekends. This was no ordinary camper van. On the roof was a large wooden box-like construction, a bit like a flat-pack from Ikea. Fixed to the roof-rack, when you released the clips, the top section could be opened out to form a floor that hung out over the edge of the car. Legs and a ladder were attached to this. As you opened the lid a tent-like structure appeared which covered the whole floor area. I don't think either Greg or Jen were born at the time but each night we were away, Maria, Anthony, Martin and I would climb the ladder to sleep on the roof. Mam would tuck us up in eiderdowns in a very comfy bed for four. Phil, the baby at the time, would sleep in the van with Joe and Ace.

By the age of three it was becoming apparent, to my father at least, that there was something different about me. My likes and dislikes were far removed from those of my older brother, Anthony, who was now six. I didn't want to go out on the green and play football with the other boys. I didn't enjoy getting into scraps. I didn't want a cricket bat for my birthday. I did want, and got, a red-lined cape that I could dance in.

Auntie Mary had emigrated to Australia and Joe regularly sent out family cine films and tapes for her to keep in touch with all the happenings in Walkinstown. Maria, the eldest at nine, Anthony and I were all encouraged to act in front of the camera and to recite poems and songs into the reel-to-reel tape recorder.

From behind the floor-length curtains in the front lounge, a three-year-old boy appears. Over a full netted underskirt, he is wearing his sister Maria's green chiffon dress, tied at the back with a large bow. On his head is a silk scarf wrapped into a turban and on his feet, little check slippers with side buttons. The music is playing, and he gracefully twirls and pirouettes round the floor with the chiffon gently rising and falling as he catches the skirt of the dress in his small hands. The expression on his face tells the audience that he is lost in a fantasy world of his own.

All this was captured on a cine film to send to Australia and, many years, later transferred to video for posterity.

On one Sunday afternoon when I was about four, Anthony and I were watching an old black and white Shirley Temple film with Ace. From nowhere I said,

'When I grow up and become a girl, I'm going to sing like Shirley Temple.'

'You won't grow into a girl' said Anthony, 'You're a boy!'

I didn't understand and looked to mother for reassurance. She said nothing. Just gave me a big hug as we continued to watch the film.

I was frequently mistaken for a girl - something that happened well into my adult life. One family holiday we were camping in Connemara in the west of County Galway. Each morning Anthony, Martin and I would go with Joe to the local farm to collect milk. It must have been the second day when the farmer said to the other two boys,

'Ah now, yer sister's a great wee lass.'

They of course fell about laughing but I was not amused, in fact I was very annoyed. My response was typically defiant. The next morning, I borrowed Mam's clip-on earrings and put on a real show for them.

One weekend when I was about five, Joe took me across the green to Byrnes the Newsagent to get his Saturday paper. Hanging above the counter, clipped to a card, I spotted a row of little black plastic dolls. They were dressed in colourful skirts and had beautiful feathered headbands. They were sixpence each and I desperately wanted one.

'Daddy, please can I have one of those?'

Joe didn't give it a second thought. He handed over an extra sixpence and I was the proud owner of a little black doll.

That doll went everywhere with me and I thought nothing of playing with it in the street. Declan Campbell and Kieran Morris, who were seven and eight, were greatly amused and set about getting it off me. I was chased into The Compound where they resorted to throwing stones at me, but no way was I losing my prized possession. In the end they gave up and threw me in the stingers. I went home with great wheals on my bare legs but, I still had my little black doll.

Dressing up was a big part of the games I played during those early years. I can remember waking early one Sunday morning after Mam and Dad had been to a dinner-dance the night before.

'There's some nice party hats on the dressing-table' said Mammy, 'One each.'

I was there first. Between the mini-bowler and the fez with a feather, I spotted a beautiful silver cardboard tiara, sparkling in the morning sunlight. I immediately crowned myself in the dressing-table mirror. Maria, who had heard the squeals of delight, was livid. She didn't want the bowler or the fez and made this quite plain for all to hear. But I was away downstairs, dressed in my crown.

It was also at that time that I first applied make-up to my face. For my birthday Joe and Ace had bought me a large box of water-colour paints from Hector Grey's. Amongst my early artistic efforts were my eyebrows in Sap Green and my lips and nails in Chinese Red – all applied with my left index finger. Both parents smiled benignly and accepted it as another of my funny personal traits.

When I first met my friend Thomas, the Doyles lived in the other half of the Parade at Number 2 - twelve more houses whose gardens backed onto ours. These only had two bedrooms, but Mrs. Doyle had her sights set on Number 46, eight doors along on our side. As soon as her fourth child Cathleen was born, in went the application and they were on their way. Bridie Doyle eventually went one better than Mother, she and Sean had eight children of which Thomas was the eldest.

Next to the Doyles at Number 48 were the Campbells – four children, Helen, Declan, Rory and Deidra. Rory was the same age as Thomas and me and joined our non-footballing club. It would be fair to say that he didn't quite have our imagination and it did take a lot of persuasion to get him to put on a frock, but we occasionally succeeded. The three of us did, however, have a lot of other things in common. As well as being the same age and all starting school on the same day in the same class, we all made our first Holy Communion together and, as it turned out, we all grew up to be homosexual. What a Gay Parade!

Chapter 3 – Brothers and Masters.

In 1963, aged eight, I was to begin the next stage of my education. I think it fair to say that, along with my fellow classmates from the Infant school, we were all a little apprehensive to be leaving the relative safety of the nuns' care.

They did their best to make it a happy day. Every child was given a paper bag full of hard-boiled sweets. Some encouraging words from Sister Equinus were followed by a final prayer, some false tears from the Sisters and a rousing chorus of Hail Queen of Heaven:

> Hail, Queen of heaven, the ocean star,
> Guide of the wanderer here below,
> Thrown on life's surge, we claim thy care,
> Save us from peril and from woe.

Then, with a real sense of peril and woe, we were lined up in a crocodile and marched off. Sister Equinus led the procession out of the school, round the back of the nuns' house and across the Long Mile Road into the unknown territory of Drimnagh Castle School. Drimnagh Castle wasn't just a name. It was a real castle and Norman to boot. Built by the English after their twelfth century invasion, it has, to this day, the distinction of being the only remaining castle in Ireland to be surrounded by a water filled moat. This is fed by a small local river, the Bluebell. Owned by various grand families through the centuries, it was eventually taken over by the Christian Brothers. They not only lived in the castle but ran a school there until the new buildings were completed in 1956. The new schools stretched for some quarter of a mile along the Long Mile Road, the primary to the right of the castle and the secondary to the left. At the same time, the Brothers moved into an impressive new house situated between the two schools and directly in front of the castle.

There were two types of teacher at Drimnagh Castle. Firstly, the Christian Brothers. These were addressed by the boys as 'Brother' and woe betide you if you forgot. Secondly, teachers from outside the Order. Unlike the British, who address their teachers as 'Sir', we were required to use the term 'Master' – more subservient than respectful.

On arrival we were taken to our classroom where we were greeted by our new teacher, Master Dalton. He was a very handsome man, about thirty, dressed in a smart tweed jacket, very fashionable trousers (narrowing almost to the point of being 'drainpipes') and shiny black shoes. He was a kindly man and I felt at ease when he was teaching us.

That was not the case in Master Hanofee's class. He took us for English and Latin. He was a big man with a narrow face and teeth that seemed to point backwards into his mouth – this may have been something to do with the fact that he played Gaelic football for County Offaly. Master Hanofee had a vicious streak and thought nothing of beating boys with his leather strap for the smallest of misdemeanours. For the first time, I felt afraid in school.

Brother Arnold, who for some reason was known as The Pig, was another man who seemed to delight in hitting small boys. One Friday afternoon, Master Dalton left the classroom for a few minutes and within seconds a riot was in full swing. I sat at the front next to Patrick Manzar and we thought we would take the opportunity to start our weekend homework. The room suddenly went silent – The Pig had arrived at the door. Despite the fact that half the class were out of their seats, it was Patrick and I who had to hold out our hands for a strapping.

What was the man's reasoning? I would love to confront him now and ask – I doubt if I would get an answer. I will never know but I will remember that Friday for the rest of my life. How could such a man, with no interest in boys, with no interest in their education, whose only aim was a psychopathic desire to inflict pain on his young charges – how could such a man become a teacher? A Christian Brother? Where was God's love and mercy in his classroom?

Surprisingly, Master Hanofee was the person who introduced me to poetry. How such a brute of a man could enthuse so much about the beauty of words is a mystery. But he did and it seemed to have a calming effect on him. We listened in silence as he read from Walter de la Mare's poem Silver:

> Slowly, silently, now the moon
> Walks the night in her silver shoon...

Then he'd have us reciting from Longfellow's Wreck of the Hesperus:

It was the schooner Hesperus,
That sail'd the wint'ry sea,
And the skipper had ta'en his little daughter
To bear him company...

The strap rarely appeared during poetry.

It wasn't that we weren't disciplined at home. We all got a slap from time to time, when we deserved it, from both Joe and Ace. I certainly drove Joe to the limit on many occasions. I remember one afternoon when we were off out on a family outing. Before Joe had started the engine Martin, my younger brother, and I were scrapping in the back of the car and got a warning. The second warning came as we pulled out of The Parade. By the time we reached the Long Mile Road (about a hundred yards) Joe had had enough. He turned the engine off and leapt out of the car but by the time he got round to my side, I was away. I was too fast for him and was fortunate that a bus was just pulling off. I jumped onto the back platform and made my escape. By the time I got home he had calmed down and not a word was said.

I also remember another day when I expected to be slaughtered. It happened some years later. Long hair was coming in and Joe wasn't happy. He tolerated it to the bottom of the ears but as mine approached my shoulders, enough was enough. I was given two-shillings and ordered to the barbers' post-haste. My hair was my pride and joy and I wasn't happy either. I felt it would be safer to go rather than argue but persuaded the barber to only take half an inch of the bottom. When I returned Joe hit the roof. He was furious and I was given another two-shillings and sent back with orders to get a short back and sides. He wasn't the only stubborn one in the family. I returned to the barber's shop and got him to shave every hair off my head, right down to the bone. I think I was the first skinhead in Dublin. When I got back to Number 30, though, I was beginning to have second thoughts – I really had gone too far. I slunk into the kitchen to be greeted by gasps from all the family. I looked at Joe and thought it only a matter of time before he went to the kitchen cupboard where he kept a black leather belt. He continued to drink his tea and didn't say a word.

That black leather belt lived in the kitchen cupboard but very rarely made an appearance. We all knew it hung there and that was enough. I only saw him use it once and that was on Martin. I don't know what he'd done but he got a walloping and disappeared howling upstairs. We could all see that Joe was not happy with himself for doing this. He stomped off down to the bottom of the garden and hurled the belt into the bushes.

It was pointless complaining at home about the severe treatment we received at school. I suppose Joe had been through the same himself and, like most parents at the time, adopted the attitude that 'if you were beaten you must have deserved it – discipline was good for you and would make you into a man.'

On one occasion he did march up to the school to complain. That was over Martin. Martin suffered from the congenital condition of albinism which meant there was a partial absence of pigment in his hair, skin and eyes. He had snowy white hair and very pale skin. On visits to the beach Ace would have him plastered in a lard-like substance and he always had to wear a sunhat. He, himself, had no sense of being vulnerable and was always up for anything. He'd frequently come home covered in cuts and bruises.

He was always getting up to mischief, or up to 'divilment' as my parents called it. This frequently resulted in his glasses being broken.

'Lamb of God, Joe' you'd hear Mammy cry. 'What's happened to him now?'

'Ah, give him a crack on the two arses.' was Joe's reply. 'That'll sort him out'.

In fact both my parents, Joe in particular, were very protective towards Martin.

A more serious consequence of the albinism showed in Martin's eyes. He suffered from nystagmus – a rapid irregular movement of the eyes from side to side. This led to difficulties in focusing and consequently problems with reading and writing. Without doubt Martin was a bright boy. I remember attending a parents' meeting with Ace when the teacher said,

'Leo will have to work really hard to keep up with Martin.'

Master Makin neither appreciated Martin's abilities nor comprehended his problems. He seemed to delight in picking on the boy, who was always in trouble in his class. He was a total bully. When Joe became aware that this was going on, it was like a red rag to a bull. He was off up to the school to give Master Makin a piece of his mind. I, on the other hand and my elder brother Anthony, were left to fend for ourselves.

There were no bags of sweets when, at the age of eleven, we progressed up to the secondary school - just a short walk along the Long Mile Road and the hand over from one set of scary brothers and masters into the hands of another.

Thomas was brighter than me and for the first time was in a different class. His experience of secondary education was different from mine in that, it wasn't the teachers he was afraid of, it was the other pupils. He did experience corporal punishment. Master Casey's weapon of choice was a short cane that, for some reason, he had gaily decorated with rings of different coloured tape. He'd ask a boy a question and if the answer wasn't forthcoming the victim would receive a crack of the cane on his hand. Master Casey would then move on to the next boy where the question would be repeated. This would continue round the class until someone gave the right answer. If he got to the last boy and still hadn't got what he required, he would start all over again with the first boy.

I don't know why Thomas was jeered at and I wasn't. Of the two of us, I was by far the more effeminate. It may have had something to do with his Sandie Shaw impression. Thomas was seen performing by one of the Brothers who thought it would be a great idea to send him round the classrooms to sing in front of the boys. I think that was when it started. Over the weeks the jeering became intolerable. Thomas began to dread the short journey to and from school and in break times would hide away.

At the secondary school we met Brother Perkins who took the weekly physical training class. He seemed quite elderly for this position but, there again, he didn't actually do anything physical himself. Not always, but frequently, the lesson began in the same way. He'd get the boys lined up in the gymnasium facing the wall bars. On the given command, we were required to perform a handstand against the bars. Brother Perkins would then make a slow progress along the line looking down each boy's shorts. If he couldn't see what he wanted, he'd gently take hold of the hem of the shorts and give a little pull. Satisfied with the results he would move on to the next boy. As an alternative to this little game, he'd line us up in front of him. Each boy would then do a handstand with Brother Perkins catching hold of our ankles – the result was the same.

I suppose we must have thought this strange, but no one thought of complaining – we wouldn't have dared! One could only say in his favour that he just looked and never laid a finger on us. His axiom was clearly 'look but don't touch.'

Chapter 4 – Anthony's Story.

Anthony's school report has to be written because of what happened several years later. My brother was two years ahead of me and generally considered academically bright. This did not protect him from the brutality of the Brothers and Masters. Secondary education, for him also, was a nightmare. How could you learn when nearly every lesson was dominated by the fear of being beaten?

The Irish strap was a version of the Scottish tawse. Some sixteen inches in length and two inches wide it consisted of three thin strips of leather sewn together around the edges. At one end it narrowed into a handle. Miscreants were instructed to hold out one hand, palm uppermost, supported by the other hand below – this made it more difficult to move the hand away during the infliction of strokes. It also insured that the full force of each stroke was taken by the hand being strapped. Older boys were often strapped across both palms at once. Then, trying desperately not to cry, you'd return to your seat and grasp the cold metal frame of the desk to ease the burning.

The man Anthony feared most was Master Dunleavy – feared, dreaded and hated. He'd sit hunched over his desk like a vulture. His skin had a pallid yellow tinge and, although only in his early forties, he was completely bald apart from a few straggly hairs that hung limply over his collar. His voice and manner emanated a cold hatred towards the boys he taught and to mankind in general. He never smiled and never spoke gently.

'Get those books out now!' he'd bark.

Every lesson was conducted in a hostile, threatening and scary manner. The strap lay on his desk for all to see and the threat of it being used was ever present.

His classroom windows looked out onto the railings that ran along the Long Mile road. If he happened to notice anyone standing there he'd say,

'That fella out there's up to no good. You boys will all end up like him. No-good wasters. Mark my words.'

He never had a kind word for anyone. Everything in his life was negative.

There were some good teachers in the school, but they too often came with a warning sign.

Brother Phelan had a passion for Gaelic but was very prone to mood swings. You could get a pretty good idea of how things were going by watching his face. He had a red complexion at the best of times and probably suffered from high blood pressure. If something annoyed him, his face would gradually turn a deep crimson. And then, the real danger sign, he would begin chewing his lower lip. When that happened, you knew the storm wasn't far away. He would suddenly fly into a rage, rise from his desk, strap in hand and head off towards some hapless boy or two. Then, as quickly as it came, it would all pass and he would become quite remorseful – too late of course for the victims. Brother Phelan liked to bring everyone out to the front of the class, to stand around him by the blackboard. Like me, Anthony was quite small for his age and would often find himself at the front of the melee. It became quite a game for the bigger boys at the back to gradually push forward until the smaller ones at the front were almost touching Brother Phelan's robes. They knew what would happen next.

'Now will you move back boys' he'd say. At the same time, he would push them back, nonchalantly placing his hands well below their belts. The whisper would then go around,

'I've a feeling Phelan is feeling!'

Another teacher who liked the 'touchy-feely' approach was Brother Lazarus. He was a much softer human being who rarely resorted to the strap and was generally liked. He taught natural science and enjoyed nothing more than to take parties of boys on long walks through the countryside and along the river Liffey. During these excursions, he could become quite intimate with some of his charges. Then, in an unholy reference to the biblical miracle, you'd hear,

'Ah-hah! Lazarus is rising!'

It was general knowledge amongst the boys that this sort of thing went on. I'm sure we didn't appreciate the seriousness of such behaviour. In some ways we looked on it as a sign that, somewhere inside these monsters, was a human being lurking. Celibacy is a terrible thing to inflict on a man and no wonder all that repressed sexuality would leak out at times. A long-standing tradition in Irish Catholic families was that the eldest son would be encouraged to become either a priest or a Christian Brother. This was not a tradition that Anthony held with, but Joe could be very domineering. And so it was, that at the age of thirteen, after two years at Drimnagh Castle secondary school and against his will, Anthony was transferred to The Ignatius Rice College in Dalkey to commence training as a Christian Brother.

Though not on the syllabus, preparation for a celibate life was very much to the fore. The motto of the Congregation of Christian Brothers was 'Noli me Tangere' which translates 'Do not touch me.' - spoken by Jesus to Mary after the resurrection. Whatever the Biblical meaning of these words was, the Brothers took them literally. They were not allowed to have any sensual feelings. Any intimacy that they might feel towards other adults of either sex, or indeed their pupils, was to be quashed. They were meant to suffer like Christ on the cross. 'Noli me Tangere' was their mantra in life and what they taught their protégées.

As intelligent, pubescent teenage boys, Anthony and his contemporaries had other priorities. Using their knowledge of Latin, they re-constructed 'Noli me Tangere' to 'Me adtingam' – 'I touch myself.' - which was much more fun.

After a year and a half of this regime Anthony left and returned to Drimnagh Castle to do his Intermediates.

He left school at the age of fifteen and over the next few years tried his hand at several occupations. He trained for three years to be an accountant and then had a spell at the paper mill with Joe. This was followed by a period in London where he worked as a housemaster in an Approved School.

On a trip home to Dublin, a meeting with an old friend led him to Burtonport, a tiny fishing village on the

Northwest coast of Donegal. Here he became involved with the Atlantis Community – so called because it was based in the old Atlantis Hotel. The group offered therapy based on its motto 'PNP' – People not Psychiatry. They put into practice the work of American psychologist Arthur Janov, as described in his book 'The Primal Scream'. This involved 'descending into, feeling, and experiencing long-repressed childhood pain.' The pain could then be released by literally screaming, which led to the group being known as 'The Screamers.'

Anthony spent nine months in all at Atlantis which, in his own words,

'Awakened a rage in me that I didn't know existed.'

Some months after his last visit to Donegal, on a wet grey afternoon, Anthony was heading home along the Long Mile road. As he passed the school railings he stopped and looked up at the windows. Suddenly it all came flooding back. In his mind he could hear Master Dunleavy.

'That fella out there's up to no good. You boys will all end up like him. No-good wasters. Mark my words.'

'That's me he's talking about' thought Anthony, 'Me and every other boy he has ever taught.'

Everything he had learned from 'The Primal Scream' welled up inside him. Instead of going home he turned into the school grounds and headed for the main entrance – thoroughly roused to anger.

As he went in old memories assaulted him - the smell of disinfectant on the tiled floors. The ticking clock. The green walls of the corridors with the crucifixes spaced out along them. Muffled sounds emanated from the classrooms. Somewhere in the distance boys' voices were singing.

As he approached the first door, he could feel his heart beating in his chest. He knocked.

'Come!'

Anthony entered to see an unfamiliar Brother sitting at the desk. Controlling his breathing, he said,

'I'm sorry to bother you Brother, I'm looking for Master Dunleavy?'

'I can't help you, son. Try next door.'

'Thank you, Brother.'

There were beads of sweat on his forehead now and as he knocked at the next classroom, he noticed his hand was trembling. He entered and found himself face to face with another older Brother. This one looked more familiar, but he couldn't put a name to the face.

'I'm sorry to bother you Brother, I'm looking for Master Dunleavy?'

'Ah now, he is in. I saw him this morning, but I couldn't tell you where you'd find him now.'

That wasn't necessarily the answer Anthony had wanted. If the man had been off sick or on a sabbatical, he could have forgotten the whole crazy idea and headed off home for tea and cake with Ace in the safety of Number 30.

The next classroom had the singers in it. There was no way Dunleavy would be taking a music class. Anthony walked further up the corridor. By now he was in a high state of agitation and decided this would be his last try. He went into one more classroom and got the same negative response. That was it. With some relief he decided that Dunleavy would have to wait for another occasion.

As he headed back down the corridor towards the exit, he came across three boys, aged about fourteen or fifteen, outside the headmaster's room. From their demeanour they were waiting to be beaten.

'Do you know where Master Dunleavy is?'

'Oh, the Monster.'

'He's upstairs in Room 12.'

So, this was it. It was all back on. Anthony retraced his steps and made his way up to the first floor. By the time he reached Room 12 he really was shaking but the determination had returned. As he stood outside the door, on the other side he heard that familiar cold voice. A shiver went down his spine but there was also a fire rising in his belly. Without knocking he barged straight in. And there he was, the Monster, sitting at the desk with his strap in front of him. Marching up to him, Anthony crashed both his fists down onto the desk – so hard that the strap leapt into the air.

'I'm a past pupil of yours' he shouted, 'and I hate your fucking guts!' With that, he grabbed the strap off the desk. Thinking he was about to be attacked Dunleavy shrank back in his chair. Anthony hurled the instrument of torture out of an open window.

The class of fifteen-year olds really didn't know how to react to this intrusion to their lesson. Half thought they were under attack and were cowering under their desks. The other half were on their feet and, as the strap disappeared, cheered and whistled in approval. Anthony turned his attention to them.

'Don't listen to any of the crap this man gives you! He's a hateful monster and you don't have to put up with his vicious bullying! Don't let him ruin your education.'

By now Dunleavy had somewhat recovered his composure and stood up.

'What's your name?'

'Fuck off!' Anthony replied to more cheers. 'If you were any teacher at all you would know my name, you bastard!'

Visibly shaken by the severity of this new verbal onslaught and the fact that most of the class were now on their feet and seemed to be edging forward, Dunleavy looked anxiously towards the door.

Anthony had been shouting so loudly that five other teachers arrived on the scene. Thinking they were dealing with a mad man they surrounded him, lifted him off the ground and carried him out into the corridor. As he was leaving Dunleavy tried once more,

'What's your name?'

He got the same reply as before.

As quickly as it came, Anthony's rage now left him. Mission accomplished, he became perfectly calm. He suddenly thought,

'I'm going to end up in a strait-jacket if I'm not careful.' Quite quietly he said, 'Put me down please. I've got no problem with you. This fella,' he said pointing back into the classroom, 'I fucking hate!'

He obviously spoke with some authority because his captors put him down. Thanking them, he adjusted his jacket and slowly made his way along the corridor and back down the staircase. Once on the ground floor he made a run for it.

There were now police sirens in the distance heading towards the school but by the time they arrived, Anthony was well away.

That was not the end of the story. Thomas's younger brother Liam, who was by this time a pupil at the secondary school, reported back that there had been several days of rebellion and that Master Dunleavy had been beaten up, though he didn't know by whom.

When Anthony made a return visit to the community in Donegal, he took great delight in recounting the story. This was the 'Primal Scream' in practice and he described the relief he felt as 'the opening of a great pressure valve'. It was not revenge in any way but a catharsis. A blow for freedom had been struck on behalf of all Catholic schoolboys who suffered under the hands of the Brothers and Masters.

Chapter 5 – Forgive Me Father.

The Church of the Assumption of the Blessed Virgin Mary had six confessional boxes, three down each of the side aisles. To keep things moving with such a large congregation, each of these boxes was a 'double'. The priest would sit in a closed compartment in the middle. On one side, behind a curtain, would be a sinner confessing. On the other side, another, waiting to confess. The priest could efficiently rotate from one to the other with minimal waste of time. If you tried to listen while you waited you could only discern mumbling from the other side of the box. Though most of the time, you could make a pretty good guess at what was being said by both penitent and priest.

Everyone went to mass at least once a week, usually on a Sunday. If you wanted to take Communion at mass, you had to have been to confession. Not to do so would be a Venial sin. You also had to complete your penances before attending the mass. Thus, Saturday evening was always a busy time at the confessional with at least four priests in attendance. Most people looked to see which priest had the shortest queue and joined the end of his line.

We youngsters were all well used to confession. We'd been doing it for years, ever since our first holy communion. Sister Equinus had trained us and we all knew what was expected. The first time though, it was with great trepidation that, as six-year olds we had lined up in the pews, waiting our turn to approach the confessional. It was only a few steps but a lonely journey for a small boy to make on his own - up to and into that dark box.

'Bless me Father, for I have sinned. This is my first confession.'

'And what are your sins, my child?'

'I was very bold to Mammy... And I killed a fly... And I ate some of my sister's sweets... And I forgot to say me prayers before I went to bed.'

It had been made quite clear to us that we had to have a list.

'And are you sorry for these sins?'

'Yes, Father.'

'And is there anything else you want to tell me?'

'No, Father.'

This would be followed by Absolution - a prayer said in Latin and at great speed. Then,

'For your penance, my son, you must say three Hail Marys and a Glory to the Father.'

Then he would bless us, again in Latin,

'In nomine Patris et Fillii et Spiritus Sancti.'

'Thank you, Father and God bless.'

There was great relief that it was over. You would first go and find a quiet spot to do the penances, then off to find your friends and compare notes.

'What did you get?'

'Five Hail Marys!'

'Five! You must have been very bold. I only got three. I'm going to tell me Mammy you got five.'

On one occasion after confession, Thomas and I saw Patrick Manzar hobbling down the street. We immediately thought of Saint Augustine. Sister Equinus had told us that Saint Augustine had to put stones in his shoes to torture himself. So, we of course thought Patrick had been told to put pebbles in his sandals after committing some terrible sin or other. The rumour going around was that he'd pinched his granny's sweets. This went on for a couple of days till we could stand it no longer. We had to find out what he had done. The truth was a bit of an anti-climax. It turned out he had a blister on his toe.

But that was all six or seven years ago. We were young teenagers now and a new and more heinous sin came to the fore. This was not one that was on Sister Equinus's list. Neither, unlike alcohol, which was a frequent topic, was it ever broached in any sermon I ever heard. Come to think of it, no priest, teacher or adult ever mentioned anything about it. Yet, all the same, we knew it was wrong, knew it was a sin and, worst of all, knew we would have to confess each time it happened.

It now became very important whom you chose as your confessor – even if it meant joining one of the longer queues. If Father Ryan was on duty, that was fine.

'Bless me Father, for I have sinned. It is four weeks since my last confession etc. etc.'

'Anything else, child?'

'Yes Father, I touched myself.'

'O.K. son. Try not to do that. Be a good boy, say three Hail Marys and help your Mammy with the dishes.'

Father Pearson on the other hand, well, that was a different matter altogether.

'Bless me Father, for I have sinned. It is four weeks since my last confession etc. etc.'

'Is there anything else you want to tell me, son? Anything you're embarrassed about?'

'Well Father… it happened only once, on Tuesday night… after I watched Batman and Robin. Mammy said "Goodnight" and… I er… I er… I touched myself.'

'Now, where did you touch yourself, son?'

'You know, Father.'

'I don't think I do, son.'

'On me mickey, Father.'

'And did you touch it for a long time?'

'Not very long, Father.'

'Are you sure it only happened the once?'

'Well… er… yes, Father.'

'And did you feel dirty?'

'I did, Father.'

'I want you to say three Hail Marys. Now that's not so bad is it? I want you to come and see me next week and tell me everything. God bless you, son.'

Chapter 6 - Foolishness.

The Doyles were a large family with a lifestyle very similar to the Donaghy's. Thomas's father, Sean, worked as a presser at Burtons' suit factory in Dublin. His mother, Bridie, like mine, spent most of her time running the house and organising the family. Both our mothers were very private women. Despite living for most of their lives a few doors from each other, I don't recall a single occasion when they went into each other's houses. Neither do I remember a time when they addressed each other by their Christian names. You never heard more than a few pleasantries if they met on the street.

'How are you, Mrs. Doyle?'

'Ah sure, I'm worn out Mrs. Donaghy. Feeding the children - it's like throwing buns to a bear!'

'And how's Mr. Doyle?'

'He's fine now. Listen to him in there, singing away. You can always depend on Sean for a good Perry Como song. Sure you can.'

Like my mother, Bridie didn't drink alcohol. When she socialized, she'd have a Pussyfoot – orange juice, lemon juice, lime juice, grenadine syrup, all shaken with ice. That's what she liked and that's what she had.

'Would you not take a sweet sherry Mrs. Doyle?'

'I won't. I'll have a Pussyfoot.'

'Are you sure?'

'I am sure!'

From the time we met in Infant School Thomas and I spent all of our free time together, but Mrs. Doyle was not happy with the relationship. She seemed to think I was a bad influence on Thomas.

'That Leo Donaghy's always leading you into foolishness' she'd say to him.

Both his parents were suspicious of anything they classed as 'girly behaviour'. Mine, on the other hand, saw my antics as entertaining. Ace would laugh and say,

'Good God Leo, you're up in the clouds!'

Bridie wouldn't dismiss me directly but, frequently when I knocked at their door, I'd be met with,

'No, no, no. Thomas's staying in. He's not playing out today.'

If I did manage to get past the front door, it was only into the hall and as we talked, you knew she would be listening to our conversations from the kitchen. I only got into their front lounge once, at Christmas, when Thomas took me in to see their tree. What happened in that lounge was private to the family and not for me or the neighbours.

One evening when she was knitting, Bridie dropped a needle on the floor.

'Holy Mother of God' she said, 'Now Mrs. Campbell knows what I'm doing!'

Why it mattered so much to her that the next-door neighbours knew she was knitting, I don't know but it certainly did.

Because of this antagonism towards our friendship, Thomas and I spent a lot of time at Number 30. The bottom of the stairs was our domain and many happy hours were passed there, just sitting and chatting away.

In the early years our favourite pastime was dressing our dolls and combing their hair. I say 'our' dolls –quite often they belonged to my younger sister Philomena and were borrowed for these sessions.

'Mammy, Leo's put lipstick on me doll and it won't come off!'

'Mammy, Leo's cut me doll's hair again!'

Thomas liked to dress his doll up as a nun, complete with head-dress and veil. The difficult bit was getting the protruding part at the front of the head-dress to stay in place. It required one of Joe's white hankies, half a dozen ice-lolly sticks and assorted bits of string. He eventually mastered it and proudly displayed his own mini Sister Equinus.

Not content with dressing our dolls, we soon progressed to dressing ourselves. I would arrive at the Doyles wearing something colourful borrowed from either my mother or Maria. Mrs. Doyle would open the door, look me up and down and say,

'No, Thomas won't be coming out. He's doing his homework.' Then she'd throw in for good measure, 'Now why do you want to be dressed like a cissy?' and, 'What are you doing with dat doll? Will yer not get out and kick a football?'

The one afternoon Thomas was allowed out was Saturday, when we went to the Apollo cinema for the Saturday Afternoon Pictures. It cost sixpence to get in (unless someone let you in for nothing through the side door) and was the highlight of our week.

Before the films started the entertainment was provided by an elderly usher we called 'Baldy'. He'd charge up and down the aisles trying to control one hundred and fifty rowdy kids all armed with peashooters.

'Who's doin' dat?' he'd shout as another pea hit him in the neck.

The chaos would only subside when the Woody Woodpecker music signalled the start of the cartoon. These were always great fun, but the main attraction was what Thomas and I were waiting for. It always provided lots of inspiration for our make-believe games.

The Metro-Goldwyn-Mayer epic Ben Hur made a big impression on us. As well as starring Charlton Heston, there were ten thousand extras, two hundred camels and two and a half thousand horses. A massive production and we couldn't wait to plan our own smaller version. Thomas and I decided to be joint emperors and the local kids would be cajoled into being our subjects and slaves. Costume was always an important part of our dramas and Mam and Maria were pestered to provide scarves, dresses, sheets and pillowslips with which we could improvise our togas and headgear.

Our story line envisaged a grand procession round the green. Being benevolent rulers, we would distribute bounty to our subjects, as we'd seen the emperor doing in the film. The lady at Sharp's Groceries was always good for this sort of thing. If we asked her nicely, she'd give us a bag of dried prunes and a few broken biscuits. These we supplemented with some windfall apples and blackberries picked in The Compound. Everything was placed in a couple of old biscuit tins which became transformed into cornucopias of exotic fruit.

We were ready to perform for the local kids. Rory Campbell was with us but wouldn't dress-up, so we put him in charge of crowd control. As we paraded round the green he called out and encouraged everyone to join in. Quite an entourage gathered, and we were able to make a grand royal progress to the church gates. There were two large pillars flanking the gates and, by first climbing on the wall, you could get up onto the top of these. I climbed onto one and Thomas onto the other. From here we could distribute the goodies in our biscuit tins to the adoring crowds below. Rory's job now was to get everyone to cheer, wave and bow to us, to show how grateful they were.

The performance didn't last long. Bridie was over like a bolt out of hell.

'Jaysus, Thomas' she said, 'Get inside the house, for God's sake!'

The dress was whipped off him and he was made to stand on the table in the front window to look out across the green at me, still standing on my pillar.

'Now look at Leo Donaghy. Doesn't he look foolish? That's what you look like. Foolish!'

We were both quite musical and often gave impromptu concerts. Instruments had to be improvised of course. On top of the church wall, along an unfinished section, was a long strand of barbed wire. When you plucked it between the sticky-up bits it gave out a melodic twanging sound which immediately became a guitar for us. This provided an excellent background for our rendition of

47

Harry Belafonte's calypso Yellow Bird. One of us would sing whilst performing suitable Caribbean swaying arms and hip movements.

> Yellow bird, up high in banana tree,
> Yellow bird, you sit all alone like me.

The other, up on the wall, supplied the barbed-wire accompaniment with…

'Bing, bing-bong, bing bong-bong, bing bing-bing bong'.

We hardly got through the first chorus and she was out.

'Jaysus Thomas! How many more times? Get inside!'

If that wasn't bad enough, climbing off the wall I knelt on a bumble bee and had my first bee sting.

Thomas was invariably invited to join us on the frequent family outings we had into the countryside. I only remember going on one picnic with his family. However, it was a memorable occasion.

Sean and Bridie got into the front of the car while Thomas and I piled into the back with his sisters Grainne and Cathleen and his younger brother Liam. Grainne was clutching a large bowl containing a partially set red jelly which swirled dangerously to and fro as Sean negotiated the bends on the country lanes up to Kilbride.

Some fifteen-minutes out of Walkinstown we arrived at our destination, an idyllic setting besides a stream.

'Right, Grainne' says Bridie, 'Put that jullee in the warter to set.' The red jelly was duly placed in the cold running stream and we kids set about playing, in and out of the water, until the picnic was ready.

All was well until Liam piped up,

'Mammy! Mammy! Grainne's trodden in the jullee!'

And indeed she had. But Bridie wasn't one to be wasting good food. Most of the grass and mud was scraped off but the rest made its way onto our plates, along with the partially-set jelly and was consumed with relish. None of our mothers was ever wasteful with food. With so many mouths to feed they couldn't be.

Bridie was not renowned for her cooking. Her signature dish was Dublin Coddle. Described in the cookbook as 'nourishing, tasty, economical and warming'. What more could a family ask for? Its main ingredients were sausages, bacon, potato and onions. Each sausage had to be cut into four or five pieces and boiled, along with the other ingredients, for a good hour. On removal from the pot, the pieces of sausage would be the same raw pink colour that they were at the start of the process. Coddle was Thomas's favourite.

You'd have to say that Bridie was a determined woman, though she didn't manage to separate Thomas and me. She did, however, get her own way in most things. Many years later Thomas took her and his Dad away for a weekend to a guest house. On arrival the landlady informed them that,

'Breakfast is between eight and nine o'clock.'

'Ah, that's great' says Bridie. 'We'll have ours at nine-thirty, and Sean'll have a soft-boiled egg.'

Chapter 7 – Granny Donaghy.

In 1965 our family was completed with the birth of Jen. Since we'd moved into the three bed-roomed house, Philomena had arrived in 1961 followed by Gregory in 1963. I was now ten and there were nine of us living at Number 30 – not to mention Granny Donaghy, who was a frequent visitor from the North.

The big front bedroom was my parents' room and Jen slept in there in a cot beside the double-bed. The two smaller back bedrooms were allocated to the boys and the girls. In our room, Anthony, who was now thirteen and the oldest boy, had his own single divan. Martin aged seven, Gregory aged two and I shared a double bed. The girls' room was slightly less crowded, except when Granny stayed. Maria aged sixteen and Philomena aged four each had their own single divans.

Bedtimes were staggered according to our ages. This meant that, by the time it was my turn to climb the stairs, Martin and Greg were fast asleep and the double bed was pretty full. Greg didn't take up much room, but Martin usually managed to sprawl his body well over his fair share of space. On the positive side, this did mean that the bed was well warmed by the time that I came to climb in. This was particularly important in winter. In those days there was no central heating. In fact, there was no heating of any sort upstairs in the house.

Martin occasionally suffered from bed-wetting and to save on the laundry, didn't wear pyjama bottoms. This allowed me to regain my territory. On many winter nights, with no double-glazing, the glass in the window was covered in ice crystals which made fantastic fairy-land patterns. Lying upside down on the edge of the bed I would place my bare feet on the window. The coldness was excruciating but I held on till I could bear it no longer. Then, swinging back round to the bed, I applied my freezing feet to Martin's naked backside. He'd never wake. He just uttered a low groan and contracted his body across the bed towards Greg, thus leaving me a nice warm space to snuggle into.

How my parents coped with seven children, including a new baby and two others under five, I will never know. Joe was at work all day, as was Maria. She had left school at fifteen and now employed full-time in Dublin at Lowe and Sons, solicitors. She was a secretary and very efficient at the typing. When the partners went off to court, she would have time to nap on an armchair in the corner of the office. Arriving home fully refreshed, she was a great help to Mother in the evenings and at weekends. The rest of the time Ace had to cope on her own.

Being so close to the schools we attended, Anthony, Martin and I would come home at mid-day for our lunch. I say mid-day but in fact the lunch breaks at the infants, primary and secondary schools were all staggered. This meant that Mammy was running a canteen in the small kitchen. I'd be eating my pudding, Anthony was rushing back to school and Martin was only just coming in through the door. In the evenings, when Joe and Maria got in from work, she would feed all nine of us together. We'd all be crammed round the one table - a proper family meal.

Apart from my mother, two other women played an important part in my upbringing. The first was Granny Donaghy and the second, my mother's sister Auntie Madge.

Granny Donaghy was my father's mother. She was born a protestant in the North of Ireland. There was no mistaking her roots as her voice sounded like a female version of the Rev. Ian Paisley. She married into a northern Catholic family but, because she'd converted to Catholicism rather than being born into the religion, was never fully accepted by her husband's family. This antagonism persisted throughout her life and even after her death. She was buried in the North, in Dungannon, with my Grandfather. However, such was the bigotry at the time, that the family refused to have her name inscribed on the headstone.

I always felt this was a sad injustice and many years later took great pleasure in etching her name onto the gravestone in a 'private' ceremony!

Though we all loved her dearly, and that included my father, she was a cantankerous woman with, it has to be said, a cruel and wicked streak. To be fair to her, she'd had a difficult life. Not only was she not accepted by her husband's relatives but my Grandfather's job, with the Irish Customs, meant that they were forever moving house around the North of Ireland. Putting down roots and making permanent friends was not easy. She had eight children and the family was always desperate for money. When we became adults, we learnt that she suffered from severe bouts of depression.

She ruled her brood with a rod of iron and my father told many stories of her own particular brand of justice. On one occasion Joe and his sister Theresa were squabbling over an old concertina that they both wanted to play with.

'I'll settle you's two!' says Granny.

With that, she grabbed it from them and, taking a large pair of kitchen scissors, cut the instrument in two, right through the middle of the bellows.

'There now,' she says giving them half each, 'You's can both play with the damn thing!'

My father was very keen on football and in later life never missed a match on the television if he could help it. As a kid, he was a good player and a member of the village youth team. They played on a Sunday and one year managed to reach the District final. Joe vividly recalled the day, though it's surprising that he lived to tell the tale.

He was helping to wash the Sunday lunch dishes, really excited as he waited for the team bus to arrive and pick him up. But, for some reason known only to herself, Granny had decided that he was not going to play that day. There was no rhyme or reason to it. He hadn't misbehaved or done anything wrong.

'But I've finished the dishes, Mammy!'

'Yer not goin' and that's final!'

The bus arrived but no amount of pleading by Joe, or the team coach, would make her change her mind.

'I said he's not goin'!'

Joe was sent to his room. But this was the day of the final and he wasn't finished yet. Stuffing his kit into a bag he crept downstairs and started climbing out of a back window.

The plan was to jump on his bike, cycle to the ground and take the consequences later.

Granny had other ideas. She'd heard him coming down the stairs and was waiting outside the window with a frying-pan. With a God almighty swipe to the head she felled him, knocking him senseless.

'I said yer NOT goin'!

She was a great trickster, especially at Halloween. Her pranks were often great fun for the kids but could, on occasions, take a very macabre turn.

One October, when the children arrived home from school, they found her hanging from a rope in the hall! She'd made the rope from an old sheet and had splattered this and herself with artificial blood to make the effect more grotesque. What in God's name would induce a mother to do that to her children? Heaven alone knows.

Joe definitely inherited some of his mother's stubbornness and he also loved a prank with the kids, but these were always great fun. When Becci, Anthony's daughter and Joe's granddaughter was about six, she came to stay at Walkinstown. Joe loved to tease her about leprechauns, the little Irish fairy folk. 'Oh' he said, 'You very rarely see them. And if you do, they can change in a flash. Change into anything they like!' On Sunday morning after going to early mass, he rushed into the house where Ace and Becci were getting ready to leave for church at a more sensible hour.

'Becci! Becci!' he shouted, 'I've got a leprechaun trapped in the boot of the car. He's very angry so I can't show him to you now, but I will when you get back from Mass.'

Off they went, pausing at the car to listen for any noises coming from the boot.

Joe had arranged with a neighbour to borrow one of his homing pigeons, a white one. Once he knew the service was underway, he fetched the bird and carefully placed it in the boot of the car. When Becci and Ace returned, very excited, he was ready.

'Now' he said, 'We'll have to be very careful. The little feller's quiet now but he won't have liked being shut up for so long.' He had Becci's full attention. 'He may have changed into anything to escape. A cat, a bird or a spider.'

With that he opened the boot and right on cue the white dove flew out and up into the sky. Becci was entranced, as any kid would be.

Granny Donaghy would often travel down from Carlingford in the North, where she lived in later years, and stay with us in Walkinstown. She remained a trickster to her dying day but with her grandchildren these pranks usually took a fairly harmless, if not embarrassing form. We all had to be on our guard when she was in residence and all have stories to tell about her.

Anthony was expecting some posh friends from the Dublin Youth Orchestra over to tea. Mammy pulled out all her confectioner stops out and laid on a grand spread.

'Please don't let Granny come in' pleaded my elder brother.

'Sure, I'll do me best' says Mammy.

But, half-way through the meal, in she comes.

'Do you know, boys' she says, 'I had a terrible accident in the bathroom today.'

'Did you Mrs. Donaghy?'

'Yes, I did. My finger went right through the toilet paper!'

She was always sending us on errands. She said to me,

'Leo, will you go over to the shop and get me a wee quarter of those nice soft sugary jullies.'

'Yes, Granny' I said and off I'd go.

On returning, she'd peer into the bag and say,

'Ah, Leo, what did you waste my money on these for? You know I hate jullies!'

You couldn't win.

Martin, my younger brother, often had to bear the brunt of her humour. He was always short of money, particularly coming up to Christmas.

'Grannie, have you got any jobs I could do for you?'

'Sacred Heart of Jaysus, Mart'n. Oi've only got enough money for the Bingo.'

He looked dejected.

'But I know where there's a grand wee job going for yer.'

'Do you Granny. Where would that be?'

'Ah, they're looking for someone over at Super Quinns to take the blind turkeys out to shite!'

She was always getting him into trouble.

'Mart'n, will you go over to the shop and get me cigarettes!'

'Yes, Granny.'

When he returned, she gave him one for going, even lit it up for him. Then...

'Joe! Joe! Come in here. D'you know Martin's smoking!'

On another occasion Maria was due to bring Peter, her new boyfriend and future husband, home to meet the family for the first time. Granny had been staying with Theresa, her daughter in California, but was due back from America on the day of the planned visit. The last thing Maria said to her before Joe took her to the airport was,

'Granny, please, please don't swear or embarrass me in front of Peter.'

In her low gruff voice, like cinders under a door,

'I wouldn't do that to you, luv!'

The day of the visit arrived and again Mammy put on one of her special teas. Peter was lovely and everyone instantly liked him. All was going well but the conversation was interrupted by a loud honking from across the road in front of the school. Granny's taxi had arrived from the airport. We all went out to greet her. There she was, already attracting a crowd of kids from the green. She was a sight to behold wearing a large high straw hat and sunglasses, a floral shirt, bright red Bermuda shorts and, drooping below the legs of the shorts, a pair of pink, knee-length bloomers that had been given to her by Auntie Theresa. The first thing she said was,

'What d'you think of these knickers, Peter?'

On the eve of Maria's wedding day, she pulled another stunt. The girls' bedroom was full as the bridesmaids, Joan Foley and Valerie Whistler were staying over. They had the two divans and Maria was sleeping on the floor between them. The girls were just settling down for the night when Granny burst in brandishing a wet toilet brush, then, as a priest would spray his congregation with holy water, she proceeded to douse them with not-so-holy water.

'In de name of de Father, and of de Son, and of de Holy Ghost' she chanted. 'There now, you's all been christened for the morning!'

Not content with that. She started beating the dressing table with the brush handle.

'Ah, you'll feel one as hard as that tomorrow night, Maria!'

Granny Donaghy died in the girls' bedroom at Walkinstown at the age of seventy-one. Preparations were made to take her body back to Dungannon, so that she could be buried with Grandad. On the arranged day some sixty or so friends and relatives met at Walkinstown, where the cortege formed up behind the hearse to begin the fifty-mile journey to the North.

Granny wasn't done with us yet! The procession of ten cars had just gone through Drogheda, a town twenty-eight miles north of Dublin, where Saint Oliver Plunkett's head lies in state in a glass box for all to see. Through the town at a stately pace and off out into the countryside. Then, several miles from anywhere, the hearse got a puncture.

Now the Donaghy's are great tea drinkers and here was an ideal opportunity for a brew-up. While some of the men set about changing the tyre, Joe heads off to an isolated cottage he had spotted back along the road.

'Good-morning to you' says he to the little old lady who opens the door. 'Were off to Dungannon to bury me mother and the hearse has got a puncture. I wonder if there's any chance you could boil a kettle for us to make tea?'

'Ah, to be sure' says your lady, 'And how many are you?'

'There's sixty of us.'

'Oh, Mother of the Divine Virgin! You's better come in and give me a hand'.

Good to her word, she made endless pots of tea and, with typical Irish hospitality, out came the cakes and scones. Granny's funeral turned into a happy family picnic.

Chapter 8 – Down in the Valley.

Auntie Madge was a complete contrast to Grannie. Softly spoken and gentle, she would literally never harm a fly. Madge was a frequent visitor to Walkinstown Parade, as I was to her house. She played a big part in my early years. She was Mother's sister and they were very close. Both were glamorous women. Madge was always smartly dressed and wore earrings that shimmered when she talked. As a kid I was fascinated by those earrings and watched them for hours, completely hypnotized.

She lived about ten minutes from The Parade and I was allowed to make the journey there on my own. Just down the Long Mile road, past the school and left at the Kokonut Newsagents. The road then led down a hill, past the left turn that went to the Drimnagh Paper Mill, where Joe worked before it closed, and on into Lansdowne Valley. There was a small enclave of houses here and the area was known locally as The Valley.

Madge lived in a small bungalow that had originally belonged to her parents, the O'Donoghues. I liked nothing better than to sit with her over tea and cake listening to stories of the past, when she and Mammy were growing up there.

'You know Leo, I remember the first time we ever saw a car in The Valley. It belonged to Mr. Holland. He lived down the drive with the big gates. Your Mam and I watched it drive by with yer man and his wife sitting in the back-chauffeur driven of course. It started up the hill and, well, they were both big people you know and the whole thing tipped up on its back wheels. Can you imagine? The front wheels were spinning away up in the air. Well, to be sure, they had to go and get ropes and horses to pull it down again. What a gas.'

One story would then lead to another.

'Ah now' she said, 'talking of cars, your Uncle Bernard's a great driver. Sure, he only ever killed a horse.'

This apparently happened when her brother Bernard was driving through a local housing estate. The horse in question suddenly leapt over the garden hedge and landed on his bonnet. The people in the house totally denied any knowledge of the creature and said it must have strayed in – nothing to do with them.

On her parents' death she inherited the family home so that she could look after her younger brother Albert, who had heart trouble and couldn't work. Albert was known as 'Gertie'. We didn't know why, except that he was a great fan of Gertrude Lawrence. He had a beautiful tenor voice and used to sing with Joe Cooghan's Ceiligh Band, The Melody Five, along with another brother, Leo, who played the piano. Albert knitted all his own jumpers – powder blue was his favourite colour. He had a little plastic bag with a zip in which he kept his patterns and needles – if anyone visited it would disappear down the side of his chair.

In 1965 he travelled over to Birmingham's Queen Elizabeth Hospital to have a heart valve transplant operation. These were early days for open-heart surgery and very sadly he didn't get through the operation. I would like to have known him better. I think we might have had a lot in common.

When Madge eventually married, her new husband moved in with her. Larry grew vegetables and sold them round the streets from the back of a small van. One morning she'd asked him in for tea and cake and their romance started and blossomed over the carrots.

The bungalow was frequently full of neighbours. Mr. and Mrs. McLoughlan - we used to pinch their raspberries. Mamie and Willie Murphy – he had a grass allergy and Mona Clinton who never came in but was always chatting over the garden fence. Then there were the Muldooneys – they were another family who kept a horse in the front sitting-room. I'd give a whistle every time I passed and it would stick its head out of the window and neigh.

Nancy O'Rourk was Madge and Aileen's cousin. Her mother, Aunt Joe, often sat out on the front steps with her legs wide apart – we used to have great fun trying to see her knickers. Two other special friends of Madge were Anna Cavanah and Annie Weekes. Annie Weekes became my godmother and had a bad toe. We'd hear...

'Ah Madge, me poor toe.' And then, a few minutes later, 'Ah Madge, I'll have to go an soak me toe.'

We heard so much about this toe but never saw it. Well, we never saw it until we went away with her for a weekend. Madge, Annie, Anna and I spent a couple of nights down at Blessington Lake in Larry's old caravan. Just after breakfast on the Saturday morning...

'Madge, would yer have a drop of hot water there in a bowl. I'm after soaking me old toe in a spot of mustard.'

Anna, Madge and I watched as she slipped of an old canvas shoe and went to work lowering a dark elasticated stocking. Eventually the toe appeared in all its glory. I don't know whether we were looking at a bunion, a hammer toe, a large callus or a combination of all three but I saw a smirk coming over Anna Cavanah's face and then her cheeks began to wobble as she tried not to laugh out loud. This started me off and in the end we both fell out of the caravan door with uncontrollable laughing. We had to run down the field to hide our shame.

They were all very hospitable people down in The Valley but at the same time, didn't like anyone else knowing their business. When Madge hung the washing out, the sheets went on the line first to make a barrier from any prying eyes. Next came the towels and hidden away on the inner line, hers and Lar's underwear.

Like Mother, she was always baking and when she made sausage rolls, she'd often add a little secret ingredient – Heinz baked-beans. Anna Kavanagh appeared one day at a critical moment. The pastry was rolled out and the baked-bean tin was open. Just in time a tea- towel was thrown over the evidence.

'What are doing now Madge?'

'Arrr Anna, I just after baking some sausage rolls with Leo here.'

Anna couldn't resist peeping under the tea-towel. Madge was furious – her secret had been discovered.

64

There were lovely musical evenings down in The Valley. Joe Cooghan would come around with his accordion and Uncle Leo would get on the old piano in the corner of the lounge. All present would be expected to do their party pieces. Thomas and I couldn't wait for Mrs. Tute's turn to take the floor. Her piece de resistance was Bless This House.

> Bless this house, O Lord we pray,
> Make it safe by night and day.
> Bless these walls so firm and stout,
> Keeping want and trouble out...

What we were waiting for was the bit with the high notes right at the end.

> ...Bless us all that one day we
> May dwell, O Lord, with thee.

Mrs. Tute attacked these lines with vigour and a vibrato that would have done any opera house proud. At this point Thomas and I would collapse laughing and get ourselves thrown out in disgrace but there was always a twinkle in Auntie Madge's eye as she ushered us through the door.

Mrs. Tute would be followed on the floor by Annie Weekes, who had also been a great friend of Grannie O'Donoghue. She was a staunch Republican and loved to sing Rebel Songs. When she stood up we knew we were in for a rousing chorus of White Orange and Green.

> In the Boal Gouty Mountains, so far far away,
> I will tell you a story that happened one day,
> About a young girl her age was sixteen
> And she carried a banner White Orange and Green.

Annie claimed to have actually been shot at by the Black and Tans. She says she and Grannie were chased across the fields with bullets whizzing over their heads.

'Sure Leo, the cherries on me hat were bouncing up and down. It was a real gas.'

The third of the 'Beverley Sisters' was Dymphna Nolan and her party piece was I Dreamt I Dwelt in Marble Halls, a popular aria from the opera The Bohemian Girl by Michael William Balfe. Madge always claimed that Balfe was a distant relative as Grannie O'Donoghue had been a Balfe before marrying. Being from an opera, Dymphna's performance was always over the top with lots of dramatic hand gestures and facial expressions. She rarely got to the end of the first chorus before the younger members of the audience were again disgracing themselves and had to be expelled.

Madge was a very religious woman, who spent a lot of time in prayer and contemplation. She was a great believer in the power of the Saints and there were several plaster replicas placed around the house. Her pride and joy, in the centre of the mantelpiece, was an eighteen-inch-high statue of Our Lady of Fatima. She had a gold crown on top of her head and her long flowing cloak was painted with a luminous green paint that glowed in the dark. Underneath, in the base, was a key you could wind up and it would play The Bells of Saint Mary's.

When Madge and Larry moved up from the Valley to a larger bungalow in Clondalkin, she was delighted to find a statue of the Child of Prague discarded in the garden. This particular saint was supposed to have a great influence over the weather. If you had an important outdoor function coming up, you placed The Child outside the front door on the night before.

'Ah, Joe' she said to my father, 'Isn't that great. That's a little miracle now. But d'you know Joe, they say it's very lucky if the head is broken off. Imagine that now!'

Joe didn't need asking twice. He took The Child by its feet and slammed it against the nearest wall – the head went flying.

'There you are, Madge' he says, 'You'll have lots of luck now!'

'Ah no' she says in a soft whisper, 'You're a gas, Joe.'

Thomas and I loved to take Madge to the cinema.

'Ah now, you won't take me to another horror movie will yer?'

'Of course not, Auntie Madge, I think it's Cinderella, or The Sound of Music.'

'That's what yer said last time.'

'You'll be fine Madge. You love the musicals now, don't you?'

'Ah, I do.'

The conversation was always the same and really we were taking her to see Dracula or some other Hammer House of Horror thriller. Once the lights went down, we had her. Sitting between us she'd grip our hands with tension and when Count Dracula's coach came hurling round the corner with a wheel hanging over the cliff she'd scream at the top of her voice, as we knew she would. It would make us roar with laughter. On one occasion she even managed to get us thrown out for making so much noise.

Poor Madge. She put up with a lot from Thomas and me but always forgave us and came back for more - we loved her for it.

Whenever a wedding was held at the Walkinstown church you could be sure that Madge would be there, along with the other women from the Parade. They'd come to see the bride and groom leave at the end of the service. When the couple appeared at the church door, whatever the bride looked like, Madge would say,

'Ah, isn't she beautiful.'

There was one local couple I remember. He had a large scar that ran down the side of his face and never ever smiled. The bride had an extraordinarily long face with a very wide mouth and horse-like teeth.

'Ah' said Madge, 'Isn't she beautiful. She reminds me of the Virgin Mary.'

Another group who always attended weddings was the local kids - Thomas, Rory and myself included. We certainly weren't there for the bride. We were waiting for the grushie. This is a Celtic tradition and the word literally means 'healthy and thriving' and was meant to get the bride and groom off to a good start. At the appropriate moment, after the photos, some kid would shout,

'Eh mister! Are you going to do a grushie?'

As the happy couple made their way to the wedding car, someone, usually the best man, would hurl a handful of sweets and coins into the air in the general direction of the waiting kids. I think its modern-day aim was to get us all out of the way and it certainly succeeded. There would be a near riot as we all scrambled for the money (we could get the sweets later). Mainly pennies and threepenny bits but you did get the odd shilling and on one happy day I managed to pick up a half-crown piece.

One of the highlights of the Catholic calendar for Madge, and for many others throughout Ireland, was the Novena to Our Lady of Lourdes at Inchicore. Inchicore, like all the other villages on the outskirts of Dublin, had long been swallowed up by the expanding city. However, it retained a village-like atmosphere and at the centre, standing in its own grounds, was the Church of Mary Immaculate - known locally to this day as the Oblates. The name came from the Monastic Order of Oblate Fathers who built and run the church. You'd hear the women on the bus saying,

'Will you drop me off at the Oblates, there's a good man.'

Behind the Church is a full-size replica of the Grotto of Lourdes in France. Built of reinforced concrete in 1930 it stands 50 feet high, 130 feet wide and 40 feet deep. Nestling in a niche, her feet surrounded by burning candles, is a statue of the Virgin Mary. Pilgrims visit the shrine all the year, but it becomes particularly busy in early February when the Novena takes place.

What a lot of the pilgrims don't know is that, housed in the bowels of the grotto, is the famous Inchicore Crib with its life-sized wax models depicting well known biblical scenes from the Nativity. This was always opened to the public throughout the Christmas festivities each year and then again on 11 February, the last night of the Novena.

We kids would usually be taken at some point or other over the Christmas period, often on Saint Stephen's Day. However, to get to see the Christmas scene again in

February was a very special treat. There was a price to pay. We'd have to sit through Mass, the Benediction and five decades of the Rosary before the priest would finally announce,

'Now, as we come to the end of this Novena, as we do every year, we're going to open the Crib. I hope all you pilgrims will take this opportunity to pay your respects to the Christ Child.'

That was the cue for the congregation to form up into a torch-lit procession which would wind its way out of the church and round the grounds to the Grotto. There followed a bit of a hold-up while the locks were taken off but, eventually we were allowed in through the wooden door at the side, into the Crib itself.

The first scene that greeted you inside, on the left, was the Inn Keeper. A six-foot high waxwork, his outstretched arms parting a multi-coloured beaded curtain – the sort used to keep flies out of kitchens. You knew his open mouth was saying,

'There's no room at the inn!'
Seated behind him on the other side of the curtain, at a small round table, were two or three of the Inn's patrons.

Moving past the Inn, a desert mural was painted on the wall. There were a couple of papier-mâché palm trees here and a lot of sand on the floor. The desert led you through to the next scene. In the corner of the building, backed by a Bedouin tent, was a small group of shepherds guarding two very stiff looking sheep.

Round the next corner you found the Three Wise Men in all their splendour and then the Nativity scene itself. The crib holding the Baby Jesus was watched over by Mary,

Joseph, one ox (with a horn missing) and one ass. Masses of straw, both bailed and loose, surrounded them on the floor.

When I recently made a nostalgic return visit, it was at the Crib scene that I bumped into Margaret, an old neighbour of my Mother's.

'Now Leo, I'm telling you,' she said in a reverent voice, 'You take a bit of dat straah and put it in the glove compartment of yer car. You'll never have an accident. Dat's God's honest truth!'

This return visit took place after a fire that had unfortunately melted a lot of the wax figures. Some had been remodelled but I couldn't help noticing that one of the patrons at the inn had become female and was wearing a nylon headscarf with a rather natty horse-shoe pattern printed on it. A couple of tailor's dummies had appeared amongst the shepherds and one of these was sporting a blonde Jimmy Hendrix wig.

The final scene, as you approached the exit, was the wicked Herod seated on a gold throne. Again, on my return visit, I couldn't help overhearing a woman say,

'Jaysus, would you look at him! The Devil to be sure! He had a wicked turn in him. May God forgive him.'

If Madge had a fault at all it was that she was not very good at time keeping. Invariably she would run behind schedule. Not just a few minutes but anything from thirty minutes to an hour and a half. When she and Larry were joining us on a family outing Joe always gave her a meeting time an hour before we were due to set off.

She quite often acted 'in loco parentis' and most of the time, the lateness wasn't a problem. However, if something important, like an elocution competition, was taking place, that was a different matter. At the age of six Ace had decided that I needed elocution lessons. She said my accent was worse than a downtown Dub and something had to be done. So, every Saturday, off I went to the Father Matthew Hall in Dublin to be taught to speak properly. I quite enjoyed the classes. I looked on them as an outlet for my aesthetic side and a good chance to show-off.

Come the day of the competition, Madge was due to pick me up at two o'clock and take me in on the bus. When she eventually arrived, it was nearly three and we had a mad dash into town. We arrived at the hall puffing and panting and were about to sit down in the waiting area when a woman came in and said,

'Will Leo Donaghy please come through.'

I stood in front of the judges trying to get my breath.

'Timothy Dan by John D. Sheridan.'

> Timothy Dan is a very rich man,
> And he keeps all his wealth in his pockets:
> Four buttons, a box, the keys of two clocks,
> And the chain of his grandmother Margaret's locket.
> A big piece of string (It's a most useful thing),
> A watch without hands, and three rubber bands,
> Five glassy marbles, some tail ends of chalk,
> A squeaker that once made a golliwog talk,
> A broken-down penknife with only one blade,
> And a little toy boat that his grandfather made.
> You'd never believe (hearing such a long list)

That there's room in each pocket for one little
fist;
You'd never believe that the smallest of boys
Could carry so much in his wee corduroys.

I got to the end without any mistakes.

'Thank you, Leo. That was very nice. You can go back to the waiting room now.'

My main rival in the competition was another six-year-old boy called Declan Smith. He lived in The Valley, just up the lane from Madge and his mother had a cat called Flicker. When the results were announced Declan got the first prize. I was pushed into second place – I'm sure it was because of my asthmatic performance.

I couldn't blame Madge for long – I loved her too much. She took me into Bewley's in Grafton Street for tea and almond buns and the competition was soon forgotten.

Chapter 9 – Boys' Games.

Despite Bridie's efforts Thomas and I would not be parted. Whilst other boys on the Parade spent their time playing football, going fishing or just hanging around, we went off in search of 'glamour'. We were ten or eleven years old and liked nothing better than to walk, talk and dream.

One of our favourite walks was off up St. Peter's Road, towards The Rise and The Goat pub. This was an area that we considered to be really posh. There were detached houses with proper front gardens – not the sort that were paved over to park the car on. We loved to go up there in search of windows with 'nice things' in them. We'd stop and stare in and discuss the people who lived there and what they did – you could tell so much from the colour and design of the curtains. This was particularly fun at Christmas when all the windows were filled with lights, Christmas trees and other wonderful things.

Someone we both thought of as really glamorous was the daughter of my next-door neighbour, Mrs. Mangan – she had a wooden leg. At least we thought it was made of wood but I'm sure it wasn't. Her daughter, Phyllis, was in her twenties and we used to follow her up the street. She had a fabulous pair of boots with white fur around the tops and high heels that went 'clickerty-click' as she walked. We were captivated by those boots and soon set about making our own. The boots themselves were easy to copy - we just turned the top of our Wellingtons down to reveal the white lining inside. It took some time to emulate the noise of her heels, but we eventually found that by tying seashells under our boots with string, we could produce a pretty fair imitation.

Shoe Shops was one of our favourite games. We collected dozens of pairs of shoes and set them out round the kitchen floor. At that time Uncle Larry had given up his vegetable round and now worked as a traveller for the Festival Shoe Company. He had a great supply of samples and was persuaded to lend them out for the Doyle-Donaghy shop. One day he brought home a box of gold rings that had been used as decoration on some style or other. We certainly put those to good use. We linked them into gold chains and turned our simple sandals into fabulous court shoes. Anyone passing through the kitchen was immediately sat down to have their feet measured. One of the two friendly assistants would then force their feet, Cinderella style, into assorted shapes and sizes of footwear.

If no-one else was around, we'd take it in turns to be the sales assistant or the customer. Being the customer was the best because we got to try on all our fabulous creations. On one occasion we borrowed a pair of shoes from my sister Maria. They were little mules with amber-glass heels and a sparkly elastic strap across the front. She loved those shoes – and so did we! They were tried on so many times in our shop and walked up and down the stone kitchen floor till eventually one of the heels broke. We got into serious trouble that day and the shop had to be closed for a very long time.

Women's clothes seemed to feature in a lot of our make-believe. If we couldn't borrow 'em, we'd make 'em. Coats turned inside out with the satin-like lining on the outside made excellent dresses. With the sleeves tied round our waists, we could lift the bottom edge like a dress whilst going up stairs, or, trail it behind us like a train when going down. On another occasion I made a dress from a circle of card that I fixed round my waist. Over this I draped a couple of mother's silk scarves. It looked so elegant and gave me great pleasure.

On the first of May each year the Feast of Our Lady was celebrated, culminating in the May Day Procession round the Green and into church. All the children would dress up. The young girls would wear their white first communion dresses and veils, with a lot of blue and white crepe paper in evidence to enhance the 'virginal' effect. The boys, of course, had to make-do with their Sunday-best.

Thomas and I weren't going to see all that crepe paper go to waste. The next day we dressed, not only ourselves, but several other kids and had our own procession round the green.

Sandie Shaw was another great influence in the sixties. Barefooted and with miniskirts made out of newspaper wrapped round our short trousers, we'd take it in turns to stand on the pillar at the church gate and perform. Pretend microphones in hand (old torches) we'd belt out 'Puppet on a String' – the year was 1967, we must have been twelve!

Then there was Eileen Reid, a Dublin Country and Western singer who made her name with The Cadets' Showband. A recent photograph shows her with her hair in a bob, but in those days, she was well known for the height of her beehive. Sitting on the bottom of our stairs, Thomas and I made beehives with our home-knitted pullovers. Pulling them up over our heads till they reached the hairline, we pulled the sleeves inside-out and wrapped them round in coils over the top. We were all set for a rousing chorus of 'I Gave My Wedding Dress Away', Eileen's hit of the day.

We even managed to turn a school trip to a football match into an occasion for dressing up and acting. Dublin Rovers were playing at Croke Park, the heart of Irish sporting life for many a year. Of course, most of the boys were very excited about the outing. Thomas and I stood there on the terraces, surrounded by a sea of green and white scarves, our heads splitting with the noise of the cheering around us – so boring! By the time the second half started, we'd had enough. We'd seen the tunnels that ran around the stadium under the seating and our active minds transformed them into the Coliseum for another rendition of our favourite Ben Hur. My coat came off and as I walked down the steps it trailed behind like a cape. We were in an imaginary world of emperors (and empresses). The cheering of the crowds was all for us, not the men running around the pitch.

A Tale of Two Cities was another film that provided great play opportunities. We avidly watched the 1958 black and white version on television. It starred Dirk Bogarde and Dorothy Tutin and was set at the time of the French

Revolution. There were aristocrats in it, who rode round Paris in their carriages – Thomas and I required no further inspiration for our fertile imaginations. A trolley, or gig as we called it, was acquired to convert into our carriage. It consisted of a plank with a set of old pram wheels front and back. Joe was instructed to bring home a large cardboard box from Clondalkin Paper Mills, where he was now working. This was attached to the plank with nails and windows cut in the sides. The local kids were again roped in as extras and this time took the part of French peasants and horses. Thomas and I, of course, played the part of aristocrats. As we were pulled past the peasantry, they were instructed to look hungry and shout out,

'Can't you help? Oh, please Sirs, we're starving, can't you help?'

We, holding lace hankies to our noses against the smell, replied,

'Drive on, drive on! I can pay nothing. I haven't enough money for my perfume!'

Oscars all round.

At the end of the game the cardboard box wasn't put to waste. It next appeared as a cocktail cabinet. Thomas and I went round Walkinstown collecting old glass lemonade bottles. You used to get three-pence back on each bottle you returned to the Kokonut Newsagent. We raised enough cash to purchase a large bottle of fizzy cherryade, borrowed a few glasses from the kitchen and opened a very glamorous cocktail lounge in the boys' bedroom.

Our next venture was The Count of Monte Cristo. We decided this had to be staged in Drimnagh Castle and at night. The Castle was strictly out of bounds to everyone at all times, let alone after dark but that wasn't going to stop us.

Beyond the outer wall with its large wooden gate was a health and safety nightmare. The castle itself was in ruins. Everywhere you looked there were fallen roofs, missing windows and partly collapsed masonry. But we'd seen the remains of several stone staircases which would be ideal for our games.

One of the older Christian Brothers kept a few chickens in the Castle gardens. After he had fed them in the evening and gone back for his own supper, we saw a window of opportunity for some reconnoitring. We discovered that the small door that was set into the main gate, was usually left unlocked.

This was what we needed to know and one moonlit night (it was probably only about half-past seven) we went for it. Creeping past the Brothers' house we reached the Castle and crossed the bridge that spanned the moat. The little door was open and there we were, inside, in what were the remains of the great hall.

There were only two parts in our drama and Thomas and I took it in turns to be the Count. We put on our costumes – a cloak for the count and a long dress for the lady in distress who had to be rescued. We lit our jam-jar lanterns with their string handles and a candle stub stuck into the bottom of each. Then, up onto the stone staircases and we were off.

'Do be quick m'lady. Come this way. Follow me.'

'Oh sir, sir! Do wait. My heart will burst.'

'There's no time m'lady. I fear our escape will be discovered.'

'But sir, I must rest a while.'

'Then sit here for a moment to gain your breath. I will stand guard.'

That basically was the script. Nothing more and nothing less but it kept us amused for hours.

Chapter 10 – Halloween.

Halloween has always been an important festival in Ireland and in fact, may well have been invented there. The Celts celebrated an End of Summer Festival when large communal bonfires would be lit to ward off evil spirits. In some parts it is still called 'Pooky Night' after the Gaelic word 'puca', a mischievous spirit.

Whilst Trick or Treat is a relatively new activity for British children, it was a well-established part of our childhood back in the fifties and sixties and, of course, provided another great opportunity to dress up. The evening of 31 October would see all the local kids out and about dressed as ghosts, witches and goblins.

'Help the Halloween Party!' was the plea as we knocked on as many doors as possible. Times weren't as affluent then and the usual contributions received into our mother's shopping bags were a few boiled sweets, or maybe some monkey-nuts. You did get an occasional apple or orange and, if you were really lucky, a threepenny bit.

All the goodies were taken home, supplemented with some home baking and the feasting would begin. Ghost stories were told, and we played frightening games like being blindfolded and sticking your finger into a dead man's eye – an egg-cup full of cold mashed potato.

Trick or Treat was strictly a children's festival but one particular year, Grannie Donaghy decided she was going to join in. Her fancy-dress, for some reason known only to herself, was a dead fisherman. She put on a pair of giant waders she'd found in Joe's shed, an oversized jumper and blackened her face with soot from the fire. There was no question of a slog round the houses to get goodies. True to form, she chased all the kids with blood-curdling cries of,

'Hand over yer monkey nuts!'

And they did.

The Halloween night I remember most was 1967. I was twelve and had recently started at Secondary school. Never ones to miss an opportunity of putting on a dress, Thomas, myself and, after a lot of persuasion, Rory as well, decided that we would forego the ghost and witch theme on this occasion and 'glam up'.

It took a bit of planning. The most difficult thing was to get Thomas's Mum to agree. After a lot of abject pleading and fingers-crossed swearing,

'I'll never do it again, Mammy,' she finally relented but she wasn't happy,

'Jaysus Thomas, would you not rather dress up as a pirate?'

Miniskirts were all the rage at the time. Maria, now nearly eighteen, was well into the fashion and had a good supply. She, along with the other sisters and mothers, were persuaded to part with blouses, scarves and high heeled shoes. Make-up consisted of some soot rubbed onto our eyebrows and a bit of lipstick. The crowning glory to our creations were the three synthetic wigs we bought from Woolies, at five shillings a piece. They were made of high-sheen nylon and had plaits. Rory's was black. Thomas's was red. Mine was blonde. Mine started with plaits but, as usual, I wanted to be different. The plaits were undone and converted into bunches tied with enormous pink ribbons.

We were adamant that we weren't going round the houses with our mother's old shopping bags. We had proper handbags that matched our outfits – we just loved the 'click' the catches made each time the bags were opened or closed.

It is true to say that a few of the other boys did dress up as girls - but they had no style and looked more like Pantomime Dames which, I suppose, may have been their aim. At any rate, they weren't a patch on us.

The three of us arranged to meet on the green at seven o'clock. We started our rounds by knocking at the doors of the Parade where we were all well known for our antics. Usually the women came to the door on Trick or Treat night and we were very well received. Maureen McCarthy was typical.

'Leo, Thomas, Rory. Sure, you'd never know it was you's!'

She roared with laughter and then her husband was called out from whatever he was watching on the television.

'Patrick, will you come and look at the boys. Ah, you look fabulous, girls.' We were greatly encouraged.

Our next port of call was Kilnamanagh Road, where our friend Pather lived, and then the houses along Walkinstown Road. The reception was the same everywhere we went. The handbags were clicked open and shut many times and began to bulge. By the time we reached the Halfway House the adrenaline was flowing, and we were really hyped up. No doubt about it, the three of us, even Rory, loved walking around in dresses.

Now, the Halfway House is a working-mans' pub and on normal occasions we wouldn't have dreamed of going anywhere near it. But on this night... well... in we went. A great roar went up,

'Holy Mother of fuck, would you look at these three gorgeous girls!'

'I'll tell you what Paddy, if my wife looked like that, I'd be feckin' well in!'

'If my wife looked like that, I'd go home more often.'

We were paraded round the bar and sat on a number of the men's laps where we were touched, cuddled, kissed on the cheek and generally made a fuss of. It gave us a great feeling. We loved the attention, all the compliments and especially the touching. Even the barman joined in.

'Can I get you three ladies a drink?'

'Thank you, we'll have orange juice.'

'Are you sure you wouldn't like a wee glass o'sherry?'

Everyone found this very funny and egged us on but we thought it would be safer to stick to the orange juice.

The men were generous too and it wasn't threepenny bits they were giving us. There were one-shilling coins, two-shilling coins and even one half-crown – a fantastic half-hour!

We were now on the Long Mile Road, which led up past the schools and back to Walkinstown Parade. Halfway along, between the primary and secondary schools, was the house where the Christian Brothers lived - an imposing building with great curved steps leading up to a double front door. This was not a place you would normally go Trick or Treating. The men who lived there generally terrified us boys. But tonight, we weren't boys. We were girls. Wearing the dresses, we were disguised and greatly emboldened.

'Let's do it' we said.

Up the steps we went and lifted the heavy knocker. We listened to the hollow sound it made, reverberating around the hall behind the door. Half of me wanted to turn and run but we could hear footsteps coming towards us.

The door opened to reveal a young Brother none of us had seen before - a handsome man, with thick black hair and a lovely smile.

'Help the Halloween Party, Brother' Thomas said.

He hesitated for a moment, glancing over his shoulder back into the hall, to see if any of the other Brothers had followed. They hadn't. He stepped out and closed the door behind him.

This was not the response we had expected. Quite obviously he was delighted to see us.

'Ah, you look great, girls' he said. 'Let's go for a stroll over to the Castle. It's not often I get a chance to go walking with three young ladies.'

With this, he put his arms round our shoulders and ushered us down the steps and round the side of the house. As we walked over to the Castle, he kept up a banter. He asked about our costumes. Where had we been and had we been well received? This was a new experience of what a Christian Brother could be like and he put us totally at ease. We got to the moat and he said,

'Now, which of you three maidens am I going to carry over the drawbridge?'

We waited in anticipation as he thoughtfully stroked his chin, looking us over while he made his choice – and he chose me! He scooped me up off the ground. His left arm supported my back and I had my right arm round his neck. His right arm was under my bare legs. As we made our way across the drawbridge with the other two boys following behind, his hand gradually slid up my thigh. Up under my miniskirt it went, coming to rest under my bottom. And there it stayed, gently massaging my buttocks.

He carried me through the little wooden door set in the main gate and into the great hall where we had played the Count of Monte Christo. Here he set me down. There were a few chickens scurrying around and we watched them for a while.

By now it was really getting quite late and we were expected home. Reluctantly we said we'd have to go and made our way back to the main road. As soon as he was out of sight the questions began.

'Did he touch you?'

'Well… er… yes.'

'Did he touch your mickey?'

'NO!'

'Did you like it?'

Oh yes, I liked it. I liked it a lot.

Looking back, 31 October 1967 was a really significant night in my young life. Up to that point I had dressed up, on the whole, for my own benefit. I enjoyed it. Women's clothes felt right on me. Yes, some adults, especially my parents, were quite amused by my antics. Others, Mrs. Doyle among them, were not.

'Foolishness!' was her verdict.

That Halloween night, things had been different. The adults had really enjoyed my performance. I'd received compliments on my clothes and my looks. They'd said I looked gorgeous. I had been cuddled and touched – and in the case of the young Christian Brother, touched quite intimately. It had been a wonderful evening and I felt, perhaps for the first time in my life, really special.

As I thought about this over the next few days, went over the events of that night in my mind, an idea began to form. If dressing up as a woman was the way to get attention from men, then maybe, just maybe, this would be the answer to a problem that Thomas and I had talked about on several occasions. Something we both knew we badly wanted. Something we didn't know how to get. That 'something' was kisses from boys!

Chapter 11 – For Real.

And so it was, at the age of twelve, Thomas and I began dressing up 'for real'. Rory was not included in this. Halloween had been his limit and, as Thomas and I grew closer together, he was now drawing apart and mixing with other friends.

Our first outings were very simple affairs, nothing more than a headscarf and a bit of lipstick. It has to be remembered that in those days, all boys had really short back-and-sides haircuts. Girls, if they went out on the town, always wore a head scarf. Thus, it didn't take much ingenuity to change sex.

The very first Saturday evening that we sneaked out of the house with our bits and pieces was so exciting. We had scarves 'borrowed' from our mothers, a small hand mirror to apply our lipstick (one of Maria's) and a wet flannel in a plastic bag to remove it after we returned.

'What are you two up to?'

'Nothing Mam, we're just going for a walk.'

'What's all the giggling for?'

'Nothing!'

'How long will you be?'

'Why's she asking so many questions,' I thought.

'Make sure you're not late back.'

The sky was almost dark as we ran across the green into the Infant School grounds. Behind the nuns' house was a shrubbery and there we planned to hide and make our transformation.

Out of sight in the safety of the bushes and with the help of the mirror, we applied our lipstick. We folded our scarves into triangles, just as we'd seen our mothers and sisters do, and tied them under our chins. The lipstick and mirror were put in the plastic bag with the wet flannel and hidden under a bush. There was nothing more to it. We both wore long Duffle coats which hid our short trousers and shirts. We were ready! We had brought one other prop with us and that was a couple of schoolbooks. These were to be held in front of our chests to hide the obvious fact that we had no breasts.

Although it was nearly dark, our hearts were pounding, and I could feel the beads of sweat on my forehead. We made our way out of the safety of the shrubbery, through the back entrance of the school grounds and onto the Long Mile Road.

The road was deserted. We linked arms, kept our heads down and set off at a fast pace in the direction of the Kokonut Newsagents. We'd practiced our walk so many times - small paces, one foot in front of the other – and now we were doing it for real. I couldn't believe it. A couple of hundred yards took us past the turn down to The Valley, where Madge lived. Once past there we felt we could slow a little. We reached The Kokonut, which was still open and there were now one or two other people around – carrying a pint of milk or the late edition of the Evening Herald. We passed them holding our breath, but no-one seemed to pay any attention to us. The plan was to keep our heads down, no eye-contact with anyone and definitely no speaking. We expected to be discovered at any second. It just had to be a matter of time before someone shouted,

'Are you's two queer?' Followed by goodness knows what. But it didn't come.

After about ten minutes walking we reached the Star Cinema, or The Rats as we called it (Star backwards). Here something did happen. We got our first wolf-whistle – from two teenage boys on the other side of the road. It was so, so exciting. We allowed ourselves a quick glance up and smiled across at them, but no more. We kept on moving.

By now the time was nearly nine o'clock. We were only allowed out on our own one night a week, usually a Saturday, and the rule was that you got home by nine thirty at the latest. Any later and there'd be real trouble and that would have been it for the following week.

We made our way back up the Long Mile and into the school grounds. Once in the safety of the shrubbery we just couldn't contain our excitement. We'd done it. We'd got away with it. As the lipstick was removed, we just laughed and laughed. Very careful checks were made to make sure that every trace of make-up had gone. The scarves were stuffed into the pockets of our coats to be returned to our mothers and we emerged from the bushes, two different people. Different, not only in our physical looks but completely different mentally. Suddenly, for the first time in our young lives, we'd found a real freedom.

With such a confidence boost we couldn't wait for the following weekend. For seven days we talked about nothing else as we tried to decide what we would do on our second outing.

Saturday night finally arrived, and we were back again in the school shrubbery. After the simple transformation we once again headed off up the Long Mile Road. I was now Maria and Thomas was Tina, the names we had chosen for ourselves.

The plan this time was to catch a bus and go a bit further afield. We reasoned that we were less likely to bump into anyone we knew – but things don't always work out as you want! It would have been too risky getting on the 50 or 56 which ran into town directly past the end of our road. There were always neighbours traveling on these routes and we were sure we would be recognised. We walked up to The Rats and caught a number 23 to Ballybough.

After a few stops we got off and, like the first night, held our books tight to our chests. We then just walked up and down. This time though, we were more relaxed and felt able to stop and look in the shop windows. We also felt confident enough to speak to each other. Neither of our voices was near to breaking so there was no reason why anyone should be suspicious. We chatted away and practiced our feminine walk and our feminine gestures. After about half an hour we caught the 23 in the opposite direction for the journey home. No problems on the bus - another successful evening. Disappointingly there had been no wolf-whistles but we did feel that we had made some progress.

Walking back home up the Long Mile we felt really happy and at ease. We'd passed The Valley turn-off and were about level with Drimnagh Castle when we saw him walking towards us. It was Willie Byrne. Willie Byrne aged twelve and in our class at school. He had his hands in his pockets and appeared to be looking at the ground. Our first thought was to cross the road, but the traffic was solid and fast moving. There just wasn't enough time. He was approaching rapidly and there was absolutely nothing we could do! We took a deep breath, put our heads down and, arm in arm, kept going. We came up level with him. Nothing happened. We walked on and for a moment we dared to think,

'Oh God, we've got away with it.'

Just as we were about to breathe out,

'Hi Leo. Hi Thomas.'

That was it - we'd been caught. Our new life was over before it had even started. On Monday morning at school we would be exposed and be the laughingstock of Walkinstown. The whole night had turned into our worst nightmare.

The rest of the weekend passed slowly and miserably. When Monday morning did finally arrive, I waited for Thomas and we made our way across the green and into school to await our fate. There was no sign of Willie in the playground. The first we saw of him was in the classroom. He was chatting to two or three boys but none of them was looking our way and sniggering. In the lunchbreak he came up to me and asked something about the next lesson. I can't remember what but there was no mention of Saturday night. By home-time we were feeling a little more relaxed.

We needn't have worried. Willie said nothing on that or any subsequent day. I don't know why he didn't snitch on us. You would have thought that with a story like that he would have been up on a soap box with a crowd round him. But no, everything was as normal. The next day we both spoke to him as though nothing untoward had happened and we both heaved a great sigh of relief. Tina and Maria would live another day.

After that scare a few weeks passed before we felt bold enough to venture out again. Neither of us considered the question of not dressing again. This was something we both badly wanted to do and having started we weren't about to give up at the first hurdle. We did make a decision though. We would have to find somewhere a bit further from home where we could change and change back more safely. This became essential when, as the Saturdays went by, our costumes became more elaborate and daring. We acquired skirts, blouses and jumpers – all borrowed without the owners' knowledge. Then came hairpieces, shoes and handbags - and of course, a more elaborate make-up box.

In The Valley, behind Madge and Larry's house, were the old derelict factory buildings that were once the home of Drimnagh Paper Mill, before it closed and moved up to Clondalkin. They were now disused and stood quite empty and isolated on a large area of waste ground surrounded by a wire fence. Thomas and I were exploring one day when we found a small gap in the wire. After checking that there was no-one around, we squeezed through, pulling the gap closed behind us. These buildings had distinct possibilities, we thought, and warranted a full exploration.

As we made our way round the main building, we came to some stone steps leading down to some sort of cellar. At the bottom of the steps was a fairly sturdy looking wooden door but on further investigation, it became clear that the padlock holding it shut was broken. A sharp tap with a brick knocked it off and allowed us to gain entry.

Once inside we found ourselves in a large basement room. The ceiling was supported by a series of rusty iron pillars that dripped water. The whole place smelt damp. The floor was strewn with all sorts of factory debris and rubbish. It didn't look very promising. Moving round we came across a door which opened into what must have been a small office area. This appeared to be drier than the rest of the place. It had wooden shelves around the walls and a small dirty window, covered in cobwebs, that let a little natural light in. This was it - exactly what we were looking for. The ideal secret changing room. Our clothes and props could be wrapped in plastic bags to protect them from the damp and stored on the shelves. It would be great not having to sneak them out of the house every time we went on an outing. We set about tidying the place up, cleaned the window, installed a mirror and moved in.

In the early days our outings were restricted to Saturday nights only. As we became bolder, we went out in the week as well. Having all the gear in the factory changing room made it so much easier. At first, it was strictly at dusk but as our confidence grew, we had trips out during the day as well. We became brave enough to talk to people. After all, our prime aim was to draw attention to ourselves, particularly from boys.

The changing became a well-rehearsed routine. Thomas and I would meet up after tea and head off down to The Valley. After checking no-one was around, we'd slip through the wire fence and then down the steps into our hidey-hole. Sometimes we carried additional items, borrowed for the evening to vary or enhance our costumes.

We were still wearing our own white vests and pants as underwear. The latter were small Y-fronts, so we reckoned we'd get away with it. We always kept our shirts on under our blouses, just in case we had to make a quick change back. We carefully folded the cuffs up and the collars down so that they couldn't be seen. We learnt to put on bras, which we stuffed out with our socks. The next advance was a pair of stockings – this was in the days before tights. We couldn't run to suspender belts, so they had to be held up with a couple of school ties looped around the top of each leg and tied in a bow. The top of the stocking was then rolled down over the tie to conceal it. Then came the dress, or sometimes a blouse with a jumper and skirt. Finally, our pride and joy, the high heeled shoes. After all the practice we'd done we were now very confident on heels.

Having dressed, we applied our make-up. As the weeks went by our range of cosmetics, and expertise in applying them, grew. From the original lipstick our box now contained a Rimmel foundation cream, mascara for our eyebrows and a lavender eyeshadow. We later progressed to false eyelashes, as these saved a lot of time in changing and changing back. And we now had a choice of lipsticks.

After the make-up came the crowning glory – our two hairpieces. We had acquired these from a Dublin Department store - acquired them for our sisters of course!

They were chignons of ringlets and were bright auburn. The colour actually didn't matter as little of them would be seen under the headscarves. They were pinned onto the back of our own fair hair where their function was to make our scarves stand out and look more realistically female.

Every stage of the transformation was carefully checked in the mirror with the help of a small torch. Our own clothes were put in the plastic bags and placed back on the shelves. We were ready.

We listened very carefully before emerging and tip-toed up the stone steps on the balls of our feet. We didn't want any clicking of heels giving us away before we were certain there was no-one around.

Having got through the fence we would set off in the opposite direction to the way we had come in. The path led around the factory, across the waste ground and down into the valley where the river Camac ran. This was a tributary of the Liffey and was rumoured to be rat infested. Although we never saw one, we were always very aware of the possibility, especially in the dark. After walking along the bank, we crossed a small bridge to the other side and followed the footpath up out of the valley onto the Dublin Road at Bluebell. The Bluebell estate must have been nearly a mile from Walkinstown. We felt at ease there. It was unlikely that we'd meet anyone we knew.

Some evenings we just went for long walks. Sometimes we went into Inchicore, where the Crib was and also a cinema. One night we stopped at a shop and bought twenty Rothmans King Sized filters, went to the cinema and smoked the lot. We liked the cinema and, in the dark, felt secure enough to take our headscarves off. This released the curls of our chignons which we could toss to our heart's content.

The evenings seemed to fly by, but we were always aware that we had to get back and changed so as to be home by ten at the very latest (the nine thirty deadline had now been extended). We wanted to stretch it out for as long as possible, so invariably we had a last-minute panic back at the den. Off came the dress. The socks were whipped out of our bras and back onto our feet. Hair pieces turned inside out and put back into their bags. Our shirts sorted out and our anoraks on. There were occasions when we had to leave our stockings on under our long grey school trousers to make it in time. Thomas was always frantic to make sure every trace of make-up had been removed and cold cream had been added to the wet flannel to help in this task.

One night when he got home his little sister Grainne called out,

'Mammy, our Thomas's got make-up on his face!'

'I haven't' shouted Thomas, as he rushed up stairs to lock himself in the bathroom.

'Ah Jaysus, Sean' said Bridie. 'What are we going to do with him?'

Chapter 12 – Sex in the City.

Thomas and I talked incessantly about sex. Though it must be said, the actual word 'Sex' was never mentioned. In the sixties it just wasn't in the vocabulary of a young Irish boy, or girl for that matter. It wasn't a word we heard our parents using. We didn't hear it at school. We didn't hear it in the films we went to see or on the television programmes we watched. 'Nuding' was the descriptive term schoolboys used at the time to indicate close physical contact and nuding was what we talked about.

We spent hours watching men and youths. We talked about their looks, their sideburns, their triangular backs, their thin waists and their meaty buttocks. We talked about the clothes they wore. We talked about taking off the clothes they wore! We wanted to nude them. We even invented our own words so that we could have open discussions in company at any time. 'Arragive' meant attractive. A tall, dark, handsome, highly desirable young man was a 'Manacancheska' – after a Mongolian warrior of the same name that we had been attracted to in a film.

We were becoming desperate, absolutely desperate, for some form of physical contact. Not necessarily sexual. We just wanted to be touched and kissed.

We weren't complete virgins. I had had my first encounter of that nature when I was only five or six. A crowd of us had gone to see a cowboy film at The Rats. Anthony, my older brother was there with his friend Thomas Morris and Thomas Morris's cousin, who was a bit older than all of us, fifteen or sixteen possibly. He sat next to me on the row and was very friendly, even shared his boiled sweets. Some way into the film he said,

'You can't see properly, can you?'

I was quite small for my age and straining a bit to see over the person sitting in front of me.

'Would you like to sit on my knee?'

I was hoisted across and onto his knee where I soon became aware of a hardness pressing into the small of my back. The next thing I knew, my little shorts were eased down around my knees and I was lifted so that I was sitting on top of the hard thing. I didn't like it. It didn't feel right but I said nothing. The film ended and we went home. I saw him a few days later coming across The Compound towards me. I turned and ran back indoors!

On another occasion, I was going through The Compound when I came across Thomas Morris and his friend Liam Roach. They had built a den and were now looking for some other form of entertainment. They offered me the choice of dancing for them or being thrown in the stingers – that was a no brainer. I had recently seen the film Salome. It wasn't the excitement of seeing John the Baptist having his head chopped off that stuck in my mind. No, far more enticing to me was Salome's Dance of the Seven Veils and here was an opportunity to perform my own version. Making my own music I proceeded to twist and turn, gradually removing every stitch of clothing on my body till I was dancing stark naked. The boys seemed to enjoy the performance and rewarded me with a little metal ring, probably from a Christmas Cracker, which I was very pleased with.

Unfortunately, the dance had also been witnessed by Mrs. Campbell, Rory's mother. Being the end house on the Parade her upstairs had a side window that overlooked The Compound. She was straight down to number Thirty where she related the whole story to my Mother, who was not amused.

Thomas McCarthy was about the same age as Thomas Doyle and me. He lived at Number 38 (Three bedrooms - parents plus Sean, Betty Maureen and Rory.) The family were country people and seemed to live on a diet of bacon and cabbage. Whilst being spotlessly clean, there was always a smell of cold cabbage soup emanating from their house when the front door was open. As twelve-year-old boys Thomas and I thought he had a fabulous bum which we were convinced was a result of his diet.

If we were lucky, we got to walk with him across The Compound to the grocery store. He would let us both put a hand down the back of his trousers, one on the left and one on the right. We got a great thrill feeling the clench of his buttocks with every step he took. On the way back we swapped sides - a very satisfying bit of nuding.

One wet afternoon in the summer holidays when Thomas McCarthy's house was empty - his father worked all day and his mother had an afternoon job for a couple of hours. The three of us saw this as a window of opportunity for some more nuding activity. Seeing as it was his house,

Thomas McCarthy took the lead. After we'd all taken our clothes off, he got a tie that was hanging on the back of his bedroom door and informed Thomas and I that he wanted to whip us! We said definitely no, this was not a good idea. However, he persisted, and threatened to stop us feeling his bum on future walks to the shops. Reluctantly we both lay across his bed to take our punishment. It didn't turn out to be a severe whipping and soon the three of us were roaring with laughter.

On another memorable afternoon during one of the school holidays, Rory, Thomas and I had been down to Urney's Chocolate Factory for a bag of miss-shapes and went back to Rory's to eat them. It wasn't long before he suggested we did some nuding. Rory and I stripped off. On that occasion Thomas seemed more interested in his miss-shapes. Rory wanted me to lie on his back and slide me mickey up and down, which I was more than happy to do. Then it was his turn to do it to me. To make things more slippery he suggested that I went to the bathroom cabinet where I would find a pot of Vaseline. When I got back to the bedroom, he instructed me to apply it liberally onto his mickey.

Suddenly, Rory's face changed into an excruciating grimace and with horror we realized that it wasn't Vaseline I was applying but rather, a thick coating of Vick Vapouriser Rub. Rory hit the roof and ran around the bedroom shouting,

'Mamma, mamma, mamma!'

I was relieved that she wasn't in the house to hear him. I'm sure he didn't believe that it had been a genuine mistake on my part - a mistake that he remembered for several days.

Mr. and Mrs. Coyle's ballroom dancing classes were held at the Father Matthew Hall in Dublin on a Saturday afternoon – the same hall I'd gone to for elocution lessons. This was an activity that I took part in without Thomas. The Coyles were always properly dressed for the occasion. He wore black trousers, a pristine white shirt and a bow tie. She had the full ballroom gown with its endless petticoats which I admired greatly. Mr. Coyle had a squint, so unless he addressed you by name, you were never quite sure whom he was talking to.

'Watch me, Leo. Watch me.' That was your signal to pay attention.

My partner was Geraldine Holmes. She was a pretty girl with long plaits that she circled around on the top of her head. She was a little shorter than me which made for a good ballroom hold. We danced well together and won several medals at competitions – we came second in the Dublin Championships, 8 to 12 years section.

If I was competing, Thomas would come along to support. At one of these competitions, held at the Ormonde Hotel, Thomas was approached by a man in the toilets. He was about twenty, thin, very handsome and had a black Burt Reynolds moustache. He said,

'Would you like to go for a drink?'
On that occasion Thomas declined the offer but a few weeks later, at another competition, the same man followed Thomas into the toilet and tried again. He got the same answer. Thomas came back to me,

'The fly's been buzzing round again!'

It was one thing nuding with our friends but even

though we longed for contact, going off with complete strangers at the age of thirteen or so wasn't on.

Another time when we nearly took the plunge, the three of us were at the Apollo Cinema and a boy of about nineteen or twenty came and sat next to us. We got chatting and before the film was over, he was inviting us home to 'have some fun'. He actually said,

'I could put some petroleum jelly on your bums and slide up and down'.

He seemed to have similar fantasies to Rory – though after the Vick incident that game hadn't been mentioned again.

We made a note of his address in Crumlin, a neighbouring estate to Walkinstown and arranged to go round the next day. We found the house but that was as far as we went. Looking up at the windows we could see that his net curtains were filthy - grey and shabby and definitely not up to the glamorous standards we demanded. We looked at each other, imagining what his bed linen would be like. It was a unanimous decision - he hadn't seen us, so we just walked on by. Our desires would have to be suppressed for a bit longer.

Although we spent a lot of time watching men, Thomas and I were also avid observers of women. By scrutinising women, we were able to acquire the feminine attributes that would be needed in our future escapades. We watched the way they walked. We noted the styles of the clothes they were wearing and the way their make-up was applied. We observed the gestures they made and the myriad of ways in which they expressed their femininity.

We noticed women were always tucking their hair behind their ears. They frequently touched their eyebrows – you never saw men doing that. When a woman wearing drop-earrings says 'Hello', she inclines her head to the side so that the earrings rattle. When a woman takes a cigarette out, she invariably taps it on the box before lighting it and putting it to her lips. The head is then slightly tilted backwards, and the smoke blown up into the air.

All these techniques needed a lot of practice, especially the walk - small steps, placing one foot in front of the other which caused the hips to gyrate seductively. We became very good at this.

In the 1959 film Some Like it Hot, we'd seen Marilyn Monroe using many ruses to display her 'feminine vulnerability'. We particularly liked the 'come-on' we called the 'high heel wobble' – one ankle gives-way on the high heeled shoe which causes the hip to drop. This in turn causes the bottom to wobble. Like the walk, this was a difficult one to master but we eventually got it.

As more and more of these observed traits were added into our performance, each outing of Maria and Tina became more realistic. When we dressed up our personas changed –we really became those two girls. Thoughts of home, school or friends completely left our minds. We were in a female world of our own making. It has to said, that we were naively unaware of the dangers our actions might have brought upon us.

Chapter 13 – New Acquisitions.

In March 1969 Thomas had his fourteenth birthday and left school. His father worked in Burtons' clothes factory in town and was able to get him a Saturday job as a messenger boy. Thomas was hard working and reliable and was soon taken on full-time, serving in the Dublin store.

Working gave Thomas a great boost to his income and I struggled to keep up with his new-found spending power. Uncle Larry was working as a milkman at this time and I used to get up early each morning to help him on the round before school. Another source of income was washing the nuns' cars, which we both did every weekend. They had two Morris Minors and we got paid two and sixpence each. If we were unlucky, we also got a helping of Sister Claude's rather solid tapioca pudding.

The dressing-up continued and we were quite adept at borrowing (and returning) all the clothes that we needed from our mothers' and sisters' wardrobes. By the Spring of 1970 our new-found wealth meant that, at last, we could splash out on proper wigs. The auburn hairpieces had served us well but were now consigned to the dustbin. One Saturday morning we set off with money in our pockets and headed into Dublin. Our destination was Henry Street and

Arnott's Department store, where we knew there was a very fashionable 'Wig Bar'.

The latest thing at that time was the now famous Ginchy Wig. They were made of fibre, pre-styled and only cost five pounds. The magazine advertising was very enticing:

> Do you really know a good wig when you see one?
> Styled easily and quickly!
> Which type naturally matches your face and colouring?
> You'll look great in a Ginchy Wig!

Thomas had also seen a large poster in Arnott's window:
No-one will ever know it's not your own!
That was it. That was what we were after.

I think we must have spun the young woman behind the counter some yarn about a fancy-dress party. Anyway, she was most helpful, and we spent a very happy half-hour with her trying on wigs of all styles and colours. We came away delighted with our purchases.

Thomas had chosen a warm chestnut coloured wig with a midi-cut style. It had short layers on top and a soft broken fringe that flicked up in front of his eyes. At the back it tapered into his neck and had long strands that hung down and round under his chin. Mine was a long blond wig that flowed half-way down my back. I wore it with a lavender headscarf, folded into a three-inch band that was tied around my forehead. The flowing mane was then divided in two, each half being brought round to the front and up under the band. Once on top I could back-comb it into a high-rise crown. All that time we'd spent combing out our dolls' hair was now being put to good use and we both looked fabulous!

Shoes had always been an important part of our costumes. Although I never talked to her about it, Maria and I had similar tastes - which was good, because she could afford them, and I couldn't. She was a size four which was fine for both Thomas and me. Mother was a size three. I did borrow hers on occasions, but they weren't as comfortable as Maria's. Peter and Maria were courting and very often went away for the weekend. Her shoes were kept in the bottom of the wardrobe behind the door in the girls' bedroom. I had to wait till she'd packed and departed before I crept in to make my choice from the pairs she'd left behind. You could depend on her leaving an old pair of black evening shoes. She rarely wore these, and they were a good stand-by. The pair I hoped she'd left were silver sling back sandals with a peep toe and kitten heels. These were my favourites and the moderate sized heel meant they were really comfortable to wear and easy to walk in.

I say they were my favourites but that was before Maria discovered Mary Quant. She just loved the black and white fashion and when Peter bought her a black and white chequered plastic raincoat, she was over the moon. When the matching shoes followed, I was extremely jealous. I would love to have borrowed that outfit but rarely was it eft in the wardrobe and, anyway, I don't think I would have dared.

Maria never noticed when her shoes went temporarily missing. I always made sure that they were clean and back in the same place in the wardrobe at the very first opportunity.

Thomas wasn't so lucky. His oldest sister Grainne was two years younger than him. He could get into her shoes, but she'd not yet reached the age when fashion was important to her – he didn't fancy her dark-tan school sandals.

He did, however, have two maiden aunts who lived together nearby and they (unknown to themselves) were a great help to him. One time he nearly came unstuck. He'd borrowed a pair of new green mules from Aunty Lily's wardrobe. Unusually, he decided that he liked them so much that he would hang on to them for a bit. What he didn't know was that Lily had brought these shoes back from a trip to Lourdes and they had rather a special significance. On a visit to the house several weeks later, she was waiting for him.

'Do you know, Thomas. Your Auntie Alice has taken my new mules and she's denying it!' Thomas was mortified.

'I wouldn't mind,' she went on, 'But I hadn't even put my foot in them. Ah, the sooner she leaves this house the better. I'm getting all the locks changed.'

Poor Alice was taking the blame and there was nothing he could do. The shoes certainly couldn't be returned now. After wearing them on a couple of nights out they were well scuffed.

Most things in our wardrobe were bought or borrowed and returned. Bras were pinched – we only needed one each. I got mine from Maria. Thomas had to have one of his mother's as Grainne wasn't developed enough yet to need one. Neither of our mothers was particularly large in this department so we found it quite easy to achieve a realistic effect and we hadn't discovered anything better to fill them with than our rolled-up school socks. Good for both for size and consistency. The bras went on over our grey school shirts, so we didn't much mind that they were second-hand.

We had, however, become very fussy about our stockings. They now had to be brand new and were purchased at Dunne's Department Store.

'Me Mammy sent me in for a pair of American Tan.'

That was the shade we usually went for. We were very tempted by the new Mary Quant styles with their bright colours and bold patterns but thought they might just draw too much attention.

With the increased cash available our make-up box had become much more sophisticated. We bought our supplies from a chemist in Errigal. This was well over half a mile from home. We couldn't risk going to the local shop. We said we were buying a present for our sisters and the assistants were always most helpful.

'And what colour lipstick would your sister like?'

We had both spotted 'Tender Orchid'. A beautiful soft pink made by Cutex, and we knew that was the one our sisters would definitely like.

My skin was so smooth that I was able to get away without wearing a foundation. Thomas, on the other hand, was beginning to shave and had a much more masculine face. He had to apply a thick beige foundation cream which he plastered on like pan-stick to get the desired effect.

We stuck to lavender shades for our eye shadow but used it more skilfully. The heavy bright blue of the Pantomime Dame was not the effect we were after. We learnt to be much more subtle, both with the colour and the amount we used - evenly applied across the lid and fading out towards the edges. We also added highlights by applying an iridescent thin white line just below the eyebrows. False eyelashes were now part of the routine. Thomas's were plain black, but mine (as usual) had to be special and were black with gold sparkle.

A small touch of rouge was added to emphasise our cheekbones and I also had to have a beauty spot. I copied this from Nula O'Donnell who read the news on R.T.E. I did it with a black eye-liner pencil, either on the top of my left cheek, or, for a change, just above my upper lip.

We loved our lipstick. We'd come a long way from those first efforts in front of the small mirror in the torchlight. It always took several attempts to get it right. You'd be almost there and then you'd be nudged – we were both fighting for mirror space.

'Oh Jaysus! I've smudged it. I'll have to start again.'

We had tried applying each other's but that seemed even more difficult.

Now though, we were much more confident, expert almost and invariably got it right first time. The secret was to concentrate and complete the task in one smooth movement with just the right amount of pressure. I thought of Ace. I'd watched her doing it effortlessly so many times and copied her routine. The application followed by rolling the lips together. Then the use of a handkerchief to take off any excess and finally, checking the corners in the mirror.

When all this was finished, we scrutinized each other by torchlight to make sure every last detail was perfect. Only then were we ready to face our public.

Chapter 14 – Thrills and Spills.

The first outing for the new wigs needed to be somewhere a bit special and Thomas had an idea. He'd seen a small advert in his father's Evening Herald:

> Town and Country Club
> Pop Night Out – Dancing 8 to 11.15
> THIN LIZZIE
> Also – Portraits
> Admission 3/-

Thin Lizzie was an Irish rock band that had been formed in 1969 and was beginning to make a name for itself across Ireland. We'd heard them on the radio and really liked their music. The Town and Country Club sounded a bit posh but so were we. We'd now been cross-dressing for over two years and saw no problem with walking into a crowded dance hall in the centre of Dublin.

The bus dropped us by The Quays, and we walked arm in arm up O'Connell Street till we reached Parnell Square. This was a lovely part of Dublin and we imagined what it would be like to live in one of the Georgian terraced houses that surrounded three sides of the Square. The Town and Country Club was just off the Square and we soon saw the queue of teenagers waiting to get it.

As well as the new wigs, we both had new outfits. I was wearing a pink and green dress that Maria had recently acquired - very glamorous with white lacey ruffs around the neck and on the cuffs. To convert it into a 'mini' I'd hitched up the skirt and secured it at the right length with the 'snakes-head' belt off my school trousers. The spare material was 'bloused' down over the belt to hide it from view. I made a note to make sure the creases were out before I returned it to the wardrobe.

Thomas had a bright hounds-tooth check mini-skirt that he'd borrowed from his sister – so short that it barely covered the tops of his stockings. With this he was wearing a black ribbed polo-necked jumper - tight fitting and clinging provocatively to his sock filled bra.

The man on the door was dressed in a dinner jacket and bowtie and looked very smart. He greeted us with an admiring look,

'Good evening girls. Welcome to the Town and Country.' He took our three shillings and we were in.

We could hear music coming from the dance floor but first we headed into the Ladies to check our make-up. Inside we found a crowd of excited girls around the large mirror doing the same thing and no-one paid any attention to us. No touching-up was needed but we did it anyway. We knew this was what girls did. Satisfied, we made our back into the foyer and headed though the double swing-doors that opened onto the ballroom.

We were in a large hall with mock Corinthian columns down both sides. This created a really grand effect – it was very impressive. At the far end on the stage the Portraits, the support group, were playing and there were quite a few girls dancing. But this was no dancing that Mr. and Mrs. Coyle at the Father Matthew Hall would have recognised. No waltzes or quicksteps here. No ballroom-hold either. The girls were dancing in small groups, in pairs and even on their own. The Coyles would not have approved of the strutting, gyrating and prancing that was taking place in the name of dance. This was the age of Rock and Roll. We got ourselves glasses of orange juice from the bar and headed into the melee.

From our position in the centre of the floor we could see that most of the lads seemed to be either standing at the bar or sitting down the sides of the hall behind the columns. This didn't surprise us. Teenage boys were very shy in those days. You could tell they were eyeing the girls up, but we knew they would need an hour or so of drinking before they plucked up the courage to ask them to dance.

The thing about the bands at that time was the versatility of the music they played. Their repertoire would include all the songs currently in the record charts, but they could also play Country and Western, Dixieland Jazz and, of course, Irish Traditional and Ceilidh music. It all made for a great evening.

After half an hour on the floor we needed to freshen up and headed back to the Ladies. As we entered, someone stood back to let us through. I didn't recognise her at first, but Thomas did. I heard him whispering behind me.

'It's Bernie!'

Bernie Mulcathy (or 'Mul-catty' as we boys rudely called her) was the daughter of the lady who worked at Urney's Chocolate factory and gave us the miss-shapes. We knew her quite well. It was too late to take evasive action, and everything seemed to go into slow-motion. I said,

'Thank you,' smiled and kept going. Thomas did likewise.

We passed face to face but there wasn't a flicker of recognition. It was a heart-stopping moment but, once through, we had to laugh.

When we got back to the dance floor it had become quite crowded and, thank goodness, we couldn't see Bernie anywhere. We placed ourselves up near the stage and it wasn't long before we were getting winks from the boys in the band. Our dancing was good, and we knew it. We returned the winks with coy smiles and little waves – it was great to flirt.

Just before the interval I gave Thomas another shock. I did a heel spin which produced a look of horror on his face. Through clenched teeth he said,

'Your zip is down, and I can see your bra over your shirt!' He was anxiously looking round to see if we were the centre of attention.

I hastily backed up to him so that he could zip me up again. Nobody seemed to have noticed and I don't think they would have thought twice about it even if they had. It certainly didn't bother me – I was so full of confidence.

The interval was announced and while they set the stage for Thin Lizzie, we headed back to the Ladies which was now nearly as crowded as the dance floor. As we stood queuing for the cubicles, we got chatting to a couple of girls about our age. Ornya and her friend Siobhan had come up from Wexford for the dance. They were both great fans of Thin Lizzie and knew all the boys' names. Philip Lynott played the bass and was the singer. Brian Downey on the drums, Eric Bell on guitar and Eric Wrixton on keyboard. Philip was their favourite and they both had his autograph. The girls were really friendly and, having once again adjusted our make-up, we headed back to the ballroom together.

The floor was now packed with both boys and girls and as Thin Lizzie was announced a great cheer went up. Their music was very loud with a strong beat which got everyone dancing. The boys were getting much bolder now and we could feel them suggestively brushing up against us, which was nice, but we were quite happy dancing in a group with Ornya and Siobhan.

Philip Lynott then announced that the group was about to release their first single, The Farmer, and this news was rewarded with another loud cheer and when the music started, we all danced away.

> Won't y'all come again,
> Won't y'all come?
> Your faces keep us warm,
> Won't y'all come?

In the end their debut single only sold 283 copies, which was a shame because we all thought it was great.

A bit later they sang Whiskey in the Jar. This, in contrast, became a big hit in both the Irish and British pop charts. A traditional Irish song about a highwayman, made popular by The Dubliners. We'd sung it many times at Madge's musical evenings and knew all the words. We'd never heard it played like Thin Lizzie played it, with a really heavy sound and hard rock beat – the singing was fabulous, and everyone joined in.

119

> As I was goin' over the Cork and Kerry
> mountains,
> I saw captain Farrell and his money he was
> countin'.
> I first produced my pistol and then produced
> my rapier,
> I said stand o'er and deliver or the devil he
> may take ya.

It had now gone ten o'clock and our Cinderella moment was fast approaching. We'd had yet another extension for the special evening but still had to be back, changed and in the house by eleven o'clock. We said 'Goodnight' to Ornya and Siobhan. We'd had a great evening dancing with them. There were quite a few wolf-whistles as we made our way across the floor to the exit, which gave us some compensation for having to leave before the end.

Dancing had become a great passion for both Thomas and me and over the next few months we returned to the Town and Country Club on several occasions. We realised that if we got a taxi home, rather than queuing at a busy bus-stop, we could gain some extra precious moments on the dance floor.

We'd make our way down to the Quays where you could always get a cab. One night we were picked up by a driver aged about thirty-five. He was a handsome man with striking black hair.

'Where you going girls?'

'Could you drop us at the Kokonut Newsagents? It's by the Halfway House in Walkinstown.'

'Ah yes' he said, 'I know it well.'

We both got into the back and were soon chatting away with yer man.

'Did you have a nice night?'

'We did.'

'And where are your boy-friends?'

'We haven't got any.'

'Ah, I don't believe that now. You're very pretty girls.'

Some ten minutes later we reached the Long Mile Road. He did a U-turn by the Kokonut and pulled up in front of Slattery's public house. We paid the fare and were just about to get out when he said,

'Could we have a little kiss before you go?'

Thomas and I looked at each other and smiled. This would be a nice end to the evening.

Thomas went first. He got out and into the front of the taxi next to the driver. I watched from the back while the two of them necked and exchanged a few kisses, nothing more. Then it was my turn. I got in the front and Thomas returned to the back seat. Again, little more than kissing took place but, after a couple of minutes, Thomas thought I'd had my share. Ever watchful of our deadline he said,

'We'll have to go now.'

He got out of the taxi onto the pavement and shut the door.

Up to this point the driver had his left arm draped across my shoulders and his right hand resting on my knee.

'Just one more kiss' he said.

His hand now started to move up my bare thigh and under the hem of Maria's pink and green dress. Sitting there on my own with this older man I suddenly felt very vulnerable. He must have felt my body tauten.

121

'What's der madder with you's?'

'I'm sorry but we really do have to go' I said and started to open the door.

In a flash, things turned nasty.

'Bastards!' he yelled. 'Fuckin bastards!'

The engine of the car had been left running and he now slammed the gear lever into first and hit the accelerator. The engine roared and we shot forward, the thrust causing my door to slam shut again. In the wing mirror I could see the look of horror on Thomas's face. He was helpless to do anything.

I too felt helpless and frightened. I didn't know if he was disappointed that I wouldn't go further, or had he suddenly realised he'd been kissing two boys? Several things were flashing through my mind. I thought, he knows, he's going to kidnap me, he's going to beat me up.

Salvation came in the shape of a red traffic light and Maimie O'Donoghue. Maimie was my mother's first cousin and lived around the corner from the Kokonut.

We had been parked only twenty yards from the lights so weren't going fast when they changed to red. He jammed on the brakes and I shot forward in my seat. As I did so I made a grab for the door handle and at that point noticed Maimie walking along the road. Wrenching the door open I screamed out,

'Maimie, help!'

'Jaysus!' she said approaching the car. 'Who's that calling my name?'

As I leapt out, he thumped me in the back and made a grab at my hair, or what he thought was my hair.

'Yer fuckin eejit!' he yelled, 'Bastards!'

I yanked up the hood of my anorak to hide my face and shot past a startled Maimie who was crossing herself for protection.

'What in the name of God's going on?' she cried.

I reached Thomas and we both legged it down the road to the Valley and the safety of the den. We kept looking over our shoulders, petrified in case he was following but thank goodness he'd decided to call it a day. Once again we had got away with it, but I did have a sore back and, more important, had lost my precious new wig.

Several weeks passed before we ventured out again. Apart from losing our confidence, I had to save up to buy another wig. The situation wasn't helped by what happened on our next outing. We couldn't face another dance night in town so settled for a visit to the Inchicore cinema. We could walk there – no taxi's needed.

In those days you always got a full programme. The evening would start with the 'B' movie. This would be followed by a cartoon or the Pathe News and then, finally, the main feature. With only one projector, there were always gaps while the reels were changed, which gave you time to go and powder your nose.

I left Thomas in his seat and went into the ladies on my own to apply some more lipstick. I probably didn't need to, but this was what it was all about. I was just about to return to my seat when the door burst open, crashing back against the wall, and in marched three rough looking girls with aggression pouring out of their faces. My exit was barred.

'Who are you's?' one of them shouted.

'What are you fucking doing in here?' said another, poking me in the chest right between my socks.

I was obviously on their pitch and they didn't like it. I tried to keep calm and said the first thing that came into my head.

'Hi girls, are you enjoying the film?

That remark was completely ignored, and they started to circle like a pack of dogs spoiling for a fight. I'd seen girls fight and knew it involved pulling hair – I couldn't bear to lose my wig again.

As I backed away towards the sinks, I put my hand out onto one of the basins to steady myself and discovered that some perverted soul (probably one of these three girls) had smeared crap all around the sink.

'Oh no' I said, 'I've got gick all over my hand!' At this, the three of them roared with laughter.

'She's got shite on her hand' they jeered but it did seem to ease the tension.

At this point Thomas came in. He'd seen the girls follow me in and was getting worried.

'What's going on here?'

Again, the question was ignored.

'Who's she?' one of them said. 'She looks like a man!'

Now it has to be said that I was a pretty boy, small build and young looking for my age. Thomas, on the other hand, was definitely more masculine looking. Something he tried to hide with the extra make-up. His interruption gave me a chance to quickly rinse my hand and regain my composure. I moved over to Tony's side by the door.

'This is my friend Tina, and that's a horrible thing to say!'

The remark came out more fiercely than I had intended but it appeared to have an effect. There were two of us now, against the three of them and they seemed to be reconsidering the odds. This, we thought, would be a good point to make a rapid exit, back to the safety of the darkness amongst the adults.

That wasn't the end of the episode. After the show, as we were walking back to Bluebell, we were horrified to hear the three of them behind us shouting a torrent of abuse. The Black Horse Inn was about a hundred yards ahead and we could see a group of people standing at the bus stop. This, we decided, was our safest option and increased our pace. As we approached the bus stop the girls caught up and, thankfully, moved on but not before they had punched me and kicked Thomas. We were physically shaking and felt very frightened.

This was another big blow to our confidence – it was dispiriting. Though on the positive side, they did think we were girls – that was good. When something like this happened, we naturally thought about whether we had the will to carry on.

'Can we do it again? Can we go on getting away with it?'

However, the lure was very, very strong. We were soon chatting away about the many exciting evenings we'd had and these more than compensated for the bad experiences.

A few days later I had yet another fright. I'd been into Dublin on some errand or other and was on my way home on the bus. Dressed in my school clothes I was sitting upstairs, on my own near the front. We had just pulled away from a stop when I heard a female voice behind me.

'Hi, Maria!'

'Oh no! What now?' I thought. 'I can't cope with another crisis.'

My heart raced as I tried to put a name to the voice and to think whom I might know on the bus who would call me Maria. Telling myself not to panic, I had the presence of mind to pull up the collar of my anorak, just turning the top over. The inside was cream, and I thought it would look quite feminine. I clutched the bag I was carrying in front of my non-existent breasts, fixed a smile on my face and turned around. Sitting a few rows back was Ornya, the girl we had met at the Town and Country Club on the Thin Lizzie night. I just managed to say,

'Hi, Ornya.'

With this she got up, came down the aisle and sat next to me.

'Sacred Heart of Jaysus, what have you done to your hair?'

I could see the look of horror on her face.

'Ohhh...' I stuttered, 'I've had it cut really short. It's a new boyish look. It's very fashionable.'

'Gee, it looks great. I nearly didn't recognise you.'

Had I started a new hair fashion for young girls? I quickly changed the subject and we chatted away about the dance and what we had been doing since. It seemed to be going alright but then she asked me why I wasn't wearing any make-up. 'Oh' I said, 'I had a rush getting into town for Mammy and I just didn't bother.'

This seemed to satisfy her, but I was beginning to sweat and wondered how much longer I could go on with the charade before she caught me out. Fortunately, we reached her stop and she had to get off. We said good-bye and she gave me a peck on the cheek.

I watched her waving as the bus pulled away. I waved back and slumped into my seat. It was all too much. I wasn't coping. There were now tears prickling my eyes and I had to make an effort not to burst out crying. We were having so much bad luck. It couldn't go on. We'd got away with cross-dressing for two years, but the last few weeks had given us some dreadful scares. There was guilt as well. What would Mam think of me if she knew? What would Auntie Madge say? Strangely there was no concern as to what God might do to me. Not for the first time, I thought that perhaps now was the time to call an end to it.

Chapter 15 – Two Nice Boys.

Despite the downs life went on and, after a long chat with Thomas at the bottom of the stairs I bounced back, I felt my confidence returning. Though, the next time we went to the cinema at Inchicore, we were a lot more cautious. We only left our seats once to go to the Ladies and this time we went together. We needn't have worried. The middle-aged lady who came out of the cubicle gave us a nice smile as she went to wash her hands.

Leaving the cinema at the end of the show we had a good look round but our assailants from the previous visit were nowhere to be seen. Linking arms, we headed back towards the Black Horse. As we passed the pub two lads, both about seventeen or eighteen, came out of the bar and gave us a wolf-whistle. This was more like it. We turned and gave them a big smile, which was enough to encourage them to come after us.

'Where are you pretty girls off to?'

'Oh' we said, 'We're just walking home.'

'Can we walk with you?'

They were both good looking, confident and smartly dressed in suits and ties, so we said,

'Yes, sure you can.'

We introduced ourselves as Maria and Tina. They were Ricky and Michael. As we set off Ricky soon had his arm round my shoulders while Michael did the same to Thomas. I was a bit jealous because, although Ricky was good looking, Michael was gorgeous, and I really wanted to walk with him.

Before we'd gone very far, both boys were nibbling at our necks and this soon progressed to kissing - kissing on the lips. This was a significant moment in our young lives. At the dances we'd frequently been pecked and nibbled at, mainly on our necks and cheeks. This was the first time we'd been properly kissed on the mouth. It didn't stop there. These boys were experienced and soon Ricky's warm wet tongue was pushing my lips apart and exploring the inside of my mouth. It felt fantastic, just what I'd always wanted, and I reciprocated each delicate movement with my own tongue – I was a quick learner and didn't need to be shown twice. I opened my eyes for a moment and saw that Thomas was undergoing a similar initiation with Michael.

The boys walked us back to Bluebell and then down into the Camac valley, kissing and cuddling every step of the way. As we crossed the river and started up the other side towards our den at paper mill, I began to get a little concerned. We were having a fabulous time with them, but our deadline was approaching. Somehow, we had to end the evening.

We reached the fence around the factory.

'I'm afraid we'll have to go now boys' I said, 'We're staying the night with my Aunt. That's her house over there.'

Thomas picked up,

'Thanks for walking us home. We've had a great time but you have to go now.' They were not keen.

'Just one more kiss.'

'Just a little bit longer, please.'

They were very hard to resist.

At this point we were both standing with our backs to the chain-link fence with Ricky and Michael pressing their bodies against us. Ricky's fumbling hands now worked their way round from my back to my stomach and, slowly but surely, were heading up towards my breasts. I really wasn't sure how much scrutiny my sock-filled bra would withstand from this sustained attack. If I had any doubt where this was all leading, I soon found out. With a smile on his face, Ricky said,

'Look at this.'

'Look at what?'

He motioned downwards. My eyes followed to where he was pointing and there, out for all to see, was his fully erect penis. To a fourteen-year-old boy who had not yet gone through puberty, it looked enormous.

'Jesus, Mary and Joseph!' was all that I could say.

'Put your hand on me mickey, Maria.'

'Oh no Ricky, I can't' I said, 'I've got to go home. I'll be in trouble if I'm late.'

'Ah, go on,' he pleaded. 'Just put it between yer legs.'

I was right out of my depth now.

Thomas was right next to me and still kissing Michael. I gave him a nudge and watched his jaw drop when he saw what was on view. Thankfully he took command of the situation. Pushing Michael away he said,

131

'That's it boys, we've got to go. Maria's aunt will be out looking for us.'

To be fair to them, they stood away and Ricky's weapon was put back from whence it came. With that we gave them a final kiss and ran off up the lane, laughing and giggling. We shouted our good-byes with promises to meet them again. When we were sure that they weren't following us, we slipped off our high heels and noiselessly made our way back to the den. Our hearts were thumping as we got changed, just in case they'd followed us. But they hadn't and we both agreed that it had been a very successful and exciting night.

When I thought about it later, I realised that this had been another landmark. The men in the Halfway House at Halloween knew we were boys when they kissed and cuddled us. At the dances the boys' efforts were very tentative – hardly qualifying as kisses. Tonight had been different. This was for real. Ricky and Michael believed we were young girls and had actually been attracted to us. The kisses were passionate. We'd touched lips and even put our tongues in each other's mouths. We had had our first truly sexual experience – our first kisses from boys.

A couple of weeks later Joe and Ace were taking the kids away for the night. The family had acquired a caravan on the side of Lake Virginia in County Cavan. It felt a bit cramped when we all went but Joe still had the tent-like contraption that fitted onto the roof of the car and we'd had a few good weekends there. On this occasion Maria and Peter were going off on their own for a couple of nights and I saw a great opportunity to be 'home-alone'. This hadn't happened before. Neither Maria nor Anthony had made this request and I could see Mam and Dad weren't keen on the idea. I had to use all my persuasive powers with promises of best behaviour. I said I wouldn't be on my own as Thomas would come and stay. With that proviso, Joe and Ace finally agreed.

Thomas was definitely up for it and we began to make plans for a night out. On the Saturday morning we stood at the door and waved them all off. Peter and Maria had disappeared on the Friday evening, so we had the house entirely to ourselves.

The first thing we did was to run upstairs to the girls' bedroom and fling open Maria's wardrobe. A feast of delights greeted us, and we lost no time in trying them all on. First, a lovely black miniskirt which I wore with a frilly, pale blue flamenco blouse. Thomas preferred it with a plain cream blouse set-off by an orange chiffon scarf at the neck. Mrs. Fallon, Peter's mother, was a great knitter and had crocheted Maria a pink mini-dress with bell-end sleeves and a plunging scalloped neckline. This didn't need a blouse – just bra and stockings. Then there was her winter coat – tweed with fur around both the collar and hemline. She wore this with a white fur hood, fixed under the chin with tie-strings that had pompoms dangling from each end. We were in heaven.

Something new we hadn't seen before was a quilted turban scarf in French green. We worked out that you placed this across your forehead and tied the ends round the back. It was a great pity that we didn't have our hair-pieces with us but we improvised with our old trick of pulling our jumpers up over our foreheads and creating a towering bouffant that poked up through the centre of the turban – this looked fabulous with the winter coat and very elegant.

After a great deal of fun, we selected our outfits for the evening. The Inchicore cinema had a new programme showing and that's where we intended to go. We knew we wouldn't be able to dress at the house. We might be seen leaving. Everything would have to be taken to the den and we would change there as usual. For the first time we took off our shirts and put our bras on over our bare chests. It felt strange to begin with but not unpleasant.

All went well and the film was great. We felt good as we emerged from the cinema in Maria's finery. We felt even better when we saw who was standing outside. It was Michael. He was on his own as Ricky was doing something with his parents that night. He was very pleased to see us, and we were soon off up the road, Thomas hanging on his right arm and me on the left. We felt comfortable with him. He was obviously less forward that Ricky and on the previous meeting had made no attempt to go any further than a kiss and a cuddle with Thomas.

When he heard we had the house to ourselves a big smile appeared on his face.

'Shall I walk you home then?'

'Yes, please.'

His parents knew he stayed out late at weekends and wouldn't wait up for him. By the time we reached The Parade, all good Catholics were indoors with their curtains closed and no-one was around. Even so, we were quite nervous as we approached the front door of Number 30. Mrs. Foley at 28 was always on the lookout for anything untoward. If she saw anything, she'd be round to Ace on Monday morning.

'Leo was out very late on Saturday night.'

We were relieved to get safely inside and lock the door. No time was wasted with coffee and chit-chat. The three of us headed straight up stairs. We decided that we would take it in turns to snog with Michael. This would happen in the boys' bedroom. The one who was not snogging would wait in the front bedroom on Joe and Ace's bed – Joe would have killed us if he'd known.

I pulled the curtains in the Boys' room and turned on the bedside light. Then had second thoughts and turned it off again – there would be plenty of light coming through from the hallway. This was going to be close scrutiny and I didn't want to tempt fate. We got Michael settled on the divan and then went next door to remove our stockings and the school ties that held them up.

And so started a night of passion. Each session lasted about twenty minutes and we got a good rest in-between, waiting for our next turn. Michael kept going throughout and must have been exhausted. He was a perfect gentleman and, apart from his jacket and shoes, kept all his clothes on. When his probing became problematical, a gentle 'No' was enough to set him off in another direction.

For sometime now we had been wearing knickers instead of our Y-fronts. Thomas drew the line at going into a shop to buy them but that wasn't a problem as Maria seemed to have drawers full. I'd borrow a couple of pairs and then, after a night out, surreptitiously wash them and swap them for new pairs. This meant I was happy to allow

Michael to let his hands wander down my back and over my bottom.

At one point I felt him fingering the elastic at the top of my knickers. He paused, but getting no resistance, slid his hand inside and gently caressed my bare buttocks – it was heaven. I tried to do the same to him, but his belt was too tight. I ran my hand round to the buckle but then had second thoughts. If I undid his trousers, he would get the wrong message. How long would it be before he started probing between my legs? Then... well, it didn't bear thinking about. I contented myself with exploring the contours of his youthful bottom through his tight trousers. After all, this was the furthest we'd ever been, and it was a wonderful feeling.

By two o'clock Michael was struggling to stay awake. It was time to draw the evening to a close. I finished my session and went back to Mam and Dad's room to find Thomas fast asleep on the bed. His wig had come adrift and was covering half his face. Not only that, his skirt had pulled up and I could see his balls protruding under the hem of his knickers. I quietly woke him and while he rearranged himself, went back into Michael. He'd done sterling work over the past two hours, but he too was now in need of sleep. We had a final kiss in the hallway, checked the coast was clear and sent him on his way.

What a great night we'd had but there was a nagging doubt. I kept asking myself,

'Does he really believe we're girls?' And I think the answer was yes, he really did. This was a time when teenagers were very naive. To get to one's wedding night Virgo Intacta was the rule and not the exception. Michael would have been quite used to girls putting a limit on his sexual activity.

If I'd wanted further proof, it came four days later. The family were sitting round the dining table having their evening meal when there was a knock at the door.

'Will you get that Leo' said Joe.

'Do I have to?'

'Yes, you do. Your mother's serving and you're the nearest.'

I begrudgingly put down my knife and fork and walked up the hall. I could see someone standing behind the glass panel. When I opened the door I nearly died – Michael was on the step.

'Is Maria in?'

My brain whirled,

'He doesn't recognise me! Why should he? He's looking at a schoolboy in short trousers with short hair and no wig – think fast!'

'Oh, er no' I mumbled, 'She's gone away for a couple of days with her boyfriend.'

As the words came out of my mouth, I knew it wasn't what I meant to say. It was the first thing that came into my mind. He looked crestfallen and I felt devastated for him.

'She's got a boyfriend? Oh, I'm sorry to have bothered you.' With that he turned and walked off down the path.

I desperately wanted to rush after him - to put my arms round him and say,

'Michael, it's alright. It's me, Maria.'

But of course, I didn't. How stupid I felt. Why had I said that – I could have just said she was out - too late now. I could only think that we would never see him again.

'Who was that?' asked Joe.

'No one. Wrong house. Some feller wanted the Mangans.'

What a disaster!

Chapter 16 – Our Day Out.

As the weeks turned to months our relationship with Maria and Tina became more intimate and special. In our heads Leo and Thomas were the false personae and the girls our real selves. The boys were an inconvenience to be endured between our outings. If we weren't out being the girls, we'd be talking about them. So much planning went on - new places to go, new costume ideas, new fashion ideas. We were now so confident that we were bold enough to step out in broad daylight. Nobody at home appeared to be suspicious of our activities. No-one asked any awkward questions, not even Bridie. We just said,

'We're going into Town' or 'We're going to the pictures.' As long as we stuck to our curfews and behaved ourselves, that was sufficient, and we were left alone.

Our next project, we decided, would be a full day out – a big step forward. Bray Head was a beauty spot that was popular with both tourists and locals alike. Thomas and I had both been there for picnics. Situated between the towns of Bray and Greystones, the hill is topped by a large concrete cross. From here there are fantastic views in all directions. However, it wasn't the scenery we were interested in.

There is only one way to the top of Bray Head and, whilst the climb is not particularly daunting, some parts are a bit steep and require some scrambling. If you went at the weekend there were always plenty of young men around. We had noticed that, if you were following a female up the path, on particularly steep sections there was a very good chance of getting a flash of her knickers. In our younger years we had thought this very rude and very funny. Now though, we saw it as an opportunity to be provocative.

We would first get the bus to Enniskerry and have a picnic down by the river. In the afternoon we would take another bus into Bray, walk along the promenade and climb Bray Head.

This was going to be our longest outing to date, and we didn't want to take any unnecessary chances. The bus-stop for Enniskerry was at Walkinstown Roundabout. Changing in the den would mean walking back past The Parade and on through the Estate. We both felt this was too risky, particularly on a Saturday when there would be a lot of locals and kids out and about. The alternative was to leave home as boys and make the transformation in the bushes by the river in Enniskerry.

If we did this, we would have to keep our outfits simple. Miniskirts were a must, as were knickers and stockings. We decided to do without the wigs and go back to headscarves – it would be very difficult to arrange and dress wigs in the bushes. Then, for some unknown reason, we decided on white high heeled shoes. The heels weren't that high but were definitely not what most people would have chosen to climb Bray Head. Make-up was discussed at length but in the end, we decided to just take lipstick – it would

140

take far too long to apply the full whack. Coming home we would take a different route via the centre of Dublin and then a bus out to Bluebell. We could then safely change out of our clothes back in the den.

Saturday arrived and was bright and sunny. I'd packed my rucksack during a quiet moment the day before and stowed it under my bed. Costume, shoes and lipstick were at the bottom, well hidden under a spare pullover. Mam made a picnic for the two of us and I borrowed Joe's primus stove and a small metal kettle so that we could brew-up tea by the river. Ten o'clock on the dot Thomas was knocking on the front door with his bag and we set off to catch the 10:36 to Dolphin's Barn. We would have to change there to get a second bus out to Enniskerry.

All went well and an hour later we were travelling through the foothills of the Wicklow Mountains, along the road known colloquially as The Twenty-One-Bends. As we approached the village of Enniskerry the road ran alongside the Glencullen River and from the top of the bus we could see kids playing along the riverbank and paddling in the shallows.

The bus came to a halt in the centre of the village, by the village tap. We filled the kettle and made our way back down to the river.

The first thing was to get changed and we walked quite a distance beyond the little beach where the kids were playing before finding a suitably secluded spot for the transition.

After removing our trousers, we swapped our Y-fronts for Maria's frilly knickers. The stockings were tied, as usual, with our school ties but we rolled over the top of the stockings just a little bit further than normal. For the climb up Bray Head we wanted plenty of bare flesh visible between the top of the stockings and our knicker-line.

I'd borrowed two summer blouses, a flowery one for Thomas and a plain apricot colour for myself. They looked great with the miniskirts. The day was really hot, and we were glad not to be wearing shirts under the blouses. Lipstick and headscarves completed the ensemble. The high heeled shoes were totally impracticable on the riverbank so, after repacking our bags, we carried them and walked back to the spot we had chosen for the picnic in our stockings.

Whilst I got the primus going Thomas laid out the food Ace had packed for us. We then sat there on the grass by the riverbank enjoying our picnic without a care in the world - Tina and Maria, two young teenage girls out for a day in the country. What could be more natural?

It would have been lovely to have gone for a paddle in the river but removing the tied-up stockings would have been too much hassle. We contented ourselves with sun-bathing. I lay there on the grass watching the little white clouds drift lazily across the clear blue sky – I felt happy.

An hour passed and it was time to move on. We carefully checked each other's costumes and, with everything packed in our rucksacks, made our way back up the bank to catch the bus to Bray.

When we reached the road, we stopped to put on our high heeled shoes. As Thomas bent over to adjust the strap, I got a flash of the top of his thigh. At this point two motorbikes roared up the road and pulled to a halt alongside us – someone else had noticed the bare flesh. The bikes were being driven by two lads in their early twenties.

'Hi girls. Where yer going?'

'Ah, we're getting the bus into Bray to meet our parents.'

'We're going that way. Would you like a lift?'

We didn't need asking twice. We'd never been on motorbikes before. Joe did have a scooter at some point, and I had ridden pillion on that, but this was something else.

They told us to climb up behind them and hang on tight around their waists. Once in position the engines roared into life and we shot off. The bikes flew along the Twenty-One-Bends road like bats out of hell. At each corner the boys leant into the bend so that we were almost touching the ground - both scary and exciting. I'm sure they enjoyed the screams coming from their passengers. Thomas was in front of me and I could see his headscarf and mini-skirt flapping in the wind. I wanted to check that my scarf was securely fixed but didn't dare let go of the waist in front of me.

In no time we were on the front in Bray. There were no strings attached to this lift – not even a kiss. We dismounted and waved as we watched the bikes roar off up the road. The whole experience had been exhilarating, not least the feel of bare flesh on the leather of the pillion seats – though I thought a little kiss would have been nice to finish it off.

Thomas and I linked arms and set off along the promenade. The sea was on our left and kids were playing on the sandy beach and messing around in the water. There were a lot of people out walking - couples with their dogs and families with ice-creams and candy floss. In front of us, right at the end of the promenade, we could see Bray Head and in the distance beyond that, the Sugar Loaf mountain – idyllic.

Suddenly everything changed. Thomas stopped abruptly and grabbed my wrist.

'Look!'

'Where?'

'In front.'

Coming towards us up the prom, some fifty yards away were Mam, Dad, Phil, Jen, Martin and Greg. Beads of sweat poured out onto my forehead.

'Oh, Jaysus help us,' I said.

I felt sick and found myself trembling. Thomas kept his cool. He did a smart right turn pulling me with him. Slightly quickening our pace, we crossed the wide grass verge and then the main road that ran parallel with the promenade. We were now outside the fairground, which was busy, and in we went. Looking back, we could see the family continuing their walk. Joe had his cine camera out and was filming the kids.

'Jaysus' I said again, 'That was a close shave.'

Thomas was laughing - hysterically, I think.

Having calmed ourselves, we walked through the crowds around the rides and sideshows and ended up at the Dodgems. We had to have a go. Climbing into one car I opened my purse and handed over a shilling to the young lad who had come over. The siren sounded and we were off. There were a lot of boys on the ride and they all seemed determined to crash into us poor helpless girls and spin us round. The yells we let out seemed to attract them even more.

Everyone was having great fun whizzing round laughing and screaming, when, out of the blue, they were all there again. Standing in a line along one side of the track - Mam, Dad, Phil, Jen, Martin and Greg. We were horrified and I again felt the beads of sweat pouring out. Keeping our heads down we steered as best we could to the point furthest from them. Fortunately, Joe wasn't filming at that point. The boys followed us and soon we were jammed in with our backs to the family. This was horrible.

Joe was now dishing out money to Martin and Phil who then started moving round the outside of the track in our direction. In a matter of seconds, they would be directly facing us.

'Will the ride ever end' I thought?

When finally the siren sounded we clambered out. I actually brushed past Martin as he rushed to get into a vacant car. I couldn't believe he didn't recognise me. He was so close. Once more we made our getaway into the crowds. We were very lucky girls.

The only thing to do now was to get as far away as possible from them. We returned to the front and set off at a brisk pace in the direction of Bray Head.

At the end of the prom we followed the Coastal Path which ran along the cliffs from Bray to Greystones. It climbed up out of the town, past a large slab of concrete. We didn't give it much attention that day, but I later learnt that this used to be the start of a chairlift which went halfway up the Head to a café and ballroom known as the Eagle's Nest. A bit further on, the path crossed a bridge over the DART coastal railway and then came to a gap in the wall on our right. This was where the real climb began. No tarmac path on the other side of the wall - just a well-worn dirt track leading up into the woods. Soon even that disappeared, and we were clambering over endless exposed tree roots. Just the sort of place a girl might easily slip and require male assistance. The high heeled shoes were totally ridiculous but that didn't worry us.

As anticipated, the climb was quite busy, and we were pleased to see a number of young men making their way both up and down the track – just as we wanted. Waiting until we were strategically placed in front of two lads I pretended to slip and 'YES' – there was a wolf-whistle!

'Do you want a hand, girls? It's very steep here.'

With our best smiles we politely declined and continued upwards.

The way up was very steep, and we needed to take regular rests. This meant we could wait for fresh boys to come up the track and, setting off at just the right moment, were able to repeat the slipping manoeuvre several times. Taking it in turns to play the damsel in distress we were delighted with the results - several wolf-whistles and several gallant lads rushing to help us to our feet.

I was behind Thomas at one point when his helper purposefully placed a hand on Thomas's buttock and gave him a heft up.

'Oh!' he squealed in mock surprise. 'You're a very bold boy.'

'Sorry, Miss. My hand slipped.'

'Yes, I bet it did.'

His friend burst into laughter which we all joined in. After all, this was what we were here for.

Coming out of the woods the path opened out onto heathland that was covered with bright yellow gorse bushes and clumps of purple heather. We were now scrambling over steeply sloping rocks and a couple more Sir Lancelots came to our rescue.

Reaching the cross on the summit, eight hundred feet above the town, the view was stunning. In front of us the Irish Sea sparkled in the afternoon sun. You could see little boats and a ferry making its way into the harbour at Dun Laoghaire. Behind us were the neighbouring cone shaped hills known as the Great and Little Sugar Loaf and beyond them the distant backdrop of the Wicklow Mountains – Joe had taught us well and we all knew the local geography.

We were ready for another rest and sat at the edge of a small group of girls and boys of about our age, perhaps a little older. Soon we were chatting away as if we were old friends.

'I like your shoes,' one of the girls said to me. 'Can I try them on?'

'Sure.'

'They're lovely. Where did you get them?'

'Brown and Thomas in Grafton Street,' I lied. It was far too posh a shop for me. 'I got them in the sale.'

'Oh,' she said, 'I must have a look next time I'm in town.'

Maria would have been very pleased.

We could certainly hold our own with girly topics of conversation. After all, we'd had a lot of practice. It wasn't long before the subject of boyfriends came up. I thought

147

about Michael and said that we'd been together for about three months, he was working today.

Thomas gave me a look but said nothing.

'What does he do?'

'He's a plumber.'

There was no stopping me. Maria's Peter was a plumber and I knew a few bits and pieces if they asked me any technical questions. But they didn't. They were more interested in what he looked like and what we did together.

It felt good, and natural, to be part of this group of teenagers – if only for a short while. They were nice and they seemed to like us.

When the time came, we made our way back down the hill together – helping each other over the difficult bits. We paused on the way to admire the view. The whole sweep of Killiney Bay was before us with Dalkey Island visible offshore of Sorrento Point. The headland hid Dublin itself but in the very far distance you could just make out Howth Head where the rich Dubs lived.

Reaching the promenade, we said our 'Good-byes' and went off to catch the bus into Dublin. However, the day wasn't over yet and had one more surprise to throw at us.

We got to the bus station in the centre of Dublin. With the curfew a good four hours away and the sun still shining, we decided to walk from here across the Phoenix Park. It was a long walk but that wasn't a problem. The park was quite busy, but we didn't see anyone we recognised. We didn't talk to anyone and no-one wolf-whistled or jeered at us.

At the Chapelizod Gate we stopped for a rest on the grassy bank. It was here, many years before, that Ace lost her wedding ring. She'd lost weight after having Maria and it just slipped off her finger. We looked around in the hope that it might miraculously re-appear – but it didn't.

Walking on away from the park we crossed the Liffey and then passed Kilmainham Jail. The route then took us up Galtymore Road and into the Drimnagh Estate – now we could do some window gazing. We loved commenting on what people had on show – an elaborate Sacred Heart with eternal flame; some bright orange nets; a white plastic swan full of red plastic roses – not very tasteful.

It was Thomas who first noticed him, some fifty yards behind - a short, overweight man of about fifty. He was wearing a drab looking raincoat, which seemed odd on such a sunny day.

'I think he's following us.'

'What?'

It was a little unsettling, but we kept our cool. There were plenty of people around and we felt quite sure we could outrun him if it came to that.

Walking on we took turns to glance back over our shoulders. He definitely was following, and he was getting closer.

'Stop! You two girls - stop!'

The voice was stern and authoritative. We stopped and turned to find him right behind us.

'You're the two girls who have just walked through Phoenix Park. I'm a detective with the Dublin Gardai and I've been watching you.'

This was scary.

He spoke with a fixed glare on his face, but I couldn't help noticing his left eye was twitching nervously. Surely he wasn't a policeman. There was no sign of a uniform under his raincoat, he showed us no warrant card and, besides, we'd done nothing wrong. This was so far-fetched that we just stood staring at him in silence.

'You stay right here while I go and get the car. Don't you move an inch till I get back. Do you understand? I'm taking you in for questioning.'

With that, he turned and started back up the road.

I could see that Thomas was quite shaken, as I was myself. We stood staring at each other for a moment, then the adrenaline kicked in – this was a chancer trying his luck with two vulnerable girls. Maybe he got his kicks from being threatening. Whatever his game, we weren't going to hang around to find out. As soon as he was out of sight round the corner, it was off with the high heels and run!

We weren't that far from home now and soon reached the safety of the den. It had been a frightening experience, but we weren't going to let it spoil the day.

Having changed we set off back up the Long Mile Road. By the time we reached The Green we were both over our shock. I said 'Goodbye' to Thomas and walked over towards Number 30. I felt contented – a sense of achievement. Tina and Maria had been out for a whole day – and without wigs!

As I went into the house, I could hear Dad listening to the football in the front room. Mam called out to me from the kitchen.

'Hi Son. Have you had a good day? There's a bit of soda bread and some cheese in the fridge if you're hungry.'

'Thanks Mam. I'm starving.'

'We took the kids to Bray this afternoon. We looked out for you both, but we didn't see you.'

'Oh yes you did,' I thought to myself. 'Twice!'

'What are you smiling at?'

'Nothing, Mam.'

Chapter 17 – Crazy Talk.

In June 1970, just after my fifteenth birthday, I left school with no qualifications. I'd become extremely unhappy in the classroom. The Intermediates were coming up, but I couldn't face the stress. I'm sure I would have done a lot better without the pervading atmosphere of terror induced by the Christian Brothers. I just could not deal with the exams, let alone progress on to the next year and the Leaving Certificate. As far as school was concerned, I was a failure. Joe and Ace were obviously disappointed but, as usual, were very supportive. We discussed it but they didn't try to stop me.

It was not a good time and I was feeling depressed. The question of finding work had been brought up but, again, there was no pressure from the family. Their attitude was that 'something would turn up.' – and something did!

On Friday evening, about two weeks after I'd left school, Thomas came home from work clutching a brown envelope. We were sitting at the bottom of our stairs - still the place where we did most of our serious talking.

'I've had this idea,' he said.

'O.K.'

'So, I went and got a brochure.'

He opened the envelope and when I saw what was inside my heart missed a beat.

'You have got to be joking?'

'No, I'm serious. We could do it. What do you think?'

'I think you're crazy,' I said.

'Crazy?'

'Absolutely ridiculous. In the first place we'd never get permission from our parents.'

'We could ask. We're not kids anymore. I'm working and you will be soon.'

'I still couldn't afford it.'

'You've got some savings, haven't you?'

'Not much.'

'We could wash the nuns' cars again... If you're really stuck, I'd help you out.'

Thomas was always very generous with his money. He'd been at work for about a year and had already had a pay rise. On more than one occasion he'd given me a sub to buy make-up and only last week had been out and bought us both our first pair of tights – they were so much better than the old stockings held up with school ties. Though, on the downside, they easily laddered and frequently had to be replaced.

'No!' I said emphatically. 'I don't want to talk about it. Let's go for a walk.'

And that was that. Well, for Friday night anyway.

Thomas was round again on Saturday morning. He was on a message for Bridie and I went with him. I'd been thinking about the previous night's conversation and wasn't surprised when he raised the subject again.

'Have you changed your mind?'

'No. Definitely not. I still think it's crazy.'

There was so much that could go wrong. I even wondered if it might be against the law – though I couldn't think which law.

'It could be fun… Think of all the boys there.' We walked on in silence.

'Think of all the kisses we'd get.'

'Think of all the kicks we'd get. We'd be murdered if anyone found out.'

'We didn't get murdered in Bray. We did it for a whole day there.'

I had to give him that. It had been great fun.

All the way to the shop and back again, he went on and on. He wasn't prepared to listen to any of my objections. In the end, to shut him up, I said,

'Have you still got the brochure?'

'Yep.'

'Well, maybe bring it round this afternoon. I'll have a proper look but I'm not changing my mind.'

The glossy brochure was full of coloured pictures of happy smiling people enjoying themselves. It certainly looked a very exciting place to be, but Thomas's idea was so scary. It literally made me tremble to think about it.

'I just don't think I could do it.'

'Of course you could. You want to do it, don't you?'

'No, I don't! Well yes… I suppose I do.'

'You know you like a challenge.'

That was true enough.

'Well then.'

We talked a lot more and by Saturday night I was beginning to warm, just a little, to the idea. I always have been a dare-devil.

'I'll sleep on it and decide definitely tomorrow.'

I couldn't get Thomas's idea out of my mind and spent a restless night tossing and turning and worrying about the consequences of saying 'Yes' to him. By morning I'd made up my mind. I'd tell him my decision after Mass.

In the end I couldn't wait that long. In church he was sitting across the aisle from me and, having got his attention and with a big smile on my face, I nodded a 'Yes'. His face broke into a broad grin. As soon as the service was over, we met outside and began planning.

The first hurdle was to get permission from our parents. After a homily on listening to other people's opinions we thought this was as good a time as any to pluck up courage and ask.

Joe and Ace surprised me by saying they thought it was a great idea, if I paid for myself and promised to look for a job the second I returned home. Joe did relent later and put a very generous fiver in the funds. As expected, Thomas had a bit more trouble with his parents. Bridie was still very unhappy about Thomas being on his own with me for more than a few hours. Sean was on his side and eventually won her round. He had to promise to take her and the other kids away for a weekend in Wexford.

And so it was, on Monday morning, Thomas walked into the travel agent in George Street and booked a week's holiday for two at Butlins Holiday Camp in Mosney. He said he was booking for his sister Tina Doyle and for her friend Maria Donaghy. Could they please send the confirmation papers to Maria's address at 30, Walkinstown Parade? He paid the deposit of two punts and 10 shillings each and it was done. We had booked to spend a whole week at Butlins posing as Maria and Tina.

Three days later the confirmation letter dropped onto the hall mat. Ace picked it up.

'Have they got it wrong?' she asked. 'It's addressed to Maria.'

I was ready with my answer.

'Oh, we had to give the names of anyone else who might be interested,' I said vaguely. 'I expect they got muddled.'

I took the letter from her hand and rapidly disappeared upstairs. My parents were totally trusting and no more was said about that.

I opened the envelope, which had the travel agent's logo stamped across the front and started to read. It said that the holiday had been confirmed and that we should pay the total amount of 14 punts each, less the deposit, at least one week before departure. That was a lot of money to find but we would manage somehow.

Having committed ourselves the excitement took over. The holiday was only four weeks away and we had a great amount of planning to do. An intensive programme of car washing took place and we did odd jobs for anyone who would pay us. Even Granny Donaghy chipped in with a punt, though I did have to take her to the Bingo. At first she said it was a loan with an extortionate rate of interest attached, but later relented and gave it to me.

Clothes of course were the top priority. Space in our suitcases was going to be a problem. We would have to pack some boys' things on top, both for our parents' sake and for emergencies. We decided that there would only be enough room to take two outfits each, one for daywear and one for the evenings. We would be able to vary these with different accessories.

My first outfit was Maria's pink and green sleeveless dress with the round neck. I'd worn it before as a mini but would now have it at its full length, just below the knees. It looked gorgeous on her and would on me too. Thomas went for the hounds-tooth check skirt belonging to his younger sister. He'd also worn this before. I remembered it being so short that it barely covered the top of his stockings. With this he chose a black skinny polo necked jumper.

We both wanted something special for our second outfits, something glamorous for evening wear. With most of our cash going to pay for the holiday, money was very tight, and we couldn't afford to buy anything new. We came up with the idea of hiring. A story was invented - something about a surprise for our sisters, and off we went into town. The hire shop was very helpful, and we came away with two fabulous outfits. Thomas's was a full-length purple dress that zipped up at the back. It had a high neck and a deep frill around the bottom. There were long sleeves with ruffs around the wrists. The yoke had a pretty line of white stitching along the neckline. It was beautiful. I found something in a similar style in a gorgeous pink. This had two bands attached to the side seams that tied in a large bow at the back.

We didn't want to cheat the shop but only had enough money left to hire the dresses for a weekend. We paid the deposit and gave false names and addresses. We realised the return date would come and go while we were away. Thomas would have his holiday pay on our return and the plan was to take the dresses back full of apologies and pay any extra due. In the end we didn't take them back at all and felt very guilty about it for years to come.

With the dresses settled we could turn our minds to accessorizing. It was the weekend of the Bingo that Granny Donaghy left behind a beautiful pure Laine wool scarf. It had been a present from Portugal and was exquisitely decorated with pink roses. I'd not had the opportunity to borrow from her before. The day she returned to Carlingford I was the first to spot it on the hall stand and immediately saw the potential – I envisaged it pinned across my shoulders and the back draped up over my head in a cowl. It would go so well with the evening dress. The scarf disappeared into my case.

When it came to the packing, there was just enough room to squeeze in an extra outfit - a blue hipster skirt and a deep white belt with a large buckle. This I'd wear with a black sleeveless round-necked jumper.

We'd recently acquired Scholl sandals from Boots. They were very fashionable at the time and would be ideal for daywear. They made a very satisfying noise as we walked in them. The Scholls and one pair of high heels each for the evenings, that was the shoe ration. Added to this were various bits of jewellery and plenty of make-up. For the first time we treat ourselves to some nail-varnish. We'd never worn this before as it took so long to apply and take off. At Butlins, we would have all the time in the world. A beautiful shade of red was chosen to match our red lipstick.

I nicked a couple more pairs of tights from Maria when the opportunity arose - no need to spend any money there. Bits and pieces were moved up from the den and put away in my suitcase which was then stowed under my bed – pushed right to the back.

As the holiday drew closer everything seemed to be falling into place. Miraculously we raised enough money to go into town and pay the travel agent – for our sisters, of course.

I thought back to when Thomas had first suggested the idea. Why had I been so apprehensive? I really don't know. This was so exciting. We were nearly there. This was actually going to happen. What could go wrong now?

Chapter 18 - Liam.

On the Monday evening before we were due to go and two days after we'd been into town and paid over our hard-earned money, Thomas appeared on the doorstep. I could tell immediately by his face that something was wrong. I think he'd been crying.

'What's happened?'

'It's Mammy.'

'What's the matter with her?'

'Come out for a walk' he said. 'I'll tell you.'

This was obviously very serious. I followed him out with my stomach in knots. As we crossed the green he stopped and took a deep breath.

'Mam says we have to take Liam with us.'

'What!'

Liam was Thomas's eleven-year-old brother. His voice was trembling.

'She says we've got to go to the travel agent tomorrow morning and book him in. Otherwise I can't go. What are we going to do?'

I was furious. For years Bridie Doyle had been against our friendship. There were times when I thought she hated me and at that moment I hated her. She believed I was a bad influence on Thomas and now she was going to spoil our holiday.

'I hope her gee catches fire!' It was all I could say. 'She's ruined everything.'

'Please don't say that about my mother,' he said, but I'm sure he was feeling the same.

'All the planning wasted!' I shouted. 'All that money.'

He walked on and I followed in silence.

After the initial anger I calmed down and caught him up. I didn't really hate her. She was a kind woman who'd do anything for anyone. Neither of us spoke – we were both deep in thought. How could we take an eleven-year-old boy with us? He'd have to see us dressing up. How would he react if he saw us kissing boys? He'd be sure to ring home and tell on us. Bridie would be down to Mosney like a shot - as would Joe and Ace.

I pictured the scene - Thomas and I standing in front of our parents trying to explain that we'd been cross-dressing for ages. It felt surreal and unthinkable. I could hear Bridie saying,

'What is this foolishness?'

I think Joe and Ace would probably have coped with me dressing-up, but I knew they would be very unhappy that I had deceived them.

Thomas did get on well with Liam. He was a kind and gentle boy. I remembered him joining in the fantasy when Thomas dressed his doll up as a nun. There hadn't been a problem then. He hadn't rushed back to Mrs. Doyle to split on us.

We'd put so much into this venture. All the effort raising the money. The cases were packed. After my initial scepticism I was now totally committed and wasn't prepared to let it all go to waste. As we walked on, in silence, I had a thought – an idea was developing.

'I'm sorry I was rude about your Mam.' I knew she didn't really hate me – she was just concerned about Thomas.

'That's O.K. You've every right to be angry.'

'Suppose,' I said thinking out loud. 'Suppose we made it a big adventure for him? Something really special. Something that we all had to keep secret. Do you think he would go along with that?'

'I don't know what he'd do. He's only eleven.'

'All kids love a secret, especially if it's from their parents. Do you think he'd tell on us?'

'I said! I don't know what he'd do.' He was still very agitated. 'We'd have to make him promise. Oh, this is dreadful.'

'Thomas, listen. I think we could get around this. He'll be really looking forward to having a great week away and he's not going to want to give that up for anything.'

'Do you think so?'

'We could tell him right at the last minute - after we've left home. Once we got there, I think it would be fine.'

I was warming to my theme.

'He wouldn't want to hang around with us, would he? He'd want to play on all the rides.'

'I suppose there'd be plenty of kids his own age. He may not want to bother with us at all.'

Thomas was beginning to catch on to my idea. I went on.

163

'We just tell him that we are playing a big game to see what will happen, but we don't want anyone else to know.'

We were both working hard now to convince ourselves that it would be O.K. As I saw it there was no other choice - either this or abandon the plan completely and go on the holiday as ourselves. Neither of us wanted to do that. Mrs. Doyle had spoken – Liam would have to come with us.

Having made the decision, we both felt a bit better.

'Look on it as another challenge,' I said. 'That's what we'll do. We've had challenges before, lots of them. We've got through them and we'll get through this one.'

The next morning Thomas called in at the travel agent. He'd stopped at a phone box and rung work with some excuse for being late. Considering it was so close to the holiday, the staff were extremely helpful.

'Sure, we can do that for you. If one of the girls won't mind sleeping on a bunk bed, we'll get you a chalet with a divan and bunks. The three of 'em will be just fine in there.'

'Yes, we will', thought Thomas.

A quick phone call to Mosney and everything was arranged. Maria Donaghy would be arriving with Tina Doyle and her younger brother Liam.

'Great now. It's all done for yer. No need to worry.'

But worry we did.

The situation wasn't helped by the younger Donaghy's. When they heard that Liam was going with us they were very jealous. Martin was roughly the same age as Liam and Phil was nine. They started pestering Joe.

'Why can't we go, Daddy?'

'We want to go to Butlins.'

'Ah' said Joe, 'Leo's saved up a long while for this. When you're older you can go too.'

'It's not fair.'

'We want to go with Leo.'

'Now here's a shillen. Go over to the shop and buy yerselves some sweeties.'

That shut them up.

Chapter 19 – The Moment of Truth.

When I woke on Saturday morning, I should have been feeling excited. Instead, as I went downstairs with my case of hidden secrets, I felt nauseous. Mam picked it up.

'Leo, you're not eating your breakfast. Are you alright?'

'Yes, Mam. Just a bit anxious I suppose.'

'Ah, you'll be fine once you get with Thomas.'

He had to work at Burtons on Saturday morning. Liam and I were going to get the bus into town and meet him at half past one at the Bus Aris terminal. We'd done our reconnaissance the week before and found a quiet little alley, around the corner from the bus station, where we could safely change out of sight. After telling Liam we would go there, get changed and then walk to the railway station. Joe offered to drive us into town as I knew he would, and I was ready with an answer. I said it's our first holiday away on our own and we want to be independent right from the start, and he accepted that.

At twelve thirty Mrs. Doyle brought Liam round with his suitcase. True to his word, Mr. Doyle was taking her and the rest of the family off to Wexford.

'Isn't it well for them, Mrs. Donaghy? I'd love a week at Butlins, wouldn't you?'

'Ah well, Mrs. Doyle, you're only young once.'

When the time came to leave, I was finding it extremely difficult to keep a smile on my face. It turned out to be quite an event on The Parade. As well as the Donaghy and Doyle clans, there was a crowd of local kids on the green and Maggie Mangan from Number 32 and Mrs. Foley from 28 were both at their doors to wave us on our way. All that was missing was a bit of bunting and a brass band. Mam kissed both of us and Dad said,

'Now you boys be very good.'

That was it - we were off. Carrying our suitcases, we walked around the corner to get the Number 56 bus into town. Sitting next to Liam there was only one thought on my mind – the moment we had to tell him the truth was getting very close. Although we had only been gone five minutes, he was already looking a bit homesick. It occurred to me that the news might just tip him over and send him running home to Bridie.

'Are you O.K. Liam?'

'Yes, thanks.'

'Are you excited?'

A little nod of the head.

We got into Bus Aris at 1:15. The sky overhead was grey and there was a drizzle in the air. We had fifteen minutes to wait for Thomas.

As we stood there in the shelter with our two suitcases, the tension was palpable. It was only two or three minutes away now and Liam would have to be told. He was still looking anxious. It was his first time away from home without his Mam and Dad and I understood that. He was dressed in shorts and over his school shirt had a russet coloured hand-knitted jumper with a darn in the elbow. He did look like a little lost boy.

We spotted Thomas coming towards us and Liam ran over to greet him. When he turned around the smile had returned to his face. He felt better now his big brother was there. I wondered how long that would last. Thomas was looking serious and I could tell that he also was anxious about the outcome of the next few minutes.

'Everything alright?'

'Yes' I said. 'I had to persuade Joe not to give us a lift into town. I'm sure he would have wanted to wait and wave us off.'

'Oh, Jeese', was all Thomas could say.

There were some tables and chairs under an awning just inside the terminal, and the three of us sat down. The moment had come. It could be put off no longer. Thomas was sitting next to Liam and he turned to face him square on. He took a deep breath and spoke, slowly and deliberately.

'Liam, we've got something to tell you.' We had his full attention. 'We're going to let you into a big secret.'

'It's going to be a great adventure,' I added for encouragement.

'But you've got to promise to keep it a secret from everyone, even Mam and Dad.'

Now he was sitting on the edge of his seat.

'Do you promise?'

'Yes', he nodded, wide eyed with anticipation.

'Cross your heart and hope to die?'

169

He made the sign across his chest.

After a short pause, Thomas took another breath and went for it.

'Leo and I are going to go to Butlins dressed as girls.'

It was out. No going back now.

There was silence as Liam's brain processed the information. We watched as his jaw dropped open. Time went into slow motion. There was a question in his eyes – but no – he said nothing. Then, quite suddenly, he burst out laughing - with excitement, I think.

We knew we were safe.

'Jaysus!' he said, 'That's great!'

'You can't tell Mammy.'

'I won't. I promise. I'll keep it secret, I promise, cross my heart.'

And with that, he jumped up and did a little jig. Thomas and I looked at each other - relief streaming into our faces. Five days of stress and anxiety were over. Five days of having to pretend everything was normal. We felt like doing a little jig as well. It was going to be alright. We got up and had a bit of a group hug.

I glanced at my watch, a quarter to two - we didn't have much time as the train to Mosney departed at 2:30. Leaving the bus station, the three of us crossed the road and turned down a side alley. There, in amongst some large rubbish bins and a drainpipe spouting water about our feet, the transformation began. It had to be quick. The glamour could come later. We were going to keep our trousers on for the time being, hoping they'd be taken as slacks. Shoes and socks came off to reveal the toenails that we'd carefully painted the night before in the new bright red varnish. We put the Scholls on our bare feet. The bras with their socks went on over our shirts with a blouse on top. No wigs, just scarves and anoraks. Finally, a little bit of eye shadow and some lipstick.

We knew we weren't totally convincing at this stage, but it was the best we could do in the time we had. Liam was impressed anyway. He'd watched the whole change in silence with his mouth hanging open.

'Jeese, you look marvellous.'

That was very encouraging.

With Liam between us, we apprehensively emerged from the alley, back into the main street as Maria and Tina.

Connolly Street station was a four-minute walk and once we got started, the three of us laughed all the way. Liam kept looking round to see if anyone was watching us – but they weren't. No-one gave us a second glance. At one point he said,

'Why are you walking so funny?'

'We're not' said Thomas. 'This is the way all girls walk.'

He tried to copy which had us all laughing again. I thought he might ask if we'd done this before but, thankfully, he didn't.

At the station I went up to the ticket office and took out my purse. The man behind the grill didn't look at all concerned.

'Two adults and one child to Butlins, Mosney please.'

He handed over three tickets and said,

'That'll be one punt and two shillings, please Miss.'

Another hurdle passed.

In the 1940s Sir Billy Butlin had decided to extend his holiday business beyond the shores of the United Kingdom and in 1948, the camp in Mosney, County Meath, opened its' doors. Mosney was an area of flat land on the coast, some 25 miles north of Dublin and conveniently situated close to the main Dublin to Belfast railway line. A loop-line was built when the camp opened, so holiday makers could get the train from Dublin in the South, and Belfast in the North, right into the camp.

Making our way onto the platform we felt as though we were in a scene from 'Some Like it Hot', which we'd watched on more than one occasion. We were Jack Lemmon and Tony Curtis. All we needed was a whoosh of steam as the train pulled in and we would shriek through it. As we waited, we gave Liam a bit of a grilling.

'Who are you going to Butlins with?'

'My sister Tina.'

'And who else?'

'Her friend Maria.'

'And how many sisters have you got'

'Three. Oh no! Four.'

'What are their names?'

'Grainne, Cathleen, Marion and Tina.'

'Good lad. You've got it.'

We boarded the train, which was quite busy and took the seats just inside the door. I sat next to Tony with Thomas on the opposite seat, grinning from ear to ear. He knew something that no-one else in the carriage knew. At least we hoped they didn't. The jollity of the walk to the station was sagging a bit and giving way to the reality of what lay ahead.

A middle-aged man came and sat down next to Thomas. He seemed to be staring suspiciously at us but probably wasn't – just my anxiety. On the other side of the carriage was a young couple with two under-fives in tow. Again, they paid us very little attention. The kids were more interested in anything edible the woman might have in her bag. Having exhausted that game, they knelt on the seats and looked out of the window.

I kept telling myself that no-one would dare say anything, even if they did think we looked odd. I didn't think we looked odd. I thought Thomas looked quite beautiful. He had on his thick purple and blue satin headscarf, which set off his bright blue eyes with their thickly set eye lashes. Though, sitting so close, I was aware of his nostril hairs – we'd have to do something about that later. The hair from his hands had been removed the night before. They were elegant hands but with a slightly awkward masculinity about them. Puberty was biting. After all, he was fifteen and seemed to be developing much quicker than I was.

The journey would take about an hour and for most of that time we sat in silence. We went through Malahide and then Rush where we'd spent several family holidays in a beach house. I tried to spot it but the railway line was too far from the shore at that point.

I was feeling quite unnerved sitting opposite the staring man – we were vulnerable under such close scrutiny without our full paraphernalia on. I whispered to Thomas,

'I wish we'd put our skirts on.'

'Too late now,' he whispered back.

At Skerries the young family got out and the man moved to the other side of the carriage – that felt better, and I relaxed a bit.

The line now ran along the coast and we had the Irish Sea off to our right. The next stop was Balbriggan and then Gormanston, the last station before the branch line split off towards Butlins - we were nearly there.

A few minutes later, with a blast on its whistle, the train slowed and pulled into the single platform that was Mosney Station. It had a white picket fence running the length of the platform with a brick built signal box in the middle. As we looked out of the window, on one side we could see the sea. On the other, the flagpoles with their billowing Butlins flags which marked the entrance to the camp - just as we'd seen in the brochure. We'd arrived. We were at Butlins Holiday Camp. The adventure was about to begin. This was it – no turning back. We now had to pull our deception off, in full public view, for seven whole days.

'Jaysus, Mary and Joseph help us!'

Chapter 20 – Tonight in the Ballroom.

As we stepped down onto the platform, the Dublin drizzle had completely cleared, and the sun was shining brightly. On the other side of the picket fence a gaily painted road-train awaited us. Puffing Billie was red and black and behind the engine were half a dozen little carriages, painted in blue with yellow tops. This was our transport into the camp itself. As we and our fellow holiday makers clambered aboard, porters loaded the luggage into the last two carriages, and we were on our way.

At a rather sedate pace the little train made its way along a road lined with the famous striped Butlins lanterns that lit up at night. On the right we could see the boating lake with its swan-shaped boats gracefully gliding to and fro. Then, on the left, we passed the amusement park with all the free rides. Liam got very excited. Next along the route was the Gaiety Theatre. I thought of the pictures in the brochure of the showgirls in their sparkling costumes and feathered head-dresses. Thomas and I would certainly spend some time there. Beyond the theatre, the orderly rows of chalets which were to be our home for the next week came into view.

Eventually the train came to a halt outside a building with a colourful sign announcing that we had arrived at the Reception Hall. Here we got our first sight of the famous Butlins Redcoats. Lined up on the steps, all with smiling faces to greet us, they looked very smart and very grown up - though in fact they were probably only a few years older than Thomas and me. They all wore bright red blazers with the Butlins badge emblazoned on the left breast pocket. The girls had white open-necked blouses and white pleated skirts. The boys had white slacks and wore a striped tie with their white shirts.

We followed them inside and while Thomas joined the queue at the reception desk to book us in, Liam and I stood waiting for the cases to be unloaded. I looked across at Thomas. With his head inclined to one side and a Veronica Martha smile on his face he looked just like a woman. When it came to his turn, the receptionist was all smiles and that was another hurdle passed. He was given a key to our chalet and directions on how to find it. We each got a programme booklet for the week ahead and enamel badges to wear. These were to be our passes into and out of camp and our free tickets for all the rides and activities.

With the formalities completed we made our way out of Reception and across to the chalets. There were a combination of single storey and two storey buildings set out in lines. A concrete path ran along the front of each row and each block was divided from the next by a wide grass verge with colourful shrubs and bedding plants running down the middle.

We soon found our home for the week. We were at the end of a one-story block. Each chalet had a front door with a little window on either side. The walls were painted in a powder blue with the doors and windows in a much darker corporation blue. The curtains had sail boats on them. With great anticipation Thomas turned the key and let us in.

The interior was very basic - about 10 feet square and furnished with a single divan and a bunk bed, separated by a sink. The candlewick bedspreads were blue and orange with the Butlins logo in the centre. Along one side were a small hanging space and a chest of drawers with a mirror over it. The toilets and baths were communal and down the chalet line in a separate block.

I suppose it resembled a prison block, which, in reality it has now become, operating as a detention centre for asylum seekers. But at the time we thought it was very pretty - our own little palace with beautiful gardens.

Liam clambered up to the top bunk with Thomas underneath. I took the divan. There was great excitement. We lay on our beds, kicked our legs in the air and laughed hysterically – we'd made it!

When we'd all calmed down, we had a look through our programmes. The front cover said, 'The Sign of a Happy Summer Holiday' and under this, on a thick blue banner, 'Butlins 70'. The inside was divided into the days of the week, with a special middle section of children's activities - Liam started there. As Thomas and I flicked through the pages there seemed to be endless things to do and see. There were fancy dress parades and sports competitions and Red Coat Shows. We could go to the cinema and the Gaiety Theatre, which we had already seen, and everything was free. There was a ballroom and an Irish Bar. Not only was there an outdoor swimming pool but an indoor one as well.

177

Then of course the funfair, which we'd passed on the way in, with its roundabout, dodgem cars and big wheel. We'd have to go on the boating lake and the roller-skating rink.

Despite all the excitement, Thomas and I both felt a kind of reticence. We'd discussed it before coming. We were very aware of how vulnerable we were and the consequences of being found out. We felt we would have to hold back a bit and not get too involved with any individual person or in any activity that might lead to discovery. We certainly didn't want to take part in any competitions that might result in unwelcome limelight. Better to watch from the side-lines and do our own thing.

The programme said that at 4:30 we should 'Meet the Recoats at the Skating Rink for a Tour of the Camp.' That sounded like a good idea. We needed to know our way around and it would be good to keep an eye out for escape routes should it become necessary. There wasn't much time and before we went out exploring, we had to get dressed in our real costumes and make-up.

I put on the pink and green dress and Thomas the hounds-tooth check skirt and jumper. He wore this with some beads around the neck. Our make-up box was laid out on the chest of drawers and we carefully applied mauve eyeshadow (not too much) and Tender Orchid lipstick. Then, finally, our wigs.

Liam sat on the edge of my divan in his short trousers, entranced by the whole procedure. He tried both the wigs on and roared with laughter at himself in the mirror before admitting that they looked better on us. We did look absolutely gorgeous and felt it too. We were now Maria and Tina and ready to face the Butlins world.

As the three of us left the chalet to explore our new surroundings, literally only seconds passed before we got our first wolf-whistle. This sent us into a state of ecstasy and Liam was amazed.

'You're getting wolf-whistles. The boys are whistling at you.' He couldn't believe his eyes.

As we made our way up the path, I did one of my well-practiced heel wobbles which led to even more excited calls and whistles. I felt a complete contentment inside my woman's shell.

After the Redcoat tour it was almost time for the evening meal. Being high season there were two sittings in the dining room. We'd been informed at Reception that we were in Slane House which meant first sitting dinner at 5:30. Tara House would follow-on at 6:45.

The smooth running of the daily schedule was controlled by Radio Butlins, complete with xylophone chimes. At 5:15 precisely...

'Bing Bong... Good afternoon campers, this is Radio Butlins. We'd like to give a warm Butlins welcome to all our new visitors and to let you know that the first sitting for dinner will commence in the dining room in fifteen minutes.'

The dining room was opposite the skating rink and looked out over the pitch and putt course. With some trepidation we entered through the double-doors into an enormous hall that was set out with row upon row of tables and chairs. It looked as though it would seat several hundred people at a time. We found our allocated places and sat down. We were going to be in close proximity to the same people each mealtime for the coming week and we knew this would be a real test. We seemed to be surrounded by new campers, all a little unsure as to the routine and thankfully, no-one paid much attention to us – once again we breathed a sigh of relief.

Waitress service was a great novelty. Although I had been to afternoon tea at the Shelbourne Hotel in Dublin with Mam and Madge, eating out for our two families meant the fish and chip shop. This was special. We felt very posh and were going to enjoy it. The meal started with soup, which was followed by a roast dinner. Pudding was apple pie and custard or ice-cream.

As the meal progressed, I couldn't help noticing the family at the next table– husband and wife with two young children. The mother had jet black hair, big staring eyes and a face that was motionless unless she was chewing food. She did this in a slow methodical way. Her red elasticated lips seemed to have a life of their own, rather like a cow chewing the cud. Those big staring eyes always seemed to be fixed on us. So much so that I began to wonder if she had become suspicious. I whispered to Thomas, but he had already become aware of her and was having the same thoughts.

The explanation came a couple of days later. We saw her out on the camp talking to someone and realised that the big staring eyes went everywhere with her. The poor woman had thyroid trouble and was really very nice when we eventually got chatting to her.

Butlins was all go from morning till night. Sixty minutes after dinner had started, we were all sitting in the Gaiety Theatre to see 'Who's Who on the Redcoat Staff' followed by 'Saturday Showtime.' This was repeated at 7:30 for the second shift diners. Then, after a short break, we were off to the Ballroom for 'Meet and Make Merry at Mosney'.

The ballroom was spectacular. Painted in blue and lit by chandeliers hanging in a row along the length of the ceiling. At one end we could see a double staircase leading up to a balcony, where you could sit and watch the dancers below. The dancing area was covered in proper parquet flooring with plenty of seating round the sides. In the middle of one side was the stage and on this the live dance band was playing under a large, golden, shell-shaped canopy, lit by pink and green spotlights. The floor was full of couples dancing to the lively music. In the centre of the ceiling was a large glitter-ball that slowly revolved, reflecting the pink and green spotlights down onto the dancers below.

The music and dancing were mainly for the older people. The quickstep was followed by a waltz and then the foxtrot. We'd done all these at the Town and Country Club but as it was our first night, we thought it better to sit at the side and watch. That was until they announced the Velita. This was an old-time dance that I had learnt at Mr. and Mrs. Coyle's ballroom dancing classes. It would have been a shame to put all that teaching to waste, and I dragged Thomas out of his seat onto the floor. The two of us dancing together was just a bit too much for Liam who, with a groan, quickly disappeared up onto the balcony. I could see him peeping down at us with an incredulous look on his little face.

It had now gone ten o'clock and when we met up with Liam outside, he was ready for bed. We took him back to the chalet but decided we would visit one more venue before turning in – after all, there was no curfew here. We made our way to Dan Lowrey's Bar which was packed with much younger people than the ballroom crowd. As we made our way to the bar to order two orange juices, someone was on the microphone singing 'The Wild Rover'. When it got to the chorus, everyone banged their glasses on the tables in time to the music.

> ...and it's no nay never,
> (Bang bang bang bang)
> No nay never no more...

The craic was great. There were no seats left, so we stood at the side sipping our drinks and absorbing the atmosphere.

We'd had a long and exciting day and by eleven o'clock both felt ready for our beds. We were just about to leave when I noticed a tall blonde boy, about twenty, heading straight for us. He came right up to me and, with a strong German accent, said,

'You are a very pretty girl.'

With no further introduction he thrust his tongue into my mouth and passionately kissed me. Nothing more was said and, with a big smile on his face, he staggered off through the crowd.

That night I climbed into bed a very happy girl.

Chapter 21 – Sunday Morning.

Whether you were home, abroad or on the moon, Sunday morning meant Mass. We weren't worried about this. In fact, Thomas and I were quite looking forward to a new opportunity of getting some attention. We'd seen the teenage boys in Walkinstown purposely choosing a pew behind a couple of young girls in miniskirts. When the girls knelt down to pray, there were nudges and smirks from the boys as they admired the pert bottoms through the taut material and the bare thighs below. Now it would be our turn.

      The programme gave us plenty of choice. There would be masses at 7:30, 8:30, 9:30, 10:30 and 3:00 p.m. Slane House were on the early breakfast shift but then we would have to fast for an hour before church. We also needed time to make final costume adjustments – we wanted to look our best. We settled for the 10:30.

      Radio Butlins made sure that no camper would be late for breakfast. At seven thirty precisely they came blasting into every chalet over the public Tannoy system.

      'Bing Bong…. Good morning campers, this is Radio Butlins. It's a lovely morning and first sitting breakfast will be served in the dining room at 8:15.'

The sun was indeed shining and, as we pulled on our knickers and bras, Thomas and I wondered what our first full day at Butlins would bring forth. Liam had planned his day which consisted of a rotation between the fairground, the boating lake and the swimming pool. He was already used to our cross-dressing and paid little attention as Thomas combed his wig and I applied some lipstick.

Radio Butlins was now pumping out music and as we made our way to the dining room, we became familiar with the Morning Song:

> Good morning, good morning, good morning,
> Another lovely day,
> For when it's wet it's fine at Butlins,
> We never let it spoil your holiday.
> Good morning, good morning, good morning,
> There's a good time on the way,
> For wet or fine the sun will always shine,
> On your Butlins holiday.

By the end of the week we knew every word backwards.

We took our places in the dining room and said 'Good morning' to all our neighbours. Before long the friendly waitress from the night before was at the table offering a choice of cornflakes or porridge. This would be followed by sausage, bacon and egg and as much tea and toast as we wanted.

We had thought that we would have to leave the camp to attend mass but no, situated behind the chalets and near the car park was Butlins very own Saint Patrick's Catholic Church. No other Butlins camp had a consecrated church on site but apparently there had been a lot of opposition to the building of Mosney. The Catholic Standard newspaper stated quite clearly that:

> Holiday camps are an English idea and are alien and undesirable in an Irish Catholic country...

Billie Butlin pacified the hierarchy by building Saint Patrick's. For the Church of Ireland and Church of England Protestant visitors, Communion was held in the ballroom at 10:15. There was no choice – that was it.

As we entered through the porch of St. Patrick's, it has to be said that we didn't pay much attention to the oil painting hanging there. Many years later I learnt that the picture was by Bonifacio Veronese - a sixteenth century Italian painter of repute and it sold for a vast sum of money.

The inside of the church was spacious with enough seating for about two hundred communicants. By 10:30 it was full. All the women were smartly dressed, and all had hats on. Thomas and I wore headscarves over our wigs. A lot of the men were in suits, or at least a jacket and tie. No concession on Sunday morning to the fact that they were on holiday.

The three of us took a pew mid-way up the aisle and, as predicted, didn't have to wait long before we heard teenage male voices in the pew behind. We didn't dare look round, but it felt good to know they were there.

The service started and followed the normal pattern that we were so familiar with. The first time we knelt down we could feel the boys' eyes drilling into our backs and I actually heard one whisper,

'You can see her bra straps.'

That's what we wanted to hear – mission accomplished.

The homily was short, to the point and totally predictable: The Lord wants you to have a great week at Butlins but don't give in to the sins of the flesh and don't spend too much time in Dan Lowrey's Bar.

When it came to taking the Communion, Liam went up to the alter rail on his own. Thomas and I sat firmly in our places, sure that it must be a mortal sin to receive the host dressed as females. It wasn't necessary - we had done our duty by attending.

At the end of the service Liam wanted to go straight off to the fairground. He promised he wouldn't leave the camp and he promised he wouldn't go to the beach on his own. We felt quite sure he would be safe. There were Redcoats everywhere you looked, and he could always ask one of them if he had a problem. He disappeared with a great yelp of freedom.

'Make sure you're back for lunch,' Thomas shouted after him. 'First sitting is at 12:15.'

Thomas and I were now free to do our own feminine things. Arm in arm we made our way to the Pool Coffee Bar. While I went to order two coffees Thomas bagged some armchairs directly in front of one of the large underwater windows into the indoor swimming pool. I returned with our drinks and sat down. Every now and then, someone would dive down, and a face would appear against the glass in front of us and wave. As soon as the boys swimming realised they had an appreciative female audience on the other side of the plate glass, they went into overdrive and the show began. The more reaction they got from us the more they performed. They'd dive down to the window, turn somersaults, pull faces and wave at us. Now this was in the days before boys exposed their backsides to attract the attention of the opposite sex but every so often, some unfortunate lad had his trunks pulled down. We looked on with mock horror as the poor victim struggled to regain his dignity - great fun to watch. Better than a night at the movies. We waved back and smiled at all the good-looking divers.

The only downside to this was that I desperately wanted to be in the water with them. I loved swimming and wanted to do my mermaid act, with my long blonde hair streaming out behind me. It was not to be, and I had to accept this.

By now we were both quite relaxed. As we sat there sipping our coffees no-one was staring at us. No-one was making comments behind their hands. We were obviously fitting in and that felt great.

We could now indulge our other favourite pastime – people watching. The Pool Bar was obviously going to be an excellent place for this as there was so much coming and going. We would have to make it part of our daily routine. Our comments on the passers-by were quite malicious but only meant in fun, and only meant for ourselves. We would have died if anyone overheard us.

We played the game 'She was here last week':

'Did you see her? She didn't glance at the pool once. She must be on her second week.'

'That one's a new arrival. Did you see how excited she got when that boy in the blue trunks swam past?'

'She must have missed the tour last night.'

We were particularly catty about the other teenage girls.

'I don't think she'll get any wolf-whistles. Her skirt's far too long.'

'She's probably going to be a nun.'

'She'll be returned unopened.'

'Look at that one over there by the counter. That dress has worn well.'

'Do you see the state of her hair? Did she come on a motorbike?'

'It looks like an exploded Weetabix.'

'What could you do with it?'

'There's only one thing you could do - set fire to it. That would sort it out.'

Then we'd both roar with laughter before moving on to the next victim. The banter was all meant in fun and I dread to think what other people were saying about us.

Before we knew it the Tannoy was 'Bing Bonging' us to first sitting lunch. When we got to the dining room Liam was already sitting at our table with knife and fork at the ready. He'd had a great morning and had an appointment at the boating lake straight after lunch with a lad he got friendly with – just as we'd hoped things would be. Thomas and I decided we'd go for a stroll around the camp and watch other people being energetic.

It was all very pleasant. We watched some young men playing football – Slane versus Tara judging by the shouts coming from the side-lines. Then, after showing our badges, had a free round on the putting green – neither of us was very good but it was fun. Most of the time we just strolled and chatted and felt feminine.

On our way back to the chalet we came to the bathroom block. I told Thomas to go on ahead and said I'd catch him up. As I started up the steps, to the Ladies of course, coming down towards me from the Gents side was someone I instantly recognised. He was a friend of Anthony, my older brother. It just hadn't occurred to us that we might meet somebody we knew.

As the adrenaline surged, I felt my heartbeat increase. I was almost face to face with him – far too late to take evasive action. Head down, I kept going.

'Maria Donaghy?'

'Jaysus help me!' I thought, 'He thinks I'm Maria.'

I doubt if it was divine intervention, but it came out spontaneously,

'Ah no, she's my cousin. Everyone says we look alike.'

'You certainly do. You're very pretty.'

I thought that was a bit forward but nevertheless much appreciated. I smiled sweetly and coquettishly tilted my head to one side.

'I know her brother, Anthony. Will you tell him Donal O'Sullivan was asking for him?'

'I will. Nice to meet you.'

'And you. Enjoy your week.'

With that, he gave me a quick peck on the cheek and was gone. He was gorgeous and I would have been quite happy to spend some more time with him but despite looking, we didn't see him again. Disappointingly he must have been a day visitor – perhaps it was for the best.

Chapter 22 – Skating Games.

Outside the dining room was a large fluorescent notice saying that, on Monday morning, the camp photographer would be coming round during breakfast to take pictures. They obviously did this at breakfast to catch as many people as possible. The notice went on to say that he'd be happy to take either family groups or individual photos. You could purchase these either framed in the traditional way or, as a miniature set in a red Butlin's key ring. This was no ordinary key ring. You had to look into the top of a tube through a small magnifying glass to see the photograph at the other end – a bit like looking into a kaleidoscope.

Thomas and I had discussed cameras and photographs at one of our planning meetings. The decision was that it would be too risky. Joe would have insisted on developing the films for us in his little darkroom at home. Even if we did manage to get them to the local chemist, Joe worked there in the photography department on a Saturday afternoon. We could imagine the conversation he would have with Mr. Curvan, the pharmacist when the pictures arrived back from the developers. Unfortunately, there would have to be no photographic record of our adventure. When we read the notice though, we got quite excited.

Surely we could get away with a key ring picture as a small memento of the holiday.

On Monday morning we were up bright and early, long before 'Good-morning Campers'. Plenty of time was needed to apply our make-up. We were extra lavish with the eyeshadow and must have used half a tube of lipstick to create the desired effect. When we got to the dining room it was obvious that we weren't the only ones to have made an effort. Even the thyroid lady at the next table had done her hair and managed a small smile as we sat down.

We watched over the bacon and eggs as the photographer made his way around the tables. People were hunching together in family groups, waving, pulling faces and saying 'Cheese' very loudly. Eventually he arrived at our table. Liam had his picture taken first. Then Thomas and I posed together with our best Veronica Martha smiles. The photographer seemed pleased with the result. He had a broad Dublin accent.

'O'il tell yer someting girls, yer's looking goorgeous.'

After a very relaxing Sunday, both Thomas and I felt that today we ought to do something a bit more active. Liam had been on all the attractions at least twice and after breakfast we allowed him to drag us off to the fairground. He'd been so good, and we felt we should spend some time with him, before heading back to the Pool Bar for the morning show.

The rides were rather modest compared with modern day standards but still great fun – after all, we were two fifteen-year-old boys. The main attraction was a large Ferris Wheel. Not quite the London Eye but it did give you a fine view over the camp and out to the beach and the Irish Sea. The other rides that caught my eye were a Merry-go-Round with garishly painted horses and of course the Dodgems. Considering everything was free the queues were comparatively short, and we were able to go on the rides as often as we liked. We loved the spinning Chair-o-Plane. Each seat was suspended from four chains and as it gathered speed you were hurled upwards and outwards. Our Scholls hung tenuously onto our painted toes.

After an hour of spinning, flying and crashing Thomas and I were in need of a coffee. Liam was already heading back to the Dodgems for yet another session and was quite happy being left on his own. We made our way to the Pool Bar via the chalet. After the battering we had taken it was important to check all our bits and pieces were still in place and looking presentable.

We had our well-deserved coffee in our favourite armchairs. The Pool Bar was certainly the best place to see and be seen but this was meant to be an activity morning.

We finished our drinks and then walked through the main building and out to the roller-skating rink. Both Thomas and I had been given roller skates as presents from our parents the previous Christmas. After hours of practice on The Parade we'd become quite proficient. We'd not been in a rink before with crowds of other skaters but were keen to try.

The skating area was rectangular in shape, some thirty yards long and fifteen yards wide. It was laid out with blue and white squares, like a giant chequer board and had a barrier railing running around the perimeter where spectators could watch the goings-on. At one end was a yellow building with benches in front of it. This was where you got your skates and put them on.

We sat on a bench and slipped off our Scholls. As I bent forward to fit my skates, my long blonde hair kept falling over my eyes. I loved flicking it back. It felt a very feminine thing to do - another attention seeking trick. Apart from that, if I didn't do it I couldn't see the laces to tie them.

We made it onto the rink, which wasn't too crowded. The skaters were mainly teenage boys and girls. At first Thomas and I held hands and skated as a pair. It proved to be easier than skating at Walkinstown as there were no potholes to negotiate. The beginners were around the outside, hanging onto the rail, so there was plenty of room in the middle to get up a bit of speed and soon we were whizzing around on our own.

We had great fun playing the 'damsel in distress' - crashing into the barrier just where a handsome lad was standing ready to catch us. If we fell, they eagerly helped us to our feet and exchanged a few words. Before long they were skating up besides us and calling out.

'What's yer name?'

'Maria. What's yours?'

'Eamon and my friend's Patrick. Your friend's got nice hair. What's her name?'

'That's Tina. I'll tell her you said so.'

Having been formerly introduced they were soon chasing us round the rink. Their game was obviously to crash into us and pinch our bottoms, which led to a lot of laughing and screaming. That's what we were there for and we loved it. As we grew more confident and speedier, we were able to do a bit of bottom pinching of our own.

When they tired of this, Patrick grabbed me round the waist and shouted out to Eamon,

'Let's make a train.'

Eamon got hold of Thomas and manoeuvred him into position behind Patrick and before I knew it, I was leading a dozen youngsters in a frenzied conga, wheeling and curling dangerously round the rink.

The frivolities only came to an end when the Tannoy 'Bing-bonged.'

'Will all Slane House campers please make their way to the dining room. First sitting lunch will commence in ten minutes.'

The boys were in Tara but followed us over to the benches in front of the yellow hut. They chatted as we removed our skates and it wasn't long before Eamon turned the conversation to the subject of our accommodation.

'Are you sharing a chalet?'

'We are.'

'Is it a one storey or two storey?'

'It's a one storey.'

'Ah, so is ours. Which block are you in?'

'I can't remember.'

'Sure, you can.'

It was pretty clear where all this was leading, and we weren't about to give away too many secrets – not after one meeting. They were pleasant good-looking boys and, later in the week, maybe we would invite them back. For now, despite his pleading, we refused to tell Eamon what he wanted to know.

There was always that awareness of vulnerability. It Was important that we had our bolt hole among the endless rows of anonymous chalets.

'That's it boys, we have to go.'

Thomas was making it clear that the conversation was over. We didn't want to put them off completely, so I added,

'We'll look out for you later.'

'Do you promise?'

'Yes, we promise, and we'll definitely be back skating tomorrow.'

By Tuesday the three of us had settled nicely into a routine. We only saw Liam at mealtimes and that was fine. He was having a great time and wasn't in the least bit bothered with what we got up to. Mosney was a big camp and there were a lot of people staying there but we were beginning to recognise faces and to be recognised ourselves. We'd say 'Hello' and even chatted to some of the boys.

After morning coffee, we returned to the rink for some more chasing games. The skating boys seemed pleased to see us and the girls now accepted us as part of the crowd. Eamon and Patrick were there again, and we exchanged names with a few of the others.

As the boys became bolder the games became a bit saucier. Now, when they chased up behind us, they'd lift our skirts and slap our bottoms. Apart from telling them that they were very naughty, neither we, nor any of the other girls, did anything to discourage this.

'Stop it Patrick. You're very bold.'

'I won't now. Yer know yer loike it.'

'I don't.'

'Yer do. Yer smiling.'

'Oow! Well don't do it so hard.'

There must have been twenty or so teenagers on the rink when one of the boys skated up behind Thomas and pinched his bum. Thomas lost his balance and lurched forward into me sending me flying. As I hit the barrier there were peals of laughter from everyone. I grabbed the rail and started to pull myself up. As my head came over the bar I got the shock of my life. Smiling directly into my face was Anthony McAvoy, aged twelve, from Number 36, Walkinstown Parade. I was speechless but managed to smile back. There wasn't a flicker of recognition from him, in fact he turned away and started to stroll off. I panicked and rushed over to Thomas.

'We've got to get off the rink' I babbled, 'Anthony McAvoy is here.'

Thomas's reaction was the same as mine and we immediately headed for the benches. I could still see Anthony. He was now standing at the rail on the other side of the rink but wasn't looking in our direction. Patrick and Eamon were over in a flash, which was good because they shielded us as we took off our skates.

'Where's you goin, girls?'

'We have to go and meet Liam.'

'Who the feck's Liam?'

'He's Tina's little brother.'

'Jeese Tina, yer didn't tell us you had a brother here. Will we see you later?'

'Ah, sure you will' we shouted, as we returned our skates and sneaked off out of sight behind the yellow building.

'Well make sure yer don't bring Liam.'

We were almost certain that the McAvoys couldn't have been at the camp for four days without us bumping into one of them. Like Anthony's friend, they must have been visiting on a day pass. But what if they were staying? That would be serious. Liam and Anthony were good friends and if they met – there was a distinct possibility that he would share our secret.

We had to know one way or the other. While Thomas went back to the chalet, I headed for the reception desk.

'Oh, I'm sorry to trouble you but I think I may have seen a friend from home. Is it possible to check if they're staying?'

'Sure, I can do that for you Miss, what's their surname?'

'It's McAlvoy.'

'Let me see now. Er… Yes, we do have a family of McAvoys…'

'Oh no!' I thought.

'…but they come from Belfast and I'd say that you were a Dub. Am I right?'

'Oh yes, you are,' I said breathing out a sigh of relief.

'You'll have to wait till you get home to see them. Are you having a good week?'

'Yes, very good,' - apart from the shocks.

'Now will you be entering the Miss Elegance Fashion Contest? The heats are on this afternoon and you can win cash prizes.'

'Oh no, I couldn't do that,' I said.

'Of course you could. You're dressed very smartly, and you've got a lovely smile.'

That wasn't a smile she was looking at – more a grimace of relief that yet another catastrophe had been averted.

Back at the chalet I found Thomas anxiously peering through the curtains. I gave him the news that the McAvoys were only visitors. All we had to do now was to find Liam and keep him occupied and out of sight for the rest of the day.

The first part was easy. The lunch time 'Bing bong' had just come over the Tannoy. Liam would now be in the queue waiting for the dining room door to open. We cautiously made our way over and, sure enough, Liam was at the front of the line with his new best friend Keiran Heaney.

We'd decided not to tell him that we'd seen Anthony – too much temptation. And we thought we had a winner to keep him out of site.

'Liam, would you like to go horse riding this afternoon?'

It was the one thing he hadn't done yet. The horses were stabled in a far corner of the camp and we'd seen them disappearing off into the woods.

Yes, he would like to go, but not this afternoon. He and Keiran had plans.

'Would Keiran like to go horse riding with you?'

'No, we're going on the boats.'

This was getting us no-where!

At this point we noticed Keiran's mother making her way through the rows of tables towards us.

'Hello girls,' she said. 'We're going to take the children out of camp for a drive this afternoon. We wondered if Liam would like to come with us? There'll be ice cream at some point.'

That was the end of the boating plan.

'We're going to set off as soon as we've had our puddings.'

'Oh, yes! Please set off as soon as possible – thank you God – thank you God.' I nearly said it out loud.

With Liam out of the way, Thomas and I were quite happy to spend a few hours locked in the chalet. We could try some new hair styles, practice our make-up, tidy our costume accessories – endless girly things to keep us amused for the afternoon.

Chapter 23 – A Change of Mood.

On Wednesday morning I was the first to wake. As I looked round the chalet in the half-light filtering through the thin curtains, my eyes came to rest on the two bras hanging on the back of the wooden door. In my mind I wandered back over the past four days. I thought of the excitement of the day we arrived. We'd certainly had lots of attention over the past few days and lots of wolf-whistles. We'd had great fun with Eamon and Patrick at the skating rink and they'd certainly hinted that things could go further, if we wanted. I thought about that kiss on the first night, from the German in Dan Lowrey's – that had been special.

This morning, as I lay there listening to the gentle breathing coming from the bunk beds, something in me felt different – quite negative thoughts were coming to mind.

'Have I got to go through all this dressing-up again – put the bra on, put the make-up on, put the wig on? Another day of pretending to be something that I'm not. Why am I doing it? Is this the way my life's always going to be?'

This was all a bit profound, but the fact of the matter was, if I was honest with myself, I was becoming bored with the whole pretence.

Liam was stirring in the top bunk.

'Is it breakfast time?'

'Almost. Are you hungry?'

The answer to my own question, 'Have I got to go through it all again?' was 'Yes, I do have to go through it all again –at least for today, and the next three days.'

But after that? I was beginning to wonder about the future. Was there going to be anything more to my life?

When Thomas started to wake, we went into the now well practiced morning routine, and I tried hard not to let the other two see that I was a bit low. Then the Tannoy started,

'Good morning, good morning, good morning,
Another lovely day...'

I didn't agree with the sentiment but sang along with the others as we made our way to the dining room.

The morning passed – another stroll round the camp, coffee and another session at the skating rink. After lunch we went to watch Liam in the outdoor swimming pool. This gave him an appetite, so we took him for a doughnut at the Pool Coffee Bar. We got our favourite armchairs in front of the underwater window and I felt my spirits beginning to lift a little.

We were quite used to the Tannoy 'Bing-bonging' throughout the day with some announcement or other – most of which we ignored. As we munched on our doughnuts the familiar sound came over the speakers. What we heard next made the three of us sit bolt upright.

'Would Master Leo Donaghy please come to reception where his parents are waiting for him.'

'What!'

My heart began to thump. I thought it was going to burst through my chest. Instantly a cold sweat broke out on my forehead and began to trickle down my face. At first, we were speechless but then the adrenaline kicked in and our minds began to race. It was so hard to take in – Joe and Ace were there at the camp. Actually there, only a few yards away from where we were sitting. Had they come for the day? If they had, they'd definitely ask where our chalet was and then head that way. They'd want to see where we were staying and how we were getting on. Would the girl on reception check the guest list?

'I'm very sorry, there's no Leo Donaghy or Thomas Doyle staying but we do have a Maria Donaghy and a Tina Doyle.'
How would they react to that information? Would they catch on or would they think there'd been a mix-up? Would Mam remember that the brochure had been addressed to Maria?

The time was well past three o'clock. Surely, we told ourselves, they wouldn't take out a day-pass that late in the afternoon. If they had the kids with them, it would be too expensive. Much more likely they were out for a run and had just decided to pop in and say hello. Once we'd got over the initial shock, both Thomas and I thought this was the scenario that made the most sense, but we couldn't be certain.

For what seemed like minutes the three of us just sat there, frozen to our seats. This really was serious - much more dangerous than the previous day's encounter with Anthony McAvoy. What on earth were we going to do? We considered the possibilities.

One, we could dash back to the chalet, do a quick sex change and go out to meet them. But it would take ages to get all the make-up off, find our boys' clothes and get dressed. They might come to the chalet and catch us in the act.

Two, we could send Liam off on his own to meet them. He could say Thomas and I were out of the camp and he didn't know where we were. Would he be able to carry that off? He'd been brilliant up to now at keeping our secret but telling lies in front of Joe and Ace? He'd be nervous and they would see something was wrong. They might want to know why we'd left him on his own and then insist on waiting until we returned. We couldn't take that chance.

The Tannoy 'Bing-bonged' again:

'Would Master Leo Donaghy please come to reception where his parents are waiting for him.'

We had to do something and do it fast.

The third possibility was to pray that they were just passing-by, hide and sweat it out until the coast was clear. That was the best answer. That was what we had to do. There would be some explaining required when we got home but we could worry about that later. It was so lucky that Liam was with us. Every other day at this time he'd been off with his friends and could have been anywhere on the camp.

The first thing was to get out of the Pool Bar. Half eaten doughnuts were dropped and we exited in the opposite direction from the Reception area.

Although we were on our fifth day in camp, we hadn't been down to the beach. This we thought, might be an excellent time to go for a paddle. The gate leading onto the sand dunes was behind the tennis courts. A commissionaire in full uniform was always on duty there, and only those wearing an enamel Butlins badge were allowed in or out - he would protect us. Joe and Ace would want to go to the beach but if they'd paid-in, the kids' priority would be the fairground and all the free rides – they could go to the beach any day. We would be safe there.

Liam insisted on going via the chalet to pick up his wet swimming trunks and towel. He wasn't going to miss a chance to swim in the sea. We dashed back and while Liam went inside, Thomas and I kept watch. And then I had a thought. Without telling Thomas where I was going, I just said,

'You two go on. I'll meet you by the beach gate in a minute.'

I just had to see for myself. Crossing to the Reception building, I peeped in through the window and, there they all were. Joe was on his feet chatting to the receptionist, a finger tapping impatiently on the counter. Mam was sitting nearby in her favourite summer dress. It was a fresh apple green, decorated with little sprigs of black, flock-velvet leaves – so soft to the touch. Standing around her were Martin, Phil, Greg and Jen – Anthony must have been out with a friend. After feeling so down that morning, I desperately wanted to rush in and give them all a big hug, but of course I couldn't do that. I told myself I was being silly, and I would be back home in a couple of days – it didn't help much. Reluctantly, and close to tears, I left them all there and made my way down to the beach.

Chapter 24 – In at the Deep End.

Thomas was a Pisces but, despite his birth sign being two fish, did not enjoy swimming at all. I think he was really a little afraid of the water. I, on the other hand, loved it. Water and swimming often played a part in our family outings. Whether it was trips to the coast at Sea Point to swim in the sea, or a drive up to a river in the Wicklow Mountains, or just a visit to the local swimming pool. I was at my happiest sitting on a rock with a towel draped around my legs to make a tail, playing at being a mermaid.

We'd discussed swimming a lot when planning our trip to Butlins. We could think of no way of getting away with it. Girls at that time wore one-piece swimsuits. How would we hide our mickeys? How would we stop our sock-breasts from floating out of the top of our costumes? In the end we decided the best thing was not to pack our swimming trunks. That way we knew we wouldn't be tempted. That was what we decided - though, at the last minute, I couldn't resist, I slipped a pair of trunks into my case. I didn't tell Thomas. It was very naughty, but I thought – just maybe.

There were two swimming pools at Mosney - the large indoor pool with the underwater viewing windows and the heated outdoor pool. The latter was surrounded by a waist-high blue painted wall which was topped with a white lattice fence. You could stand on the outside and watch the goings-on in the water. At each end of the outdoor pool were two circular paddling pools. These had beautiful white, four-tiered fountains in them. Kids were allowed to climb up these and had great fun with the water cascading down over their bodies.

Thomas and I had to watch from the outside of the enclosure. I was so envious of a particular young girl who climbed right to the top of the fountain. She sat there on the fourth tier in her green bathing cap, which was decorated with starfish and seaweed. I wanted to do that. It should have been me sitting there - Queen of the mermaids, looking benevolently down on all my mermaid and merboy minions.

We would have loved to go into the enclosure. Just to sit and watch all the activity. But it was too dangerous. As the week progressed and the boys got bolder, it was clear that their games were becoming more boisterous. Despite the lifeguards many a girl was captured and thrown in at the deep end – occasionally fully clothed. We couldn't risk that happening to us.

Liam, like me, loved the water and had been swimming every day, at least once. He went in both the pools and the previous day, on our unplanned visit to the beach, had swum in the sea as well.

By Thursday afternoon and after our walk on the beach, I was desperate to get into the water. Thomas had gone off somewhere with Eamon, Patrick and some of the other girls. I said I would stay and watch Liam swimming. I'd join them later.

Once again, I was standing outside the blue wall looking in at Liam and Keiran splashing around in the pool. They were having a great time. The afternoon was so hot and sunny and after ten minutes or so, I could stand it no longer. I went back to the chalet, locked the door and drew the curtains. My case was under the divan and, right at the bottom, under my dirty clothes, I found my swimming trunks.

After taking the wig off and carefully removing every trace of make-up, I got undressed and put on my togs. I looked carefully at myself in the mirror. Under my wig I had a short boyish haircut. Looking back at me now was Leo Donaghy. I was sure no-one would recognise Maria. Anyway, I was prepared to take that chance.

Before leaving the chalet, I made quite sure that the coast was clear - at that time in the afternoon most of the campers were sunbathing or indulging in some activity or other. I could hear cheering in the distance and remembered a rounders match was taking place somewhere - Slane against Tara no doubt. With a towel draped round my shoulders I took a circuitous route back and, for the first time that week, went beyond the blue wall, through the gate and into the enclosure. It felt so great to be on the other side of the fence looking out.

The pool was crowded and there were two lifeguards patrolling up and down, blowing their whistles when the games got too rowdy. There were people both in the water and around the outside that I recognised, but no-one was paying any attention to me. They were far too busy enjoying themselves.

Liam was still in the water. I could see him chasing Keiran. I crept along the side until I was close and, with the lifeguard looking in the other direction, bombed in beside him.

As the water enveloped my body the sensation was indescribable – like a thousand champagne corks popping. I felt as free as Aladdin's genii released from his bottle. With the cold water tingling on my face and scalp I ran my fingers through my hair – my own hair, free from that tiresome wig.

It took Liam a few seconds to catch-on but when he did, he squealed with delight and immediately tried to drown me. The pool was too packed to actually swim more than a couple of yards but that didn't matter. Keiran accepted me as another friend of Liam's and the three of us had a great time chasing each other and playing hide-and-seek.

The two paddling pools were full of smaller kids but, having got this far, I wasn't going to miss out on the chance of climbing to the top of one of the fountains. I'd made it to the second tier when the whistle went. The stern voice of one of the lifeguards directed me back into the main pool by and watched until I was back in the water. At least I'd tried.

About an hour had passed, when I suddenly noticed Eamon and Patrick had appeared at the pool in their swimming trunks. My first thought was, where's Thomas? I anxiously scanned around the outside wall for his face – he would certainly recognise me and would not be pleased. He wasn't there. This, I thought, was my cue to make a quick exit. If I stayed any longer the boys might just happen to push me in. If they didn't recognise my face, they would certainly recognise the screams as I hit the water. No point in taking unnecessary risks. I was now worried that Thomas might be back in the chalet. I hadn't decided yet whether to tell him or not. I had a quick word with Liam, who wanted to stay longer and asked him not to say anything. Then, as Eamon and Patrick dived into the deep end, I climbed out at the shallow end and made my get-away.

Again, I took a long route back to the chalet and stood for some time at a distance to make sure I wasn't being watched. The curtains were still closed so there was a chance that Thomas wasn't back. I made a dash for the door and went inside – it was empty. After locking myself in, I threw the wet trunks into the washbowl and stood there drying myself. The swim had really lifted my spirits.

I started to dress - first my school-boy vest and then my sister's knickers. I wasn't in a hurry. I had the chalet to myself and I was enjoying a little peace and quiet after the noisy pool. I lay on the bed in my underwear, relaxing. The wig was on the chest of drawers and my sock-filled bra was hanging on the back of the locked door – I'd finish dressing later.

The peace didn't last long. I was shaken from my revelry by a loud insistent knocking on the door.

'Hello girls. Are you in there?'

'We're coming in to get you.'

It sounded like two or three boys outside the chalet, obviously up to devilment.

There was another knock and I saw the door handle being tried. Then, to my horror, a hand appeared round the curtain of the open window. I watched as it searched about

211

looking for the Yale lock. Instant action was needed. With one hand held over my breastless-vest I leapt off the bed and rushed to the door. Giggling and screaming I shouted,

'No, no, you naughty boys. You can't come in.'

I put the snip on the door and checked the lock. The hand was still through the window, so I gave it a good slap and pushed it back out.

'Go away. I'm not dressed. I'm in the nude.'

This produced gales of laughter and catcalls.

'Don't be such a spoilsport.'

'Let us in. We promise we won't look at you.'

I managed to get both of the windows shut without revealing myself. It went quiet for a moment and I had a peep through the curtain. Outside were three boys in a huddle, discussing what to do next. I recognised two of them from the skating rink. They decided on one more try.

'Could we come in when you're dressed?'

'Just for a little chat now.'

It would have been nice to accept their offer, but I couldn't risk coping with three of them on my own. Things might very easily go too far.

'Sorry boys. I'm going to have a little nap. I'll sees you all later.'

They were only being playful, and we had been asking for attention all week. You couldn't blame them for trying. I heard them moving away, still laughing and shouting back,

'See you later.'

I collapsed back on the bed smiling to myself and thinking about what might have been. Ah well, the week wasn't over yet.

When Thomas got back to the chalet, I was dressed but stupidly, I'd forgotten about my wet trunks which were still lying in the washbowl. He spotted them immediately and was not pleased. He was upset more than angry - sad that I had gone behind his back and broken our agreement not to bring our swimming things. Concerned also that it might have led to us being discovered. There was nothing for it but to sit back and take the telling-off I deserved. I didn't dare tell him about my visitors.

Chapter 25 – If You Go Down To The Woods.

Friday - our last full day at Butlins. The adventure was coming to an end and I can't say that I was sorry. Deep down I had a strong sense that my cross-dressing days might be coming to an end. I would have to have a long chat with Thomas when we got home. But that was for the future. Today we would enjoy ourselves.

A glance at the programme showed lots of finals were taking place during the morning – table tennis, darts, billiards and the inter-house cricket. They weren't for us and we pretty much followed our usual routine, including coffee and doughnuts in the Pool Bar and a final chase with the boys on the skating rink. There'd been hints from Eamon and Patrick about exchanging addresses but sadly, that wasn't going to happen.

In the afternoon the highlight was the 'Che Che Final'. The programme said 'A competition to find the most cheerful, charming and chubby girl on Camp. Open to lasses over sixteen and under sixty.' We decided to give this a miss but did pay a visit to the ballroom to watch the 'Dandy Debonair Final – A competition to find the most genial, pleasant, gay and immaculately dressed gentleman on Camp.'

The climax of the day was to be the Gala Dance in the ballroom. After dinner we gave ourselves plenty of time to get ready. We both wanted to look our best. Locking ourselves in the chalet with the windows shut and the curtains drawn we set to work. The purple and pink evening dresses were laid out on the divan. After washing we put them on - Thomas spent ages arranging the large pink bow at the back of mine, it had to be just right. As I helped him into his dress and zipped him up, there was a twinge of guilt - the dresses were supposed to have been back at the hire shop four days ago. Ah well – what's a girl to do?

Liam had been ready for ages – a lick and a promise at the chalet sink, the last clean shirt from the bottom of the case and his school tie. That was it and he was done. Waiting patiently on the top bunk with his legs dangling over the edge, he was passing the time reading the evening's programme.

'What's Oh Revor mean?' Thomas took the programme from him.

'It's Au Revoir. It's French. It means goodbye.' He read on out loud.

'The Redcoats say their farewell to you on behalf of the staff. God bless you all and a very safe and pleasant journey home tomorrow. We look forward to seeing you all again next year.'

'I don't know about that,' I said.

'The evening concludes with Auld Lang Syne followed by Goodnight Campers and the National Anthem.'

While Liam practised his French, we turned our attention to make-up. He'd seen this routine several times now and just left us to get on with it. I'd spent some time before dinner dressing the wigs, so they just had to be slipped into place. Then, apart from the final checks, we were ready for our night out.

As we left the chalet, we were greeted with dance music drifting through the evening air from the direction of the ballroom. The party was already underway with the brass section of the band clearly on top form. We joined the other campers heading that way.

The Ballroom was packed with our fellow holiday makers dancing, chatting and laughing and, no doubt, taking a last opportunity to exchange addresses with new-found friends. The Redcoats were on a three-line whip. They were everywhere - round the edges of the Ballroom, up on the balcony and on the floor dancing with the campers. Three were on the stage at the microphone harmonising a chorus of Bye-bye Blackbird. Some lusty singing was also coming from the dancers - not quite in tune with the group on the stage but it all added to the atmosphere.

We found three seats together and Thomas and I joined the melee on the floor for our first dance. After that we barely sat down. We loved dancing to the live music from the band. Eamon and Patrick were hovering nearby. They looked very smart in their jackets and ties with their hair Brylcreemed back. They were clearly trying to muster the courage to ask us to dance. It was painful to watch, so we went over and dragged them onto the floor for a slow waltz. They didn't know the steps but that didn't matter. It just felt nice to be that close to them. They were perfect gentlemen and kept their hands in strict ballroom hold – too many adults around for them to wander below the waist.

At one point we even managed to get Liam out of his seat for an awkward threesome. He much preferred watching, so we kept him plied with large pink lemonades and crisps and let him be.

Mid-way through the evening the House competition result was announced. We'd paid very little attention to this but cheered along with the rest when our House, Slane, was pronounced the week's winner. Doug, who was apparently our appointed captain, went up to the bandstand to collect the trophy.

Then came the final of the Miss Elegance Fashion Contest. Despite Liam's urgings we had declined to enter though, looking at the final six, I was pretty sure we could have made it into the top three.

It was a great evening, but inevitably the time came when the lights dimmed and the compare announced the Last Waltz. Everyone in the Ballroom came onto the floor. Liam had to be dragged but eventually joined us. You couldn't dance properly – there was no room. Everyone just shuffled around in time to the music. Then, as the dance came to an end, coloured balloons came floating down from a large net suspended from the roof.

As the band struck-up the familiar tune for Auld Lang Syne, the crowd miraculously formed itself into two large circles, one inside the other and, linking arms, joined in the singing.

Then, led by the Redcoats, who were now lined up across the front of the stage, we went into the final chorus of Good-night Campers.

Good-night campers, I can see you yawning,
Good-night campers, see you in the morning,

You must cheer up or you'll soon be dead,
For I've heard it said,
Folks die in bed.
So we'll say good-night campers, don't sleep in your braces,
Good-night campers, put your teeth in Jeyes,
Drown your sorrow,
Bring the bottle back tomorrow,
Good-night campers, Goodnight.

With a roll on the drums the mood changed. Everyone stood to attention with their arms at their sides and sang the British National Anthem. This was followed by another drum roll and the Irish Anthem.

Sinne Fianna Fail ata faoi gheall ag Eirinn.
Soldiers are we whose lives are pledged to Ireland.

The campers burst into loud applause and a rousing cheer. The lights came up and it was all over.

It was certainly 'Good-night campers' for Liam, he was exhausted. Having seen him safely back to the chalet, Thomas and I thought we'd end the night and the holiday at the Disco Bar. The club was not sophisticated like today's venues but, it was dark and had coloured lights and a D.J. – 'Twist and Sway with your Favourite D.J.' it said in the programme. When he took a break, everyone headed over to the Juke Box, which was free to use.

When we arrived, the place was crowded. Thomas and I pushed our way to the middle of the floor and danced away to Connie Francis who was bursting out of the speakers with 'Who's Sorry Now.' No Waltzes or Quicksteps here. After the dance we got a couple of lemonades from the bar and stood by the Juke Box.

We'd only been there for a minute or so when Thomas nudged me. We were being eyed-up by two men from across the room. I say men because they were obviously in their early twenties, several years older than Patrick and Eamon. We had seen them around the camp during the week. They were very good-looking but hadn't paid any attention to us – up to now.

We went into our well-practised routine - shy glances across the room followed by whispered exchanges, then, a little smile in their direction. They got the message and it wasn't long before they came over to the Juke Box and went into their routine.

'Hi girls. I'm Martin and this is my friend Gary.'

'Hi there' said Gary,

'Are you having a nice time?'

We were now! Martin was very handsome. He had black hair with long, well-trimmed sideburns down each side of his face. I couldn't help noticing his beautiful blue eyes and fell in love immediately. I was pleased to see Thomas was edging towards Gary, who was equally good-looking.

'Would you like to dance, girls?'

Honky Tonk Women by the Rolling Stones was playing now. This was another of our favourites, so we didn't need asking twice. There were no ballroom niceties here. Their hands went straight to our buttocks and remained there.

After a couple more up-beat numbers, the D.J. put on a 'slowie' and off we went smooching round the floor with Martin and Gary pecking our cheeks and nibbling at our earlobes – heaven!

Gary made the next move.

'Would you girls like to go for a walk down the Horse Trail?'

We knew what that was code for. The Horse Trail, as we were aware, was an unlit path that led from the stables, through the woods and down onto the beach. We'd followed Liam on his horse ride so knew exactly where it went and how dark it would be at this time of night. We glanced at each other with a look that said,

'It's our last night. Let's take a chance.'

So, arm in arm with the boys, we left the night club and set off in the direction of the stables.

As we approached the wood the lights and sounds of the camp were becoming distant. Soon, apart from a little moonlight filtering through the canopy, it was pitch black. I became aware of the isolation and wondered if this had been a wise decision. We were completely on our own, in the dark, with two young men whom we'd only just met.

We came to a small clearing around a large old oak tree. Martin guided me towards the trunk while Gary took Thomas round the other side. At least it was a little lighter here.

How naive of us to think that this was going to be another Ricky and Mike encounter. I thought back to that night in Walkinstown - Mike's gentle fumbling and his willingness to stop when I said 'No'. These boys were four or five years older. They were more experienced and more aggressive in their approach. It soon became very apparent what their intentions were.

I didn't like the way Martin was now clawing at my neck and shoulders. I didn't like the way his body was thrusting against mine and I didn't like the way his tongue was pushing to the back of my throat – I was almost choking. None of this was pleasurable. It was painful and a bit frightening. The situation was rapidly getting out of control.

Martin now began to explore more of my body. He was pulling up the back of my dress and then I felt his cold right hand slip into the back of my knickers where it started to massage my buttocks. Any moment now he was going to pull my knickers down and discover the awful truth.

When I glanced over my shoulder at Thomas, I could see that Gary was taking things a bit slower and they were still enjoying kissing and cuddling. I had to warn him what was happening, and I had to do it quickly.

If I needed any more evidence that these boys meant business, it soon came. Martin had removed his hands from my knickers and was undoing his flies. I looked down to see the biggest erect mickey I'd ever seen.

'Come on Maria, I won't hurt you. I'll only put the tip in.'

'What? No, you can't.'

We had to get out of there. I said the first thing that came into my head.

'You can't, Martin... I'm pregnant!'

He grunted derisively,

'Then there won't be any problem, will there?'

I tried again.

'No, no, it wouldn't be respectful to the child.'

Now he just laughed at me.

'Martin, she really can't.'

It was Thomas. Hearing the panic in my voice he appeared from around the tree by my side. He spoke firmly. Martin took a pace back, but his face showed he wasn't about to give in.

I had a final try.

'Alright' I said, 'but not here. It's getting cold and I don't want to lie on the ground. Let's all go back to our chalet.'

To my relief the boys looked at each other and smiled. They had no objections to that suggestion. The tension eased and the still erect penis was returned from whence it came. Arm in arm we made our way back up the path towards the lights of the camp.

The place was noticeably quieter than it had been earlier. A few late merrymakers were loitering by the main buildings, their voices and laughter floating to us through the night air. The chalet areas seemed deserted too, but there were some lights on behind the drawn curtains and that was reassuring.

I'd gained us a bit of time and I now knew what we had to do - an escape plan was forming. I led Martin towards the Tara chalets, the opposite direction to our own Slane accommodation. Thankfully the other two followed without question. Thomas was bright and I guessed he'd catch-on.

Chatting away, with the occasional encouraging kiss, I led the party left and right through a maze of pathways into the heart of Tara territory. Somewhere near the centre I stopped outside a toilet block. Each of the camp's toilet blocks was set between two rows of chalets. You could enter and leave from either side. I said in girlish fashion,

'Just wait here for a minute. We're going to powder our noses.'

Thomas now knew the plan. Reassuring the boys that we would be back soon, he gave Gary a quick peck on the cheek and followed me up the steps.

I knew the they would never dream of entering a Ladies toilet. Calmly we went inside, our high heels clattering on the cold stone floor. No-one else was there. Standing in the dim lighting we banged a couple of doors, waited and then flushed one toilet followed by a second. I removed my noisy shoes and Thomas did the same. Then, under the cover of the running water, we silently crept out of the door on the other side of the building, down the steps and away.

Barefoot we ran through the remaining rows of Tara chalets, across the sports green and into the safety of Slane country. Neither of us spoke – we were too shocked. I wouldn't feel safe till we were back in our own chalet with the door locked and the snip on. Avoiding the main paths, we wound around the backs of the blocks till we reached home. Thomas opened the door and, without putting the light on, we crept inside.

In the darkness we sat on the divan for several minutes, listening for any noise. But the only sound was the gentle breathing coming from the top bunk. We were safe. Normally at this point the two of us would have collapsed in a heap of laughing, but not tonight. This had been so scary. We sat there in silence. I'm sure Thomas was thinking, as I was, that the evening could easily have ended very differently.

Chapter 26 – After the Ball.

'Good morning Campers' broke into our sleep for the last time. The holiday was coming to an end. We ate breakfast, collected a few shillings for our waitress and said 'Goodbye' to the thyroid lady and her family.

Back at the chalet the evening dresses were carefully folded and placed at the bottom of the suitcases. Our boys' clothes were placed on top, ready for the change. At Reception Puffing Billy was waiting to take us and our luggage on the short return trip to Mosney station.

It was no surprise to find a gang of smiling Redcoats waiting to wave us off. We smiled and waved back but you could tell everyone was feeling flat - that empty feeling you get when a good holiday is coming to an end.

I was feeling a mixture of emotions as we climbed aboard the Dublin train and took our seats - certainly a great sense of achievement but also a great sense of relief that it was nearly over. I was also very aware that the necessity of finding gainful employment was looming ever nearer. Our great adventure was over – back to reality with a bang. As the train pulled out of Mosney the three of us sat in silence - each with his own thoughts. Every day had been full of fun, laughs and sex. We had taken every opportunity to give the boys a glimpse of our knickers and in return had received the attention that we so craved. Each day had ended in a clean, dry chalet where our clothes could be put away and our wigs brushed and our bras hung neatly on the back of the door - so far removed from the damp dark basement that was our changing room at the paper mill.

Yet, for me, there had been a downside to all this. It was so hot under that blonde wig and I hated not being able to swim every day. Then, the constant stress of hiding a secret – acting the part of a girl every waking moment of the day. Not being able to be totally myself. The falsehood of it all was beginning to worry me and as I sat there on the train, there was a lump in my stomach, and I couldn't help feeling sad.

I tried to keep positive. You could only say that the week had been brilliant, and we'd certainly got our kisses from the boys. We got cuddled as well and we got our socks felt. We nearly got a lot more than we bargained for. That, surely, was the point. The boys wanted more from us than just kisses and cuddles, and I was beginning to realise that I too wanted more from the boys – a lot more.

I looked across at Liam who was also deep in thought. No doubt his mind was on the hours he had spent in the swimming pool and at the fairground. His week of freedom was coming to an end and it showed on his face. He'd been fantastic and taken the whole adventure in his stride. And, as far as I know, from that day to this has never uttered a word to a living soul about our big secret.

Liam, eleven years old and soon to be twelve. It wouldn't be long before he was a teenager and taking an interest in girls. Then he'd be courting, get married and having children of his own. That's what life was all about - procreation, producing the next generation. I couldn't see myself being any part of that. Perhaps I should be? Perhaps I'd got it all wrong? I tried to picture myself out on the town with a girl on my arm, taking the male role. The trouble was I didn't feel like a male. I didn't even look like a male.

My schooldays had come to an end and I had to find a job. Maybe I'd come to the end of my dressing-up days? I certainly felt that I might have. I looked at my watch. We'd soon be arriving in Dublin. That train was carrying us away from the fantasy land of Butlins and back to the reality of everyday life. But what was my reality? Who was this person who liked dressing-up in women's clothes? I felt very confused and quite alone. Perhaps it would make more sense when I was back in familiar surroundings, with my family around me. I felt a tear pricking at the back of my eye.

We left Connolly Street Station and made our way back to the alley where it had all begun a week before. At least it wasn't raining as we changed into our jeans and T-shirts. The bras and wigs were stuffed right to the bottom of the cases, under our dresses. We said good-bye to Maria and Tina and were soon on the bus back to Walkinstown.

The welcoming committee was out on the green to greet us. Thomas and Liam were ushered off to Number 46 and I was left alone with the family. They were all excited and wanted to know every detail of what we'd been up to. I felt guilty at feeling so miserable. I gave them all a hug and tried to put on a brave face.

The conversation very quickly came round to their visit to Butlins.

'We came down to see you on Wednesday afternoon' said Joe. 'Did you not hear them calling you over the Tannoy?'

The lies seemed to come very easily.

'No Dad, we didn't' I said with an amazed look on my face. 'I think we were on the beach and in the sea all that afternoon. You couldn't hear the announcements from there.'

'Ah, the kids were very disappointed but never mind. Did you's have a great time?'

I showed them the programme and told them about everything we'd done. There were some extra bits, like,
'We went swimming every day - sometimes in the sea and sometimes in the pool.' Quite a lot was left out. I'd bought the kids some little Butlins souvenirs and they went down well. And that was that. The interrogation was over, and it was time for tea.

Before I knew it, Monday morning had arrived, and I had to find myself a job.

Chapter 27 – Nuts and Bolts.

Finding work wasn't nearly as difficult as I'd anticipated. With the employment section of the local paper spread out on the kitchen table I was spoilt for choice. Joe had highlighted several of what he considered to be suitable vacancies, but I wasn't sure we were on the same wavelength. There were plenty of sales assistants and factory worker jobs advertised but I wanted something a bit different - something with at least a little bit of glamour involved in it.

In the Catering Staff section, I spotted a vacancy for 'a part-time table waiter at Slatterys Bar Lounge and Cabaret Club'. The word 'Cabaret' was what caught my eye, not the word 'Waiter'. Perhaps I thought I might end up on the stage taking part. It was enough to make my mind up that this was the job I would apply for.

Slatterys Club was just up the road in Terenure, about two miles from Walkinstown. I would be able to walk to work. It would be ideal. I made the phone call and a few minutes later had my first job, as a part-time table waiter.

I was to start the following Friday evening and, at the appointed hour, reported to the bar manager for training. This wasn't very extensive.

'Go to a table and get an order. Bring the order back to the bar. Take the order back to the table and get the money. Got it?'

Friday night was the big night of the week at Slattery's when a 'star turn' would appear in the cabaret spot. I'd seen the posters around town and was quite excited that I was going to see Eileen Reid in person. Back in the days when we used to copy her Beehive, she was the lead singer with the Cadets Band. In 1968 she left the band to go solo and was now a star in her own right, appearing in the cabaret lounges around Dublin. Thomas and I loved her music.

I went into action and took my first order up to the bar - three pints of Guinness and shorts for the ladies - all neatly written on my little pad. When the order was ready, I went to pick up the tray. The bar was high, up at my shoulder level and I completely misjudged the weight of the loaded tray. The whole lot went crashing down to the ground.

'Fucking eejit! Get it cleaned up.'

I did as I was told.

Slatterys was soon heaving and table orders were coming at me thick and fast.

'Hey, young feller, it's me next.'

'Would yer ever get me an order.'

'Jaysus, I'm parched. Would yer get yerself over here.'

The bar-staff were pulling pints as fast as they could, but you now had to queue with the other waiters to get your order dealt with.

About two hours into the shift I was standing in line, next but one to the bar, when the lights dimmed. Two bright spotlights came on highlighting the small stage where the band was already set up.

'Ladies and gentlemen,' came a voice over the speaker system. 'Would you please welcome to Slatterys, the dazzling Miss. Eileen Reid and the Melody Makers.'

Thunderous applause greeted her and naturally I turned to the stage. She looked fabulous. Her blonde hair was up in the highest beehive I had ever seen, and she was wearing a beautiful silver lame dress decorated with black swirls. Her high heeled shoes were to die for - I was very envious.

At that point it became my turn at the bar. Someone grabbed my hair.

'For fucks sake, will yer wake up!'

It was the man who had earlier called me an eejit. In spite of my small stature and mild disposition, there was no way I was going to be treated like that.

'Don't you dare pull my hair!'

'Well in that case you can fuck off.'

So, I did just that. I took my tray into the back room and hurled it into the corner with a satisfying metallic crash. I put on my duffle coat and stormed out of the club. My first employment had lasted two hours and fifteen minutes and I got no pay. Worse than that, I didn't get to see Eileen Reid perform.

When the Drimnagh paper mill closed, Joe applied for and got the job of stores' manager at the new Clondalkin paper mill. In this position he had dealings with Bernard Curtis who was in charge of the stores at Blackwood Hodge on the Long Mile Road. As well as this, my Uncle Leo, Ace and Madge's brother, also worked at Blackwood Hodge in the office. Over the weekend some strings were pulled behind the scenes and I was taken on - my second employment in seven days.

So, it was on the following Monday morning that I made the ten-minute walk up the road to take up the position of junior storeman. No glamour here. I arrived in a clean white shirt and tie, but this was soon covered with a dowdy brown coat that nearly came down to my ankles. There were brown buttons down the front and a breast-pocket for my pencils.

Blackwood Hodge was an earth-moving equipment company. They were agents for J.C.B. and Yale Forklift Trucks. I looked around my new workplace. It was a large room with a counter at the front. Behind this were row upon row of shelves loaded with hundreds of boxes containing millions of parts. Nuts, bolts, gaskets, washers and every manner of thing that went into the making of a J.C.B. earth digger and a Yale forklift truck – not a feather or bauble in sight. At the back of the room, behind all the shelves, was the dispatch desk and beside this, a pile of flattened cardboard boxes waiting to be folded into shape. Alongside the boxes was a large roll of brown paper suspended on a spool contraption. On the desk I could see scissors, sticky-tape and a ball of string. This, I was informed, was to be my domain.

Uncle Leo worked in the office next door, separated from the stores by a glass partition. He gave me a little nod but didn't leave his desk and come through to welcome me – perhaps he wasn't allowed to.

Farmers, builders and the like would come to the front counter to buy spare-parts for their machines. In the main, my job was to deal with telephone orders that came into the office next door. The office-boy, Francis, would bring me a docket:

'Two cylinder-head gaskets, one hundred stainless steel rivets and a pound of nut washers.'

I'd search among the shelves for all the items on the list and take them to the dispatch desk where I'd wrap them, place them in an assembled box and post them out to the customer.

My searching frequently took me past the front counter where some rough countryman would be waiting for his order. I quickly learnt that this was a dangerous place to be. There would be a wolf whistle and I'd turn bright red with embarrassment. Each time this happened, all six members of the office staff stopped working and looked up. From the very first day I was the centre of attention and I hated it.

I also had to deal with requisitions that came from the adjoining workshops. The men were supposed to come to a hatch with a docket but invariably came right into the stores. They could usually find the parts they needed quicker than I could and weren't prepared to wait.

It wasn't long before the bullying started. I was fifteen years old but looked more like twelve. Damian Keogh was about twenty-eight and worked in the paint shop. He'd come up behind me and force me to bend over the dispatch desk. With his hands holding my arms down, he'd then simulate sex with me to roars of laughter from the other men. I didn't have the strength to get him off me and just had to put up with the humiliation.

Daley Lynch was another fitter who was always in and out of the stores with a docket. As I took it from him, he liked to grab my nipple and twist till I screamed. Again, getting the attention of everyone in the stores and office who took no notice of my plight. Apparently, this sort of behaviour was considered normal in the initiation of young new staff.

One day Keogh came up behind me and grabbed my chest in a vice-like grip. I managed to get an arm free and hit out at him. I say hit out, but it was a very puny blow which had no effect. The punch I got back sent me reeling across the floor. This time he'd gone too far, and I went straight to the office to speak to the store's manager. Mr. Curtis seemed annoyed that I was making a fuss. In truth he probably didn't know how to deal with the situation. Eventually he said he'd have a word with Keogh but the only effect of this was to increase the taunting. This was worse than school and I became desperately unhappy. I felt there was no-one I could talk to without appearing totally foolish.

It would be unfair to say that all the staff there were cruel. There was a lot of ignorance about. No one seemed to see the seriousness of the trouble I was in and certainly no-one spoke up for me. They all took the easy way out and looked the other way.

When I started at Blackwood Hodge my wages were £7 a week. On the Friday I went home with my first ever pay packet, I said to Joe,

'How much should I give Mammy?'

He thought for a second and said,

'I think £5 would be good.'

I suppose I was a little disappointed. It seemed an awfully big chunk to hand over, but I knew he was right, and gave Ace the money without further thought. I was left with two pounds to show for a week's work and stress.

During lunch breaks, when most of the lads were out in the yard kicking a ball around, I ate my sandwiches in the store. I'd then spend the rest of the lunch hour familiarising myself with the layout of all those shelves and boxes. I started tidying the drawers and putting new labels on where the old ones were worn away.

Someone else who spent the lunch hour indoors was Joe Murphy. He was about forty, had worked there for some years and was now a senior storeman. He was a nice, gentle man and because of this was also subjected to a lot of stick from the other workers. I suppose there was an affinity between us, and we started spending our lunch hour together. One of the things we talked about was art.

I'd started to take a serious interest in painting at the age of eight when I was in Master Dalton's class at Drimnagh Castle – I loved that man. The only male teacher I ever felt any connection with. One afternoon he read us The Little Match Girl by Hans Christian Andersen - a sad story about a young, poor girl who dies on the street and is carried to heaven by her dead grandmother. He then set us to paint a picture about the story. I'd obviously been inspired because he declared my painting to be the best in the class and let me off weekend homework - my first recognition in the art field.

I was further encouraged by Peter, my future brother-in-law. He also enjoyed painting and bought me my first art book – Painting Sunsets by Violet Parkhurst, price ten shillings (I still have it today). On page twenty-nine was a desert scene with a mauve and pink swirling sky rising over the darkening sand dunes. There were cacti and palm trees, almost black, silhouetted against the skyline. I spent hours copying that picture and the finished painting was one of my first serious pieces of work. Madge, of course, praised me in whatever I did. When she saw my picture she said,

'My God, would you look at the talent in that child.'

All very encouraging.

Madge also inspired my next effort. She'd been to see the ballet Giselle and related the story over a cup of tea.

'Ah, she was beautiful, you know. She died of a broken heart. Then she comes back to life with a group of fairies. They were lovely, all dressed in pink tutus. They try to kill Giselle's boyfriend but her great love manages to save him. Ah Leo, you would have loved it. Beautiful, just beautiful.'

This was the picture that, after a lot of persuasion, I took into work to show Joe Murphy. I hid it well away until we were alone in the lunch break. It was a nice painting, only fourteen by twelve inches but born out of my imagination. There were the six fairies dressed in their pink tutus and in the foreground, Giselle, in a contrasting white tutu. Behind them all was a backdrop of pale-green forest trees bathed in moonlight. Joe seemed very impressed and immediately offered to buy it. I didn't know what to say but he insisted and gave me seven shillings and sixpence – my first commission.

One afternoon, two months after I'd started in the stores, Francis came through to say that Mr. Curtis wanted to see me in the office. I could see him through the glass partition. He looked very serious and I wondered what on earth I'd done. I needn't have worried as he wanted to offer me a small promotion to work in the office. Business was doing well, and they needed another clerk to work alongside Helen and Francis on the card index system. There would be ten shillings a week pay rise and the possibility of some overtime. Mr. Curtis had obviously noticed my diligence - or perhaps he felt guilty about the bullying.

Working on the stock index system was just as boring as the stores. All the dockets coming through from the workshops and front desk now had to be recorded onto cards that were then filed alphabetically. We also recorded all the incoming stock. I still had to go back to the stores and workshops to chase up missing dockets, so the bullying continued unabated. At least I didn't have to wear that horrible brown coat in the office.

At the end of November, the Christmas decorations were dragged out from a cupboard at the back of the stores. The office staff set about putting up paper chains and a very artificial looking Christmas tree. This was placed on the front counter, along with a box labelled 'For the Staff'. I never discovered if anyone put anything in it – I certainly didn't get a penny.

All the talk in the office was now about the imminent Christmas Dinner Dance that was to be held at the Intercontinental Hotel in Ballsbridge. It didn't sound the sort of evening that I would feel comfortable at, especially as all the workshop men would be there and a lot of alcohol would be drunk. Helen and Francis had both been before and tried to persuade me to go. With a certain amount of trepidation, I finally added my name to the list on the noticeboard. Uncle Leo would be there with his wife Marion and I thought I would be able to sit with them for protection.

It would be good to dress up in a suit, as opposed to a frock. I bought a pale grey tweed jacket and some navy slacks. I already had a beautiful pink shirt and a navy tie with pink spots that would match the shirt. When I showed her, Mam said,

'You just know how to put things together. You look lovely and I'm very proud of you.' That made me feel good.

On Friday 18 December, a week before Christmas, Joe dropped me at the Intercontinental and I felt pretty confident as I walked in through the revolving door. I'd purposely left it a bit late and the party was in full swing. Everyone seemed to be drinking cocktails, but I went up to the bar and asked for an orange juice. Joe Murphy was there ordering something with a cherry and a pink umbrella in it for his wife Mary. He invited me over to his table to meet her. Mary shook my hand and said how pleased she was to meet me.

'I've heard so much about you from Joe' she said. 'Your clothes are lovely. You look so stylish.'

I liked this woman. She was saying all the right things. I spent some time at their table chatting with them both but, as I moved on to join Leo and Marion, I couldn't help overhearing her say,

'He's really beautiful. He looks just like a girl.'

I suppose she meant it as a compliment and a few months earlier I might have been delighted if someone had said that to me. This was the wrong time. It ruined the evening for me.

The Christmas dinner was good – turkey with all the trimmings, and the lively cabaret that followed did lift my spirits. By eleven o'clock though, things were all getting a bit raucous. Most of the workmen were now gathered round the bar and had another hour of drinking in front of them before the coach arrived to take them to their homes. I was relieved that Leo and Marion had had enough and accepted their offer of a ride back to Walkinstown.

With another working week to go before Christmas, I can't say I was looking forward to the festivities. I would have to make a great effort to put on a happy face in front of the family. It would mean a few days away from work and I badly needed that break. I had hoped that after leaving school my life would take a turn for the better, but the reverse seemed to be happening. The only thing that gave me any pleasure, that made living worthwhile, was my close friendship with Thomas.

Chapter 28 – A New Wig.

Thomas bought himself a new wig. He went on his own – I knew nothing about it. He'd seen it in Arnott's window, a full-length blonde and just couldn't resist the urge to go in and buy it. This happened some weeks after I'd started at Blackwood Hodge and I hadn't had the time, or perhaps hadn't had the courage, to talk to him about my feelings after Butlins - my feelings that Maria and Tina were reaching the end of their lives. Now it was too late. He had a new wig and wanted to go out and show it off.

'At least one more outing' he pleaded.

'One more outing?' I questioned.

'Let's see how we get on.'

That gave me a little bit of encouragement. It must have crossed his mind that we couldn't go on for much longer. I felt we were really pushing our luck. There had been some very close escapes at Mosney. It didn't help that I felt so low. Not only was there the bullying at work but the dressing-up didn't seem right anymore. I felt like half a person. All I could see ahead, if we carried on, was a miserable existence but Thomas was very persistent and, in the end, I gave in.

'Oh, go on' I said. 'Let's do it.'

When I saw the wig, I had to admit it was fabulous and I had great fun dressing it. With masses of back-combing it frizzed up beautifully and gave Tina a completely new look. We would wear our evening dresses from Butlins – Thomas the full-length purple and me the full-length pink with the bow.

The Garda Club in Harrington Street was a great venue and considered to be one of the top entertainment hotspots in Dublin. It had a ballroom with a proper sprung dance floor and live bands regularly played there. Thomas and I had been a couple of times over the past year, but we preferred disco nights to the ballroom dancing. The place was similar to the Town and Country Club but with the added attraction of lots of young single Gardai. Looking back, it is strange to think that we were at our boldest in a room full of policemen. If this was to be our last outing, the Garda Club would be a great venue.

Two days later Thomas came back with a surprise for me. He had booked one night bed and breakfast at the George Hotel in Great George's street, not far from the Garda Club - a twin room in the names of Miss Tina Doyle and Miss Maria Donaghy. We wouldn't have to worry about getting home after the dance. He was very excited at the prospect and I couldn't help but be enthusiastic. We both told our parents that we were going to stay over at Patrick Manzer's – more lying.

On the night of the disco we got changed in the den. The nights were drawing in and it was quite dark when, fully dressed, we set out to get the bus into town. There was a chill in the air, but nothing was going to make us wear anoraks over our evening dresses. We would just have to freeze.

We went upstairs on the bus and got a wolf whistle from the conductor – a good start to the evening. Thomas took a window seat near the back and I sat down next to him. Halfway into town the bus stopped at The Coombe. The amber light from a streetlamp just outside the window shone in through Thomas's blonde wig. His face became surrounded by a golden haze. The light also showed up a blonde fuzz all over his face. As I sat looking at him, I realised Thomas was no longer a boy. Almost overnight, it seemed, he had become a man. I don't know why I was so surprised. He had always been more advanced than me physically. I knew that he now shaved his face daily and the hairs on his legs required frequent attention. But it wasn't only that. He was more mature in many ways. Unlike me, he enjoyed his work at Burtons. Some nights he would go to the pub with his work mates – something I would never contemplate. I put the thought out of my head and concentrated on the evening ahead.

The bus dropped us near the Four Courts and, carrying our overnight bags, we made our way along the Quay to the Ha'penny Bridge. On the other side of the Liffey we walked up through Temple Bar and into Great George's Street where we located the George Hotel. In we marched, bold as brass, and registered. Miss Tina Doyle and Miss Maria Donaghy – no problems so far.

Our room was on the second floor. Simply furnished but clean and with a large, well-lit mirror for us to put the finishing touches to our make-up. Thomas looked out of the window and gasped. He was looking across the road at

'Weaver to Wearer', the Burton's shop where he worked. He hadn't realised that the George backed on to Burtons. The curtains were quickly pulled shut. The shop was closed, of course, so I don't know why he was so shocked. It made us both laugh.

The Garda Club was only a short walk up the road and when we arrived it was buzzing. The ballroom was full of eligible young men. Most of the girls were in long evening dresses and all the boys smartly dressed. One or two were still in uniform, presumably just come off duty. Apart from this, if you hadn't known, there was nothing to suggest that most of the men and boys there were either already policemen or training as cadets.

One of our favourite singers, Stevie Wonder, was blasting out of the speakers and, after the requisite visit to the Ladies, we were soon in the thick of it, dancing and singing along to 'Superstition'.

> There is superstition, writing's on the wall,
> There is superstition, ladder's bout' to fall.
> Thirteen-month-old baby broke the lookin' glass,
> Seven years of bad luck, the good things in your past.

After Butlin's, we had the confidence to go up to boys to ask them to dance and not wait for them to come to us. We had plenty of choice that night and set about making the most of it. Thomas was in great form and I could see Tina drawing many admiring glances. I felt pleased he was so happy.

Later, we were having a drink at the bar with two lads, when the D.J. introduced 'Lola', by the Kinks. This was our song. Grabbing the boys, we headed back to the dance floor. The lyrics were quite remarkable for the time – a song about a man falling in love with a transvestite, a song about Thomas and me:

> Well I'm not dumb but I can't understand,
> Why she walked like a woman and talked like a man,
> Oh my Lola, lo-lo-lo-lo Lola,
> Lo-lo-lo-lo Lola.

As we danced my partner held me close, thrusting his hips against me in time to the music. I had to smile. If he only knew all that separated his chest from mine was a bra and two old school socks.

'What are you's laughing at' he said.

'I'm not laughing.'

'You sure is.'

I spun him round to avoid answering the question.

Although we had started the evening dancing together, by the time it ended, Thomas and I had danced with half the police force in Dublin.

We left the club around eleven and, still feeling high and having no curfew to worry about, decided to walk back to the hotel the long way round. We made our way across to Stephen's Green and then down Grafton Street, which was still lively. We mingled with groups of young people and couples looking in the fashionable shop windows and listening to the buskers and poets outside Bewley's coffee shop – for a small sum of money they would perform a poem of your choice from their endless repertoires. We felt very much part of the scene as we walked arm in arm down towards the Liffey.

As we approached the O'Connell Bridge, where we intended to turn left back to the hotel, we spotted in front of us the unmistakable figure of Ulick O'Connor. He was in his early forties and making a name for himself as an author, poet and playwright and, perhaps more-so, for his controversial appearances on Gay Byrne's 'Late Late Show'. Everyone in Ireland watched this and he was instantly recognisable.

We quickened our pace and halfway across the bridge drew level with him. He noticed us and spoke. This was very exciting.

'Hello girls' he said. 'And where would you be going?'

'We've been dancing at the Garda Club and we're just off back to our hotel.'

'Well, you can't go home without a little kiss, can you now?'

We were now over the bridge and coming up to Eason's bookshop. He came between us and with an arm round our shoulders, edged us both into the doorway. Without further ado, he planted several romantic kisses onto the faces of two star-struck fifteen-year-old boys. What a special end to the evening - being kissed by a famous man. We felt so good as we said good night and made our way back to the George Hotel.

The next morning, as soon as we woke, we realised that we hadn't brought a change of clothes with us. We would have to go down to breakfast in our evening dresses. This produced gales of laughter from the two of us. Breakfast was included and we weren't going to miss out. So, on with the make-up and wigs and down the stairs for a grand entrance into the breakfast room. It was quite crowded, but no-one seemed bothered. A young waiter showed us to a table for two and handed us the breakfast menus. All around us people were sitting in T-shirts and jeans. We couldn't help giggling. One lady at a nearby table did keep looking over but I think it was the noise we were making that got her attention, not what we were wearing.

I thought I would be very ladylike and just ordered some brown toast and a pot of tea. Thomas, on the other hand, was hungry and went for the full Irish.

'I'll have a fried egg with two rashers and two sausages... err... black and white pudding and err... some fried potatoes. Thanks very much.'

The waiter wrote it all down and disappeared off to the kitchen.

'Thomas' I said, 'you're supposed to be a lady. That order's enough for a hungry docker.' We both roared with laughter again.

After breakfast we packed our bits and pieces, paid the bill and headed for home. Sitting on the bus my mind played over the last twelve hours. We'd had a good night out - one of our best, no doubt about that. We both looked fabulous and had received lots of attention. There had been no scares. For the first time in weeks I had forgotten about work and enjoyed myself – we hadn't stopped laughing from the moment we left the den.

Then my thoughts returned to the question of Thomas's manliness. That morning he'd spent some time shaving before we went down to breakfast. He couldn't continue to hide his changing body. In no way could he go on getting away with being Tina. It had to stop before something went badly wrong and we landed ourselves in real trouble.

As for me? I'd come to a decision. This time my mind really was made up. It was over. I could not go on with it any longer. What is Maria I thought? She's a wig, some make-up and two socks stuck in a bra. That wasn't what I wanted in life. I knew now that I needed something more than just kisses from the boys and, as Maria, that was not going to happen. From the Halloween night back in 1967 we'd had nearly three years of fun and fantasy. Now was the right time to end it - the time to finally say 'Good-bye' to Maria and Tina forever.

Chapter 29 – The Cremation.

I dreaded telling Thomas about my decision but when the moment came, he took it surprisingly well. He was an intelligent boy and deep-down, even though he'd just bought the new wig, he'd already come to the same conclusion. There was no discussion, no argument, just an acceptance that this was the right thing to do. It had to be done and it had to be done now.

We paid one last visit to our den at the old paper mill. Despite the dinginess and the dampness, it held many happy memories. Whilst we'd borrowed a lot of our costumes we had also, over the years, accumulated quite a collection of our own clothes and accessories – all carefully folded and stored in plastic bags on the den shelves. These all had to be disposed of.

We collected a pile of wood and old scraps of paper and, out of sight behind a wall, built a bonfire. Thomas struck a match and we waited and watched in silence as the kindling crackled and the flames grew higher. Then, piece by piece, we ceremoniously dropped all our costumes into the inferno – one by one our beautiful frocks, skirts, blouses and underwear were committed to the flames.

High heeled shoes and make-up had been wrapped in plastic bags to be dumped later in a litter bin. As the fire engulfed each new offering, we watched as three years of our life went up in smoke.

Not a word was said. We took it in turns to feed the hungry flames. The hardest part was destroying the wigs. Thomas had only had one outing in his new blonde creation, but it had to go along with the other items. He held it high above the fire on a stick and then slowly lowered it into the flames. The acrylic sizzled and crackled and melted, eventually disappearing into nothing. It was done.

The occasion was very sad but at the same time, very cathartic. We had watched as Maria and Tina were cremated. They would play no further part in our lives.

Chapter 30 – Veganin.

As the months went by, work was an ever-present evil in my life. Things at Blackwood Hodge were not good. Some days the bullying was almost intolerable, and I felt so miserable. Joe could see there was something wrong, but I couldn't bring myself to talk to him about it. He'd worked so hard to get to where he was and bring up seven children. He'd always stressed to us the importance of a good education.

'When I went to the interview for my first job at the paper mill' he said, 'they asked me to do fractions and I couldn't – I was mortified.'

He got the job anyway but went straight to night school to better himself.

And so it was, at the age of sixteen, I started a night school course to take my Intermediate Certificate. I had a real struggle with the classes. Any thought of teaching brought back the nightmare of the Christian Brothers. After three terms my efforts brought me five miserable passes at Grade D. I should have been proud to have gained the Certificate, but it seemed to have the opposite effect and my self-esteem plummeted to even lower depths.

One of the side effects of my depression was that I was putting on weight – comfort eating, I suppose. The pounds piled on and, to my disgust, I became quite obese.

I tried to cheer myself up by going into town and buying a new coat. All my peers were wearing overcoats that were double-breasted with wide lapels and a single vent up the back. I wanted to be part of this new fashion but couldn't even get that right. Despite knowing exactly what I wanted a very pushy salesmen convinced me to purchase a single-breasted coat with narrow lapels.

'It really suits you sir. This double-breasted lark is on the way out. You'll be ahead of the fashion game. Believe me, sir.'

And I foolishly did.

To make matters worse, my very fat bum stuck out of the single vent at the back. Even Thomas teased me about that. Every time I went out in that coat, I would pull the collar up as high as it would go to hide myself.

In another desperate attempt to 'normalise' my life, I thought I would try taking a girlfriend. To be honest, it wasn't my idea. Carol Marcetti kind of forced herself on me at the church social. She lived around the back of Walkinstown Parade and Thomas and I had known her for years. What we didn't know was that her family was of Italian extraction – we used to innocently call them the Mulcatties. She obviously fancied me, and we went to the cinema a couple of times. Despite sitting in the back row, nothing much happened between us. We did hold hands but even that was an effort on my part – it just didn't feel right. Despite my reticence she persisted for at least two months and was rewarded with nothing more sexual than a peck on the cheek.

The affair came to a head on Christmas morning 1971. After mass Carol came around to the house with a beautifully wrapped present for me and insisted I opened it on the spot. Inside was a silver linked identity bracelet with both our names engraved on it. I had nothing for her and felt very embarrassed. I made some terrible excuse to get rid of her. I said something about wanting to be alone and then rushed round to the newsagents which I knew was open until one o'clock. There wasn't much left in the way of presents but I came away with a cheap gold bracelet with a pearl on each link. When I took it round to her in the afternoon she was not impressed – and neither would I have been. I was not asked to stay and left her house with the distinct impression that our relationship had come to an end.

In the Spring of the new year I tried with another girl. Again, it wasn't me who initiated the contact. A boy I knew from church was taking two girls out for a meal and he asked me to make up a foursome. The venue was in Dublin and quite posh, so I thought I'd better make an effort. I dressed in my Christmas dinner-dance outfit, the pale grey jacket and navy slacks. Fortunately, the evening was warm enough to leave my new overcoat at home.

The girl's name was Dymphna. I bought a box of chocolates and went around to the house at seven o'clock to pick her up. Dymphna's mother opened the door and immediately took the chocolates off me.

'Tanks very much' she said, 'Dat's very kind of you.'

That was the last I saw of them, though I did tell Dymphna that they were meant for her. She was dressed in a tight-fitting lemon dress that showed off her developing figure. Again, I tried to do and say the right things and told her that she looked very nice. She smiled but didn't return the compliment.

Dymphna was a shy girl and I was relieved when we got to the restaurant and met up with the other couple. They were very much at ease with each other and chatted away all through the meal whilst Dymphna and I said very little. The silence continued on the journey home and when I dropped her off, she gave no indication that she would like to meet up again – I was very happy with that.

Over the following months, though it didn't seem possible, things at work went from bad to worse. I was now waking at four or five o'clock each morning with a great lump in my stomach. I lay there just dreading the hour when I would have to get up and go into the office. This wasn't just feeling under the weather. Although I didn't know it at the time, I was suffering from a deep clinical depression. I'd lost interest in everything. I couldn't bring myself to pick up a paint brush. I didn't want to look at the fashion pictures in Mam's magazines and I didn't want to go to the beach when Joe suggested a run out. At work I was making silly mistakes and they were being noticed. I just couldn't concentrate and came home each night with a banging headache.

I did discuss matters with Thomas, but he was having problems of his own. Thomas, who eighteen months before had walked out so confidently in his new blonde wig, was now suffering from a degree of agoraphobia. Although he wasn't bullied at work, in the streets near home he was being regularly jeered at. He'd acquired the name 'Nancy' and was mortified by it. He started to adopt strategies to avoid those taunting him. The dark winter mornings and evenings became his best friends. In the lighter months, he'd often make himself late so that when he left the house the coast was clear. He'd take a long route to the bus stop, through the school grounds, to avoid people on the streets. We were both in a bad way.

We poured out our problems to each other at the bottom of the stairs. It did help a little. Neither of us felt we could talk to our parents. I think I was afraid that Joe would have been straight up to Blackwood Hodge to sort things out – I couldn't face that. For both of us home was a refuge. Once inside you could put the day's problems behind and be yourself. There seemed to be nothing for it but to struggle on.

One Saturday night, after a particularly bad week at work, I could take no more. By evening I was sitting alone in my bedroom, in the dark. Joe and Ace were watching television downstairs. The Late Late Show was on and I could hear them laughing. The kids were either out of the house or already asleep – I don't remember. I was sitting there thinking,

'I just want to go to sleep and not wake up.'

Over and over again the thought kept coming into my mind.

'I just want to go to sleep and not wake up.' I felt completely alone and helpless. You can only fight those feelings for so long and now, I was at the end of my tether – life held nothing for me. I could see no future – only endless bullying and misery.

255

I went quietly downstairs, through the kitchen and into the new bathroom extension at the back of the house. On the wall beside the bath was the cabinet where Mammy kept tablets and things. I opened the door and took out the tube of Veganin I knew she kept there for the occasional headache. I put it in my pocket. Then, I went back into the kitchen and made myself a cup of warm milk. Joe and Ace were in the next room. I went in and kissed them both.

'Good-night Dad.'

'Good-night Son.'

'Good-night Mam.'

'Good-night Love. Sleep well.'

As I made my way back upstairs the tears began to flow. I sat down on my bed sobbing and put the bedside light on. The label on the thin red tube read 'Veganin - maximum two tablets every four hours.' I unscrewed the metal cap. Inside was a short coil of cotton-wool that held the tablets in place. I pulled this out and put it on the bedside-table next to me. I suppose the tube held about twelve tablets and it looked as though a couple of these had been taken. I removed the first tablet and placed it on my tongue, took a sip of milk and swallowed. Then the second tablet, then the third. One by one, I placed all the remaining tablets in my mouth and swallowed them down with the warm milk. When the last one had gone, I put the cotton-wool back into the empty tube, replaced the cap and threw it in the waste-paper basket. I got undressed, got into bed and fell asleep.

Chapter 31 – A New Day.

The next morning, I woke at about eight o'clock – something was different. I felt fresh after an excellent night's sleep. For the first time in a long while I felt happy – happy to be alive. My first thought was,

'Thank God that I haven't caused my parents the pain and hurt of my suicide.'

I got dressed feeling positive. Nothing had changed but somehow, I knew this was going to be a turning point.

The first thing I did was to remove the evidence of the previous night. I retrieved the Veganin tube from the wastepaper basket and hid it – I'd drop it in a bin after mass. A few days later I heard Ace calling,

'Has anyone seen my Veganin?'

I just smiled to myself.

'Do you want me to go to the chemist to get you some more?'

The bullying at work didn't get any easier but I did cope with it better. My thoughts were much more positive and rational. I was able to ask myself,

'Why am I still working here when I hate it so much? What's stopping me leaving?'

At that time, I could see no clear way forward but at least I was thinking along the lines of making a change.

Thomas and I weren't socializing with each other as much as we had been – inevitable, I suppose, after the death of Maria and Tina. The chats on the stairs were becoming less frequent and our long walks a rarity.

It seemed to need an occasion to get us together. When Maria and Peter got married, Thomas was of course invited. We both dressed up to the nines and had a great time discussing all the wedding outfits and hairstyles, and what we would have done with them – just like the old times.

We had a great night out at the cinema when Cabaret was released. It became my favourite film of all time and I thought of the great games we would have had in the past. I could see my bedroom turned into the Kit-Kat Club. There would have been a lot of argument as to who played Sally Bowles. We'd probably end up taking turns.

In the early summer we had a weekend away together. We stayed at a small hotel in Athlone, right on the edge of the Shannon River. Since the demise of our alter egos, Thomas had stopped shaving and now sported a mop of hair and a handsome beard. He looked very much like the footballer George Best.

As I no longer wanted to dress in women's clothes, it was more difficult for me to express my feminine side - I still felt that need very strongly. In the hotel bedroom Thomas did allow me to play with his long hair. I teased it up into a very respectable bun on the top of his head and we roared with laughter.

We had two good days - nothing special. We walked a lot, down along the river and through the town. We window shopped but didn't buy anything. Mainly we just chatted. Very much at ease with each other, but there was no mention of the past. When we went to the bar before dinner Thomas was drinking pints, whilst I was still on the orange juice. I don't think I would have been served with anything stronger as I still looked like a twelve-year-old. Also, he'd started smoking – 'Major Cigarettes', which were manufactured in Dundalk, close to Dublin. Wherever we went he now carried the green and white box and frequently lit up.

We remained very good friends, but it wasn't quite the same. He spent more time drinking with his work mates and I became friendly with two boys who lived on the other side of the church. Padraig McCarten and Niall Stack were into fishing and I started to join them on the riverbank. After a couple of these expeditions, they invited me to go with them on a camping weekend.

Curracloe is a long, wide stretch of sandy beach in County Wexford. When we arrived, we set the two tents up on the flat grass behind the hillocks that bordered the beach. The boys had done this before. We would all sleep in the larger tent and the smaller second tent was to keep the stores in. They also put up a washing line to dry our wet swimming trunks on. The shoreline was an idyllic setting and the weather was perfect. We spent the first day just messing around on the beach and in the sea.

On the second afternoon I was in charge of cooking tea on the small primus stove we had with us. Padraig and Niall were down on the beach. I had a pan of chopped meat and diced vegetables sizzling away when I became aware of a man standing behind me. He was about twenty-four and had a pack on his back.

'That smells good.'

That was enough encouragement for me. He seemed nice enough and was hiking on his own.

'You're very welcome to stay and have some with us.'

When Padraig and Niall returned from their swim, they were not well pleased. I could hear them muttering in the tent as they got changed.

They were even less pleased when I invited the man to stay the night with us. His name was Breandan and I thought he was very good looking. The tent was big enough for the four of us, but I soon realised I had made a wrong decision. A frosty silence descended as we climbed into our sleeping bags. Niall was on one side with Padraig next to him. I was next to Padraig and then Breandan alongside me.

We settled down for the night, but it wasn't long before I detected Brendan's arm moving into my territory. I felt this wasn't the time and place for that sort of thing. Had I been on my own it would have been different, but I didn't want to upset the boys any more than I had done. I turned on my side, away from him, and pretended not to notice. He didn't persist.

By the next morning our visitor had obviously got the message and didn't stay for breakfast. As we packed up the camp, the boys were speaking to me, but I sensed that the atmosphere between us had changed. I was the guest at their camp and it really hadn't been my place to invite a complete stranger to join us. There was nothing I could do about it and I wasn't surprised not to be invited on any more of their fishing trips.

Chapter 32 – Meet the Coles.

It was Thomas who came up with the idea of going to Benidorm – which made me feel good. He hadn't deserted me completely and we would be able to spend some quality time together. We were both still searching for some glamour in our lives and the brochures offered this in abundance – Sea, Sun and Sangria. Luxury hotels with your every need catered for - pictures of sun-tanned bodies with smiling faces, both on the beach and lounging around the hotel pool - waiters carrying trays of exotic cocktails and in the dining room, tables laden with sumptuous food. Every picture was meant to entice you and it certainly did.

Neither of us had been abroad – unless you counted Northern Ireland. Very few people had at that time. It all looked very exciting. We'd have to save every penny we could, as this was going to cost considerably more than a week at Butlins. It was hard work, but we managed it.

There were no dresses or make-up to pack in the suitcases, but I did have a fetching pale blue cowboy shirt with epaulettes and fringes on the breast pockets. I was looking forward to wearing that.

The Aer Lingus flight from Dublin to Alicante was leaving at ten o'clock in the evening. This was the first time anyone in the Doyle or Donaghy families had been on a plane and everyone turned out in force at the airport to see us off. Joe was now into cine film and was in his element. People were staring and we all felt a bit embarrassed. I think they thought we were film stars.

'Come on now Sean, move next to Thomas and I'll get you in the shot.'

'Ah, yer don't want to break yer camera on me, Joe'

Bridie was standing with Mother.

'Isn't it well for them, Mrs. Donaghy?'

Ace, looking slightly aloof, just nodded.

There had been no suggestion that Liam should come with us this time – Thomas wouldn't have stood for it. She still gave the impression that she would have preferred it if Thomas was going away with another friend rather than me. She was pleasant enough when we spoke, but I always detected an edge in her voice.

It was a relief to pass through to the customs. They weren't allowed to follow, and we were now on our own. After a few minutes browsing in the Duty-Free shops we made our way down to the gate, where our fellow travellers were gathering – some already in their shorts and T-shirts and some decidedly merry.

When the boarding announcement came, Thomas and I waited for the rush to pass before joining the end of the queue. Walking out across the tarmac we could see that both families had now made their way up onto the viewing platform and were waving vigorously in our direction. We waved back.

At the top of the steps we were greeted by a young air hostess wearing the smart Aer Lingus uniform – jacket and skirt in Connemara-green, and a shamrock emblazoned necktie.

'Failte ar bord.'

We'd both passed our Intermediate Irish and knew that meant 'Welcome aboard.'

'Go raibh maith agat,' we replied, 'Thank you.'

We found our seats and through the small plane window could just make out Joe and Ace and the Doyles still on the roof of the terminal building. This was undoubtedly a big event for them all, and no-one was going anywhere till the plane disappeared into the night skies over Dublin.

As we sat there waiting for the plane to taxi, I became conscious of a feeling of unease in my stomach - a feeling I recognised. Surely it wasn't the old depression surfacing again? I had no reason to be depressed. I was just about to depart on an exciting holiday with my best friend - a week away from work. I told myself it was just a bit of anxiety about flying.

I wasn't helped when a very heterosexual looking man took the third seat next to me. I wanted to talk to Thomas about the air hostess's bun and fluttering eyelids. He'd already mentioned her pill-box hat, but the third man put an end to that conversation.

The flight to Alicante took over three hours and as the time progressed, my anticipation of a glamorous week on the Costa Blanca was becoming a little jaded. The cabin was noisy, with a lot of alcohol fuelled banter filling the air from take-off till landing. There was also a lot of cigarette smoke drifting around the back of the cabin – including a large contribution from the Majors that Thomas seemed to be chain smoking.

From the airport we had to take a bus into Benidorm. This took nearly an hour so when we finally reached our destination, with the clock going forward an hour, the time was nearly four in the morning and we were exhausted.

Even at that unearthly hour the hotel looked sumptuous. We walked through the grand entrance hall, past luxurious settees and coffee tables with exotic flower arrangements on them and joined the queue at the marble reception desk. After booking in we took the lift up to the fifth floor where our room was situated. This was equally impressive.

Inevitably we compared it with our chalet at Mosney. This was so much more spacious and had marble floors and its own bathroom with fluffy white towels and little bottles of free shampoo. We even had a private balcony looking out to sea, with two chairs and a table with an ashtray – Thomas immediately lit up again. This was luxury. This was the glamour we were both looking for.

We hadn't paid much attention to our surroundings on the journey from the airport. In the light of day, I was in for a bit of a shock. Why had I imagined we were going to stay in a small Spanish fishing village beside the sea? Why did I think that the streets would be full of senoritas in beautiful flamenco dresses and matadors on their way to the bull fight? Once again, I had set myself up for disappointment. The truth was that Benidorm was completely built up with hotels and office blocks and you had to cross a four-lane highway to get to the beach. The beach itself was full of sun-loungers and umbrellas hiding other package tourists like ourselves. It was disappointing but it was warm and sunny. Despite that flat feeling in my stomach, which was still there, I was determined to make the best of it.

On our first evening in Benidorm we met Gary and Yvonne Cole at the hotel bar. He was a handsome man in his early thirties with a very masculine moustache. He worked at Cammell Laird's shipyard in Birkenhead, where they lived. Yvonne was a secretary at the Cadbury's chocolate biscuit factory in Morton on the Wirral. She wore pounds of make-up and a long necklace of red plastic popper-beads – as big as cherries. Her glasses were very Nana Mouskouri, in fact, wearing her hair in a long bob made her look very much like the singer.

Thomas was becoming quite a raconteur. He was much more outgoing than I was. Sitting at the bar with a pint in one hand and a cigarette in the other he was in his element and kept the three of us entertained for the next hour or so.

Being from Merseyside the Coles were inevitably into football and the subject soon came up in conversation. Gary couldn't understand why Thomas and I weren't in the least bit interested in the game. When he asked if we supported Everton or Liverpool, he got blank stares. Even more so when he asked who our local team was. Even Yvonne knew that in Birkenhead Tranmere Rovers was the team to follow and Gary had high hopes for them. We did tell them about the ancient Irish game of hurling though we knew very little about individual teams and their prospects.

On that night I had my first ever experience of alcohol. I was seventeen and never a drop had passed my lips. Gary saw this as a challenge and wouldn't hear of me drinking orange juice. He insisted I tried a Bacardi and Coke – a typical Spanish triple measure. By the time I got to the bottom of the glass I could barely perch on my bar stall.

The barman kept coming over and whispering in my ear,

'You's-a very pretty.'

He obviously thought I was a girl. In the past this would have been flattering but now, it felt intrusive and I wanted him to stop talking to me and go away.

By the end of the second glass I literally couldn't stand and desperately needed to lie down. The barman was still taking an interest.

'Ah, she canta holda the drink eh?'

I wanted to hit him.

Thomas helped me back to the bedroom. He made sure I was comfortable and then went straight back down to Gary and Yvonne in the bar.

By the next morning we had two new best friends. Tony said he'd like to spend more time with the Coles. They'd been very pleasant the previous evening, so I was happy to go along with that.

We met up after breakfast and I noticed that Yvonne was now wearing a different set of popper-beads. Again, they were red, but whereas last nights had been crimson, these were more ruby. I noticed also the subtle change in her lipstick which perfectly matched the beads. It turned out that she had quite a collection. Each set was a different shade of red and each set had its own matching lipstick.

In the afternoon Yvonne dragged me off to explore the old town. I'd rather have gone walking with Thomas, but he and Gary were ensconced by the pool bar and nothing was going to shift them.

The old town was more like the Benidorm I'd imagined - a maze of narrow streets with lovely bars, cafes and shops. There were a lot of tourists enjoying the sunshine though I still didn't spot any matadors. Everywhere was decorated with red geraniums and brightly coloured bougainvillea - authentic Spain.

Yvonne headed straight into a shop selling beads and jewellery - there was always one more string, one more variation that she had to add to her collection. Having made a choice, the next challenge was to find the matching lipstick. I was quite used to choosing jewellery and make-up and have to admit that I enjoyed the girly afternoon. In the days of Tina and Maria, Thomas would have enjoyed it too.

When we went into dinner that evening Gary had arranged a table for four so that we could all sit together. I did enjoy their company, but I didn't want to spend the whole holiday with them – the truth was I didn't want to share Thomas. He obviously didn't feel the same and wasn't bothered at all.

After the meal we went up to the lounge. The lascivious barman was on duty again, so I was pleased when Yvonne suggested we sat at a table. She was wearing her new beads which were carmine-red.

I joined in the conversation but insisted on drinking orange juice. It was very pleasant but by 11 o'clock I'd had enough and wanted some time on my own. I made my excuses and hoped Thomas would follow suit - he didn't. I left the three of them ordering another round of Bacardi and Coke.

Thomas had said he would be up shortly but when he did appear, some thirty minutes later, it was to borrow money.

'We're going to a club and I'm a bit short.'

'Help yourself' I said.

He took a thousand pesetas and disappeared with the promise that he'd cash a traveller's cheque the next day. Why was he going out now, I wondered? Didn't he want to have a long chat with me about Yvonne and Gary and the other characters around the hotel? That's what we'd always done in the past.

At two in the morning the door opened again. He didn't put the light on, but I woke anyway.

'Sorry' he said – crashing into a chair and roaring with laughter.

I turned over and went back to sleep.

The next morning, I left Thomas in bed and went down to breakfast on my own. Gary and Yvonne were already there at our new table.

'You missed a great night, Leo. You'll have to come with us tonight.'

I didn't think so. I really needed to spend some time with Thomas, just the two of us.

When he eventually appeared, looking the worse for wear, he just missed the Coles who had gone off to the pool. I felt he owed me one after the previous night and I think he knew I was upset. When I suggested spending the day on the beach he readily agreed. We got our swimming things and headed across the highway to the sands. This was more like old times. We went for a swim then sat sunbathing. Later, after a bit of lunch, we went for a long walk along the beach and made rude comments about everyone's swimwear.

After having Thomas to myself all day I was happy to spend the evening with the Coles.

'That's a lovely shade of burgundy, Yvonne. Are they new?'

On the Thursday night the four of us had paid to join a 'Typical Spanish Barbecue and Entertainment', laid on by the travel company. We boarded a coach outside the hotel and were driven up into the hills to an old Spanish hacienda. When we arrived, we could see a crowd of people sitting at long bench tables. These had been set-up in a courtyard that was surrounded by olive trees that twinkled with fairy-lights in their branches. Waiters were pouring Spanish red from glass carafes with long, thin spouts.

We found a space that would take the four of us and were soon tucking into some very dubious looking meat, followed by some very scrawny chicken. There was plenty of bread and salad on the table and a seemingly endless supply of the red wine which the waiters delighted in pouring from a great height into the throats of the laughing tourists.

The company was in good form with plenty of craic – fun, entertainment and enjoyable conversation. I got talking to a young girl from Sheffield called Sharon. She was the life and soul of the party - very glamorous and good looking. I was suddenly quite envious of all the attention she was getting from the people around her, especially the boys.

Back at Butlins it would have been me in that position but sitting there watching all this happening, I began to get that old feeling of 'not belonging'. I wasn't part of all this jollity and wanted to go back to the hotel. But I had no choice. The festivities continued late into the night.

The next evening was our last. We had dinner with Gary and Yvonne in the hotel restaurant and then sat chatting over coffee and drinks in the bar. Despite being the last night I was exhausted after the Barbecue evening and wanted to go to bed. Yvonne looked as though she'd had it too. When Thomas and Gary suggested a night on the town – their euphemism for a bar crawl, we both groaned. They were happy to go on their own, so Yvonne and I said our good-nights and went up to our rooms – Yvonne carrying a last glass of red wine.

It felt good to be alone. I drew the curtains and arranged some soft lighting – just the two bed-side lamps with a couple of my cravats placed over the shades to enhance the effect. We were lucky to have a quiet room with no background thumping from the local discos. I took off my shoes and lay back on the bed.

The peace didn't last for long. Someone was knocking on the door and then a voice I recognised.

'Are you awake?'

It was Yvonne. She'd had a fair bit to drink during the evening and when I opened the door, I noticed that the last glass of red wine was now half empty. She invited herself in, made her way to the bed and sat down. After taking a slug of wine she placed the glass down on the marble floor, patted the bed and said,

'Come and sit here, Leo.'

Reluctantly I sat down beside her and was immersed in her Tabu by Dana – not a perfume I would have chosen. This, combined with the alcohol fumes, was quite overpowering. She obviously wanted to chat and moved even closer to me.

At first, we talked about the holiday and then a bit about Ireland. She and Gary had never been and of course I said they would be very welcome, and we would show them around if they ever visited. The conversation then got a bit more intimate. Staring directly into my face, she said,

'You've got beautiful eyes.'

She now started to stroke my hair with her right hand.

'It's not fair, Leo, I have to wear make-up and glasses to show mine off.'

Her left hand now moved onto my thigh and it was quite clear where all this was heading. As she leant forward and tried to kiss me, I pulled away.

She was obviously irritated by my response to her overtures.

'I suppose you'd rather kiss Gary.'

That was a shock.

'No Yvonne. Why would I want to do that?'

'Oh, come on' she said, 'You know you're a homo.'

'A homo?'

I didn't know what the word meant. Retrieving her glass from the floor, she staggered to her feet and made for the door.

'You're no fun. I'm going to bed.'

The next morning at breakfast, the previous night's episode had clearly been forgotten and all appeared normal between us. Our busses back to the airport weren't leaving till after lunch so the four of us spent the last morning together at the pool bar and, of course, exchanged addresses.

'You must both come and stay with us in England' Yvonne said. 'We live in Claughton Village. It's beautiful. There's a windmill nearby on Bidston Hill. There're lots of parks to visit and we're close to the River Mersey.'

'It sounds lovely,' I said.

'It is Leo. We're very lucky.'

The imagination took over, and in my mind, I was there – walking across the village green to the babbling brook; sitting on the bank and watching the sails of the windmill turn in the gentle breeze.

This was a place I wanted to visit.

Chapter 33 – Idyllic Birkenhead.

Five months after our trip to Benidorm, Thomas and I were back at Dublin Airport. It was a Friday afternoon in November and our destination this time was Speke Airport in Liverpool. Yvonne and Gary had been good to their word and invited us both over to spend a weekend with them. The flight was short, and we were soon over the mountains of North Wales and heading north up to Liverpool. As the plane started its descent into Speke, I looked out over the Mersey Estuary. Was this the river Yvonne had been referring to? It was considerably larger than I had imagined and certainly not a babbling brook.

Gary and Yvonne were there to meet us, and we were soon on our way to the beautiful village of Claughton. Any further delusions that the Mersey was akin to a tumbling Irish stream were dispelled as we went under it. Travelling through the two-mile long Mersey Tunnel that connected Liverpool to the Wirral, the Mississippi came to mind.

We finally emerged at the other end where Gary paid the fee of one and sixpence to a man sitting in a little green booth. We were now in Birkenhead, the main town on the Wirral Peninsula. First impressions are often wrong, but this wasn't the rural idyll I had expected from Yvonne's description. Birkenhead was an industrial town built around Cammell Laird's shipyards, where Gary worked. Across to my left I could see the long sheds and towering cranes laid out along the Mersey – not a tree in sight.

The streets reminded me of downtown Dublin. We drove past the outdoor market where traders were closing for the night, and then took a left turn into Conway Street. This was a long straight road that seemed to go on forever, with row upon row of terraced houses stretching out on either side of the main road. No sign of green pastures or a windmill.

After about a mile we reached the grand entrance to Birkenhead Park. This triumphal structure with its eight columns and three arches did look impressive, and beyond the gates we could see grass and trees. Yvonne proudly told us that it was the first public park in Britain and had been the inspiration for Central Park in New York. We were very impressed and thought that we might now be heading out into the countryside.

The road skirted the north side of the park, but we were still passing yet more rows of terraced houses on our right. Gary took a left fork and there it was, a road-sign saying, Claughton.

'Nearly there,' said Yvonne cheerfully.

We passed the Birkenhead Park Rugby Club on our left and then slowed to take a right turn into Palmerston Avenue. The car came to a halt in front of Number 15. We looked out at the terraced house that was home for Gary and Yvonne. This was the beautiful village of Claughton – not a blade of grass in sight.

They both made us most welcome. I would have loved a cup of tea, but the alcohol was out – I accepted a small sherry. I didn't want to appear unsociable but couldn't face the offered Bacardi and Coke. The Croft's Original Cream didn't taste anything like Mam's trifle – more akin I thought to a small glass of cough mixture. But it was only a small glass and I drank it without disgracing myself.

We were soon reminiscing about the Benidorm holiday. I hadn't completely given up on my country village image and asked where the windmill was.

'Oh,' said Yvonne, 'We'll take you to see that tomorrow.'

Saturday was a bright and sunny day. After a long breakfast the four of us set off for Bidston Hill, where the windmill was situated. A five-minute walk past more terraced houses and we came to a parade of shops. This was Claughton Village proper. As the shops ended the houses became semi-detached and a few trees appeared along the roadside.

As we crossed Tollemache Road Gary pointed out his old school. The sign just inside the railings said 'Tollemache Secondary School for Boys.'

'That's Tolle,' he said. 'Great school.'

Another hundred yards beyond the school railings and the scenery changed completely. We had arrived at Bidston Hill – there was a painted wooden sign telling us so. The main road continued on but diagonally to the right was a well-trodden footpath that led into open countryside. Taking the path, we walked across heathland and into a small wood of conifers – this was more like it. The path climbed up to a footbridge which took us over a sunken road that was lined on both sides with rhododendrons. On the other side of the bridge, up on a hill in front of us, was the famous windmill. The sails were still complete, though chained. It certainly was an impressive sight.

We were now on a sandstone ridge that stretched out as far as the eye could see - standing on great slabs of sandy coloured stone, surrounded by gorse bushes with their acid- yellow flowers and the many silver birch trees from whence Birkenhead derived its name. The walk continued along the ridge until we came to the Bidston Observatory and from here an exhilarating view of the Irish Sea spread out before us.

The outing had certainly shown us another, more appealing, side of Birkenhead. That evening we were to be further impressed by the famous Merseyside hospitality.

Yvonne and Gary took us to the Saturday night 'do' at Our Lady's Social Club on Park Road North. We sat around on comfy settees in the Members Bar. There was a television at one end of the room showing a football match – a local team judging by the enthusiasm of the members. I could hear snooker balls clunking nearby. It was a pleasant atmosphere and I felt relaxed and comfortable chatting to the locals. Being two good Catholic boys from Ireland, they made a real fuss of us. I accepted a sherry but then managed to get myself an orange juice from the bar without Gary noticing. It was a good evening.

By the time Sunday afternoon came and we were getting ready for the journey back to Speke, an idea was beginning to form in my head. I realised that over the weekend, I hadn't once thought about Blackwood Hodge. Despite the initial disappointment over Claughton not being a country village and the Mersey not being a babbling brook, I was feeling happy – the first time for a long while. As we set off in the car for the airport, I said,

'I think I'd like to move abroad.'

What I meant was, that I'd like to move to England. Yvonne's reply was spontaneous.

'Well, you'd be very welcome to come and stay with us till you got settled. Wouldn't he Gary?

'Yes, we'd love you to come. I'd have you drinking pints in no time.'

We all laughed but it felt to me like a genuine offer from them both - an offer that I would have to give some serious consideration to. I sat there quietly imagining the prospect of never ever having to go to Blackwood Hodge again. That brought a smile to my face. In the late afternoon sun, even the terraced houses with their drab net curtains looked quite elegant and inviting.

Chapter 34 – Time for a Decision.

When I returned to the office at Blackwood Hodge on Monday morning, the idea of moving to England was still very much on my mind. Birkenhead wasn't an ideal place, but everyone had made us so welcome and there was an offer of accommodation.

Leaving home would be difficult. I adored my parents and I knew Mam and Auntie Madge would be upset by my leaving. I wouldn't be the first to fly the nest. Maria had moved out the previous year when she married Peter, but they were living quite close, on the Tallaght Estate. They were always popping home. I would be going abroad, and this would mean I wouldn't see my parents for weeks, possibly months.

On the other hand, although I wasn't as seriously depressed as I had been, it still lurked below the surface and I felt there was very little meaning to my life. There had to be more to living and I wasn't going to find it, whatever 'it' was, in Walkinstown.

The other big problem with leaving would be finding a job in England How would I earn a living? I certainly wasn't going to work as a card index filer. As the days passed, I tried to think about what I was good at. What did I enjoy doing?

At school I had spent a lot of time drawing and painting. This was the only subject I had achieved any success in and I'd actually won a prize. But it never occurred to me that I could make a career out of it. Then there were the feminine things - clothes, colour, glamour. Was it possible that I could become a designer, go into the fashion world? That would certainly be exciting.

One of my friends, Peadar McCarthy, had an aunt in the fashion trade. I'd met her once at his house. Kathleen Barron was a glamorous woman who designed women's clothes. I spoke to Peadar and he arranged a meeting with his aunt. He took me to her house, and we talked over a cup of tea. She listened very patiently to all I had to say and at the end of the conversation had one piece of advice.

'The best thing for you,' she said, 'would be to enrol at the Sybil Connolly School of Design in Dublin.'

Well, I thought, that would be an alternative to emigrating. I could still live at home and it would get me away from Blackwood Hodge. It had to be worth a try.

I found the number in the telephone directory and rang. Apparently, it was the wrong time of year to enrol full-time at the school, but they were running evening classes which I would be eligible to attend.

'Come at seven o'clock on Thursday and bring your portfolio.'

Portfolio? What was that? I had no idea.

I went to Grafton Street at the appointed time and without much formality was taken to a classroom, where several other students were hard at work. A woman, presumably the tutor, put me to work on pattern cutting – this was a complete mystery and there was no instruction. I watched the person next to me and tried to copy what she was doing. Later in the class, the tutor showed me some booklets with drawings of unclothed models in different poses.

'I want you to trace these and then draw some designs on them.'

This was more like it. I drew some designs and by the end of the session thought I had achieved something. The tutor only gave them a cursory glance. There were no words of encouragement to a new student. That was disappointing. I thought my ideas were quite imaginative.

The next week it was back to the pattern cutting. It went completely wrong and the tutor was not impressed.

'You can't go on without mastering pattern cutting' she said. 'I really don't think this is going to be for you.'

I begged to differ. This was only my second week, but she wouldn't have it and said there was no point in attending the class any longer. I was amazed by her reaction and very upset. It was definitely her lack of teaching skills rather than my ineptitude that I hadn't mastered the pattern cutting. I was sure that with proper instruction I would have got there but she wouldn't change her mind. I left without even knowing her name.

So, it was back to option one - emigration. In the back of my mind I thought,

'When I get to England, I'll enrol in a college there.' I was very determined to make something of my life, and despite the Sybil Connolly woman's opinion, design was something I knew I had the flair and imagination for.

Over the next month or so all the arrangements were made. I was to go to England and move in with Yvonne and

Gary Cole in Claughton. It was October 1973, I was eighteen years and four months old and leaving home for good.

Maria and Peter had recently acquired their first car, a green Opel Cadet with the registration plate 519 ZJ. They were very proud of it. When they said they were planning a trip to England to see Peter's sister, I jumped at the offer of a lift. They were happy to go via Birkenhead, which meant I wouldn't be departing on my own.

My last day at Blackwood Hodge was Wednesday 3 October. I'd worked there in the stores and office for three years and one month. Ace made a cake which I took in and the office held a collection. I left with a five-pound book-token and a reference from B. J. Curtis (Parts Manager). I must say he was most magnanimous:

'To whom it may concern.
Mr. Leo Donaghy has been employed by this Company from 2 September 1970 to 3 October 1973. He worked in our Spare Parts Sales Office and was responsible for the progressing of customers' orders, operating Kardex System etc. etc.
We have always found him honest, an excellent timekeeper and most efficient in all his duties. He has an excellent personality and we have no hesitation in recommending him to any company. We regret very much losing his services, but he is leaving of his own accord.'

Neither the reference nor the book-token made up for the three years of hell I had gone through.

As the departure date drew nearer the inevitable doubts began to surface. I was far from sure that I was making the right decision. This wasn't like going on holiday. This was something much more grown-up and permanent.

When the day did finally arrive, I gritted my teeth and tried to smile.

Joe drove me to the port at Dun Laoghaire with Mammy and Auntie Madge. Peter and Maria followed behind in the Opel with all our luggage. Dad kept up a cheerful banter but the rest of us were very quiet. When the time came for me to board the ferry it was so difficult to say good-bye and I think we were all fighting to hold back the tears. I hugged them for a long time and said I'd be back soon.

I joined Maria and Peter in their car to board the ferry to Holyhead. While they found us some seats in the lounge I went up onto the open deck. I could see Ace and Madge on the sea-wall that stretches out from the port and we waved. Joe had disappeared to find some vantage point to film the departure for posterity.

It wasn't long before, with a blast of its horn, the ferry started to pull away. Ace and Madge, arm in arm, set off along the wall, keeping pace with the boat. I was standing on deck looking down on their diminutive figures. One can only imagine what they were thinking as they looked up at me and occasionally waved. Although I was eighteen, I really did only look about twelve – and at that minute, that's the age I felt.

I tell myself it's the stiff breeze that's making my eyes water – but it's not. Deep down inside me there is a pain. Deep down I want to jump ship and go home with them for tea and cake in the kitchen at Number 30 and pretend nothing's happened.

The ferry reaches the end of the sea-wall and Ace and Madge can go no further. This really is the moment when they have to let me go. We wave one last time and I watch them standing there till they disappear into the distance. I stay on deck for a bit longer as the Sugar Loaf Mountain comes into view to the South. The memories of so many childhood picnics with the family in the Dublin Mountains come flooding back, as do the tears. I have to remind myself that I'm not going for good. I'll be back in a month or two to see them all. As I make my way down to the lounge, I'm so glad Maria and Peter are there.

The crossing went smoothly and as the Welsh coastline came into view, we all went up on deck and watched as the ferry steered into the port of Holyhead. A stiff breeze was blowing the falling raining into our faces and it was hard to make out the distant peaks of the Snowdonia National Park in the cloud cover.

Once disembarked we set off up the old A5 that ran across Anglesey and on up the Welsh coast towards Birkenhead and Liverpool. Peter had only recently passed his driving test and I could tell he was a bit anxious driving the new car. We made steady progress and eventually, following Gary's instructions, found our way into Birkenhead and Claughton Village. I began to recognise some landmarks and, after a couple of wrong turns, managed to direct Peter into Palmerston Avenue.

Gary and Yvonne were waiting and made us all most welcome. They'd invited Peter and Maria to stay a couple of nights before moving on to Barton where Peter's sister lived. Again, I was most grateful to have their company to help me settle into my new life.

We had arrived on the Friday evening and, after a lazy Saturday, Gary had arranged a night out at a Liverpool night club. The weather had changed and as we piled into his car it was pouring down. There appeared to be a problem with the wipers, and we had to drive with the window down to allow Gary to periodically pull on a bit of string he had attached to the wiper-blade to clear the screen. We were relieved to get into the Mersey Tunnel and shut the window.

The night club was as I expected - loud music, flashing lights and a lot of alcohol being consumed. It really wasn't my scene, but the others all seemed to be having a good time and I tried to join in. I kept thinking,

'This time tomorrow Peter and Maria will have gone, and I'll be on my own.'

When a man came up to our table and asked me to dance, I was very embarrassed. He thought I was a girl and must have thought me very rude when I refused. How different from Butlins! I couldn't wait till it was time to leave. Thank goodness it had stopped raining and we didn't have the charade with the string and open window on the way home.

Sunday morning arrived. Maria and Peter packed the car as Yvonne cooked breakfast. I could tell they were anxious to be on their way - they had a long journey ahead of them. As soon as we'd finished eating, we said our goodbyes and went outside to see them off. Once again, I had to fight back the tears as the green Opel Cadet made its way up Palmerston Avenue and turned the corner out of sight – they were gone.

Chapter 35 – Monday Morning.

Monday morning - a new week and a new life. Yvonne directed me to Price Street where the Birkenhead Dole Office was situated.

It was a large plain room with cubicles along one side and rows of orange plastic chairs. The windows were too high to look out – rather like a schoolroom. I sat on one of the chairs and found that it was firmly fixed to the floor. As I waited for my turn in one of the cubicles, it amazed me to see and hear the aggressiveness shown, by both men and women, to the staff who sat behind thick glass partitions. At some of the windows I could hear shouting and swearing but the people behind the desks seemed to take it in their stride. They just stared ahead, stony faced - I felt sorry for them.

When my turn came, I took a seat in the free cubicle and tried to move my chair forward up to the partition. Again, the chair was fixed to the floor. I was sitting in front of a middle-aged woman who, quite frankly, looked bored. It was nine thirty in the morning and she looked as though she'd been on duty all night.

She was writing and without looking up said,

'Can I help you?'

'I came from Ireland on Friday and I'm looking for a job.'

She looked up for the first time and peered at me over her glasses.

'How much money do you want?'

It hadn't entered my head that someone might offer me money. That wasn't what I was there for. I had money.

'I don't need any, thank you. I've saved up forty pounds.'

This was something she'd not heard in a long while - someone who didn't want money. Someone who didn't swear at her and someone who said, 'thank you'. She was quite taken back and actually smiled at me.

'What do you want to do?'

'I eventually want to be a dress designer.'

'In the meantime, you need to earn some money. Just a minute.'

She'd come alive and was on my case. After ruffling through a cabinet behind her she produced a file. Then she picked up the phone on the desk and dialled.

'I've got a nice young boy here from Ireland. I think he would be ideal for you.'

I was to go the next morning to Saint John's Precinct in Liverpool, to a shop called Temple Jensen's.

'It's a fashionable young gentlemen's clothes shop. The area manager, Mr. Terry Hymes, will interview you. And...' she went on, 'the Mable Fletcher College is quite near the Precinct. You could enquire about a fashion design course for next term.'

I think I made her day. She certainly made mine. I walked out of that office a foot taller with a host of exciting new possibilities before me.

On Tuesday morning I made my way to Birkenhead Park Station and took the Merseyrail, three stops to Liverpool Central. From there it was a short walk to Saint John's Precinct where I located Temple Jensen's on the ground floor. The window looked amazing - full of fascinating clothes specifically designed for young people. I could see patterned shirts with long wide collars; knitted jumpers of all colours; trousers with no pleats at the front, tiny waists and legs that flared out at the bottom covering the shoes. A manikin was wearing a powder-blue tank-top jumper with a matching cardigan. I'd never seen a twin-set for men before. It was exhilarating just to look at.

I went inside and was met by the shop manager, who was expecting me. He said that he was going to interview me, and I'd meet Terry Hymes later. It was a very short interview, but I assumed I'd got the job as he said Gary would confirm the appointment later. He looked me up and down, shook my hand and put me to work in the trouser section.

Ten minutes later, I was kneeling on the floor straightening the trousers, when a tall, ruggedly handsome man in his late thirties came and stood over me. In a broad Scouse accent, he said,

'While yer down dere doin' nuttin', could yer do a little job for me?'

A gale of laughter arose from the other assistants. It was Terry. He gave me a big wink and ruffled my hair. Unlike the rest of the staff, I'd no idea what the implication of his remark was but I could tell by his smile that he was a nice man – I liked him immediately.

There were four other guys working in the shop - all youthful and all handsome. Terry liked to employ young gay men, or 'chickens' as he called them. They were all very friendly and helpful. The morning passed quickly, and I soon felt at home and began to enjoy the work. Among other things, I learnt about the hundred per cent mark-up on clothes. I also learnt that staff got a good discount, which was great for me with my love of fashion.

Working in the shop was the first time I'd ever heard another male being referred to as 'she'. Alex would say,

'See that one over there, she's camp.'

Or Max would ask,

'Is she gay?'

To which the reply came,

'Is she gay? She invented it!'

And then,

'I've been with that one. She's built like a donkey.'

Chris wasn't gay but he was quite happy joining in the banter. Being the only heterosexual on the staff, he came in for a lot of stick from the others.

'Hey, Chris. Would yer like to be a chick with a dick?'

'Yer wha?'

'You know, a trannie.'

'Yer cheeky queen.'

He took it in good faith, but the gay boys didn't have it all their own way. Chris could give as good as he got.

Max was a little overweight and was always on some diet or other.

'It's no good' he moaned, 'nothing works.'

'Have you tried shutting yer gob?' was Chris's advice.

Another time, when the boys were discussing their sexual preferences, Chris waited for the right moment to exert his masculinity.

'I like to get a bird on the end of me dick and spin her round.'

This produced shrieks of false shock from the others and cries of,

'Oh, you are awful!'

Despite his heterosexuality, Chris frequently came up to me in the storeroom and kissed me on the lips.

I'd never knowingly met other boys like this, apart from Thomas of course. We always thought we were the only two in Ireland - in the World. Now I was surrounded by them. I had heard the word 'gay' before, but I still didn't quite understand what it meant. However, if it meant being like these boys, I loved it.

One lunch hour, after I'd been at the shop for a week or two, I walked up to the Mable Fletcher College and arranged an appointment with the Head of the Art Department. Not only did I now know what a portfolio was, but I actually had one. Admittedly it wasn't very large – just the few design sketches I'd done on my short stay with Sybil Connolly and a few extra pictures of my own. However, it was better than nothing and the tutor seemed impressed. So much so that he provisionally offered me a place at the College. Then came the bad news. I would have to apply for a grant. Further research revealed that this would only be possible if I'd worked and paid National Insurance contributions for five years. It was a blow, but I was feeling positive. It would only be a temporary set-back. If that's what it took, I would work for five years and then apply again.

Four weeks after starting at Temple Jensen's, Terry asked if I would transfer to a new shop they'd recently opened on the first floor of the precinct. It was coming up to Christmas and they were getting busy. The manager there wasn't gay, but he was a friend of Terry's who worked as a club comedian at night. He was good fun. This was a smaller shop and there was only one other assistant, Brian.

Another new word I'd picked up was 'Camp' – not only a new word but a whole new concept. Brian was gay and Brian was camp. His antics and the way he spoke did remind me of a bus conductor Thomas and I used to watch on the run into Dublin. He'd spin the handle on his ticket machine and, in an affected manner, slink up the aisle lisping,

'Any more faiss, pleeth?'

This was Camp behaviour.

Brian was twenty-six and I'd watch him in idle moments grooming. He'd lick the third finger on his right hand and smooth both eyebrows. Then he'd pat both his cheeks to bring up a little colour, carefully check his coiffure in the mirror and adjust any individual hairs that might have strayed out of place.

When a customer came in, he'd swing into action. With his left hand clasped across his chest and the right hanging limply by his side, the wrist turned out, he would saunter over to greet them. The movement was something to behold and fascinated me - akin to a model on the cat-walk. One foot would be carefully placed in front of the other producing a smooth forward motion – the legs being the only part of his body that moved. If no sale took place, he'd turn back to me and, dramatically holding the trouser rail with one hand, and sporting a face that looked as though he was sucking a lemon, say,

'Miserable cow.'

I liked Brian and we got on from the start.

About a week after the move upstairs, he and I were sitting in the staff room having our lunch – cheese on toast from Sayers Bakery, which was conveniently situated around the corner from the shop. He casually said,

'Has Terry Hymes approached you yet?'

'Approached me? About what?'

Smoothing his eyebrows,

'You know he's gay?'

'Gay' was now firmly fixed in my vocabulary. I'd soon gathered from the lads at Temple Jensen's that it referred to boys, like Thomas and myself, who liked to look at men. I was very naïve and really didn't understand the full sexual connotation. Brian went on,

'And I'm gay too.'

I actually said to him,

'What does that mean?'

He looked at me with a broad smile on his face.

'It means I'm a homosexual. And you are too.'

I didn't know what to say. Of course, I knew that I was attracted to men, but to be told directly to my face that I was a homosexual. It came as a shock. My mouth went dry and my mind went blank.

'It's nothing to be ashamed of' he said.

At that point a customer came in. With the manager out, we were not supposed to leave the shop floor unmanned. Brian shot off his seat to deal with them. I sat there on my own for several minutes trying to get my thoughts together. Trying to understand what it meant. Could it possibly be true? Could I really be a homosexual?

Brian came back.

'Miserable cow.'

He pulled up his chair and sat directly facing me. 'I know a club where they meet. I can take you there.'

I couldn't believe my ears – a club where gay men met.

'What do they do there?'

'What do you think they do? They have wild passionate sex.'

He must have seen the look of horror on my face and burst out laughing.

'No, I'm teasing,' he said, patting me reassuringly on the knee.

'Do they kiss?' I asked.

Another customer came in and he swept off again, calling back to me over his shoulder,

'And the rest!'

Chapter 36 – The Bears Paw.

Nine o'clock on a Saturday night in early December and I was standing outside Liverpool Central Station waiting for Brian. The plan was that we would go to Casey's Bar opposite the station and have a drink there. Then, at ten o'clock we would move on to the club.

This was going to be an entirely new experience for me, and I was very excited. I remembered Thomas had once heard a rumour at work that there was a gay pub in Dublin.

'Ah, Davy Byrnes, dat's where all de queers go.'

The next evening we were in town, we went to explore. As we got to the door it opened. Inside the bar was full of men. They were ordinary men dressed in ordinary clothes. It could have been any pub - but what did we know? We walked on past. A few minutes later we went back again but were still too scared to go in. Now, after a drink at Casey's, I was walking with Brian on my way to a real gay club.

The route took us down Matthew Street, past the famous Cavern Club where the Beatles had started their career. Any other time I would have loved to have gone in but not tonight. On we went down a couple of alleys and there it was. The sign over the white double door said, 'The Bears Paw'.

A woman in high white boots with a man on each arm knocked three times on the door which swung open. They were greeted by a handsome man who motioned them in. I was exploding with a mixture of emotions – excitement, anticipation and fear. I was anxious that I wouldn't be admitted. I was eighteen but still looked so young. Brian took my arm. He'd been before and knew the doorman.

'Hiya Allen, this is Leo.'

I just managed a quiet 'Hello' and we were in. We followed the trio down a dimly lit flight of stairs to where a man, sitting behind a small table, was taking money. Brian knew him as well. We paid and signed the registration book. Brian signed as a member and I signed as his guest – not putting my correct address, as I'd been instructed. Then, down some more stairs and we were in. I had my first glimpse of a gay night club.

I immediately spotted two young men in their twenties. The Bee Gees were heading the pop-music charts in those days and these two, with their long dark hair and beards, were dead ringers for Barry and Maurice Gibb. The incredible thing to me was that they were kissing - kissing in front of a room full of people. But no-one was taking a blind bit of notice. I don't know why but it didn't feel right. I thought I'd walked into a scene from my favourite movie, Cabaret. I was in the Kit-Kat Club in Berlin, surrounded by the debauchery of the 1930's.

I could hear an organ playing, and in an alcove to my right, seated at the keyboard was a lovely smiley lady of about fifty. I later learned that her name was June and she was a regular on Saturday nights at the Bears Paw. She was surrounded by a group of men singing 'You Made Me Love You'. They'd all linked arms and were swaying in time to the music - having a great time. Somewhere in the distance I could hear the beat of a more modern sound. This was coming from the disco, up on the next floor.

The room before me was full of men, and a few women, of all ages. Some were holding hands, and some were embracing - happy, laughing, confident people. Brian was behind me, encouraging me forward through the throng towards the bar. It was coming up to Christmas and everywhere was decorated with sparkling lights and gold and silver tinsel. I thought I was in fairyland.

We made it to the bar and Brian ordered a beer. I had my usual orange juice. I couldn't bring myself to look around in case anyone thought I was queer. I just didn't get it and sat staring into my drink. Brian chatted to a few people, but I could tell that somehow, he wasn't at ease in this environment - which surprised me. In the coming weeks, as I got to know him better, he confided that he hated being gay. He wanted a normal life with a wife and kids – but fate is cruel.

We finished our drinks, chatted a bit more and then Brian left. I was now on my own in a room full of men. I was beginning to feel a little more at ease and managed to turn on my bar stool to absorb the atmosphere. I just wished Thomas had been there beside me – I'm sure we would have been hysterical.

By the time I had drunk three orange juices I needed the toilet. Up a small staircase I could see the signs, 'Ladies' and 'Gents' and, unlike Butlins, I went into the Gents.

Checking myself in the mirror, I heard the toilet behind me flush and then a very camp Liverpudlian voice said,

'Hello dear, I think you need the ladies Ladies.'

It had happened before, being mistaken for a girl. I said,

'I don't think I do.'

'Ohh, bona. You're a pretty one. What's your name?'

'I'm Leo.'

'Hello Leo, I'm Alex but I'm known to everyone as The Duchess.'

I thought, I'll never sleep tonight.

The organ music had now stopped leaving the pounding of the disco. I followed the sound across the bar and up a flight of stairs. This second room was quite dark apart from the flashing disco lights. In the middle was a small wooden floor full of men dancing with each other. Fascinated, I watched for a short while but felt uneasy standing there on my own. I desperately wanted to join in but didn't have the confidence to ask anyone to dance. Again, I wished Thomas had been with me. We would have been in the middle of it all dancing our hearts out.

Returning downstairs, I went back to my seat at the bar. I wasn't aware of it, but I must have been staring at someone. A young lad came up to me and said,

'Wha yer looking at? 'Ave I got a telly on me 'ead?'

I was mortified and started to apologise, but he roared with laughter and took my hand.

'Yer alright, gel. I woz only jokin.'

I needed a drink and was just about to order yet another orange juice, when one came sliding down the bar cowboy style, stopping right in front of me. I looked in the direction it had come from and came eye to eye with a very handsome man leaning on the bar. He smiled, removed the cigarette from his mouth and waved. I plucked up courage and went over to thank him. He introduced himself,

'I'm John, from Australia. Everyone calls me John the Australian.'

That seemed logical and I soon learned that in the gay world most people were identified by some sort of pseudonym. He gathered that I was new on the scene and set about enlightening me as to what was what.

'The Bear's Paw attracts a better type of queen. You know what I mean? You don't get any riff-raff in here. All the rougher sort go down to Sadies in Wood Street. Now...' he went on, 'there's an unwritten law that if someone offers to buy you a drink and you accept, it goes without saying that you've just agreed to sleep with them.'

He must have seen a look of shock on my face and burst out laughing.

'Don't worry kiddo, seeing as it's your first night I'll let you off.'

I don't think it would have taken much persuasion to get me to take up the offer.

John the Australian had made me feel very special. He was good looking, and I liked his easy-going manner. This was an important moment. I was now a man. Not a pretty boy dressed up as a girl. I was a man, whom another man had found attractive - attractive enough to buy a drink. The significance of what had just happened was not lost on me. It made my night.

Chapter 37 – Fecking Old Sante.

Although I'd been living in England for less than three months, this was by far the longest time I had been away from home and the family. Ace wrote letters weekly with all the gossip, but I was desperate to see them all. I was determined to get home for Christmas. Flying from Speke Airport was out of the question, but I had saved enough money to purchase a ticket on the night ferry crossing from Liverpool to the North Wall in Dublin. I even booked myself a cabin.

Christmas Day that year was on a Tuesday. By offering to do all the overtime in the lead up, I managed to persuade Gary to let me have Christmas Eve off. He said I could take a few days as long as I was back for the start of the January sales.

Presents were going to be a problem. I couldn't go home empty handed but after buying my ticket funds were very low. Brian came to the rescue. He'd recently started to run a catalogue. After spending a lunch hour perusing the glossy pages, I settled on a metal plant holder for Mam, Old Spice aftershave for Joe and a Cussons Gift Set for Auntie Madge – My Fair Lady bath cubes and talc. I'd get some chocolates on the boat for Larry. This could all be paid for in

January, in instalments. Another lunch hour in St. John's Market provided plenty of bits and pieces for the kids.

On the evening of Sunday December 23rd, I made my way into Liverpool and caught the bus from the Liver Building, out along the Dock Road to where the B & I vessel 'Munster' was tied up at the quayside. We sailed at 10 o'clock at night and wouldn't be docking till 7 o'clock the following morning.

I was tired and needed to get away from the lively 'Christmas spirit' that pervaded the upper decks. I made my way down to the cabins. My romantic image of a stateroom on the Queen Mary was soon shattered. I was surprised, not only by the smallness of the space but by the fact that it contained four bunks. On the wall opposite the door was a tiny sink but no porthole – we were probably below sea-level. I undressed, cleaned my teeth and got into one of the lower beds.

About 1.30 in the morning I realised my mistake. The door burst open and the room was flooded with light as three burly Scousers entered. I got such a shock. I leapt up and banged my head on the bunk above.

'Ar-right mate! Sorry to wake yer.'

I had booked a berth and not a cabin.

There followed a few minutes of loud whispering and stifled laughs as the cabin filled with alcohol fumes and smoke from their cigarettes. They climbed onto their bunks without undressing. Eventually the light went out and peace returned.

I was the first awake next morning – excitement I suppose. I got dressed by the glimmer of light that shone under the cabin door and left the Liverpudlians to their snoring.

Up on the open deck the air was fresh. Although it was still dark, I could make out to the right, the flashing lights on the tall Poolbeg Chimneys, part of the Poolbeg Electricity Generating Station. They were local landmarks and told me we were entering the mouth of the Liffey.

At 7 o'clock on the dot we pulled into the North Wall and, despite the early hour, Joe and Ace were on the quayside waving madly. An emotional reunion followed. I couldn't believe how much I'd missed them. They both thought I looked well, and Ace was sure I had grown. I had grown – not so much in stature but as a person. In the short period I had spent in England I had become much more confident in myself – much more grown-up.

We drove back to Walkinstown and the moment I walked through the door it was Christmas as it always had been. The house was full of kids and excitement and it was only 8 o'clock in the morning.

After breakfast Joe went off to work. He'd already started his Christmas Cold - an annual occurrence. Throughout December he worked every hour God sent. As well as Monday to Friday at the paper mill, Saturdays were spent behind the photographic counter at Curven's Chemist – there were seven stockings to fill. He was always exhausted by Christmas Eve and 'the cold' was the result. Before leaving he downed his special remedy – a Beecham's Powder dissolved in warm red lemonade.

I knew that Thomas would also be working, and I wouldn't see him till after mass on Christmas Day. We had written to each other several times over the previous months. I had told him about my new job and new friends. I'd even mentioned visiting The Bears Paw – but no details. There was the possibility that Bridie would see the letters, and I could just hear her voice,

'In God's name Thomas, what's all this foolishness?'

There was so much more I had to tell him - I couldn't wait.

By late-morning the house was full of delicious baking smells. While Ace prepared the open mincemeat tart, I worked on the pastry lattice that would go on top. Then there was dough to knead – both brown bread and the traditional Irish Soda. She also had a trifle to prepare and a Bakewell Tart. The Christmas Cake was finished and on display on the sideboard. It was always made in November – late October, after mass, you'd hear the women saying,

'Have you got your fruit in?'

Everyone knew what they meant – Christmas was on the way.

After a break Mam started on the turkey. This was always supplied by Larry and had been hanging over the bath for the past two days. The giblets were set aside to make the gravy and also for Joe to spend a mad ten minutes chasing the kids round the house, brandishing the bird's gizzard and gobbling frenetically – all part of the Christmas tradition.

Although Janette was the only one who still believed in Father Christmas (she was nine that year) none of us were going to miss out on the stocking tradition. In the Donaghy Household socks were used – the biggest you could find in the airing cupboard. The first ones there got Joe's fishing socks. The rest made do with the boys' school socks, with the grey and yellow stripes across the top. At bedtime these were neatly laid out, not on the ends of our beds but around the lounge. We each had our own places – where Mam used to put out our clean clothes for Mass on Sunday mornings. Mine was on the armchair in the bay window, next to the Christmas tree.

In the evening Joe started reminiscing about Christmas's past, when we were all toddlers.

'You used to come creeping downstairs to see if Sante had been and I'd tell you's, "He won't come till you're all asleep." Then your Mam and I would just get to bed, and you'd be at it again. I tell yer, that fecking old Sante, if I could get me hands on him, he'd be sorry!'

We eventually made our way up to bed - all except Joe and Ace. One other ritual had to be followed. Madge and Larry went to Midnight Mass in Clondalkin with Larry's father. After Mass, usually about one in the morning, they would call down to Walkinstown for a cup of tea and supper. They didn't have to worry about being woken at first light like Mam and Dad, but it had become a Christmas tradition and Joe and Ace wouldn't have had it any other way.

Christmas morning at Number 10 was like every other Catholic household with young kids – an early start, stockings and presents, and then everyone off to mass. This had to be before breakfast because of the fasting rule. After a long homily on abstention, everyone was starving. Ace went to work – a full fry with rashers, black and white puddings, fried bread, mushrooms and tomatoes. The special Christmas treat was a small piece of white steak (pork fillet) on each of the nine plates.

I'd had a quick word with Thomas at the church and we'd agreed to meet after lunch. This was a quiet time. Ace was ushered into the lounge to watch the kids play with their toys, while Joe did the washing-up entirely on his own. He would then cut the Christmas Cake and take Mam a cup of tea with the first slice – that was the tradition.

Thomas knocked on the door at 4 o'clock and we set off on a long walk. It felt good – like the old days when we'd wander round the houses, looking in the windows and making comments.

I had so much to tell him. Things that I knew he would find hard to believe – like two men with beards passionately kissing in public. I still found it hard to believe myself, but I had seen it with my own eyes, and a lot more besides. With each new revelation his jaw dropped open, and his eyes came out on stalks, then we'd both roar with laughter. I had to keep repeating myself and assuring him that every word was true. He made me describe The Bears Paw in great detail – he wanted to know everything about the place and everything about the people who went there.

We went on to talk about work, and about Terry and his chickens. I told him I was a chicken. When I got to my conversation with Brian, the one about being homosexual, he became more serious. He listened quietly but said nothing. I didn't push him. I remembered how shocked I had been at the revelation. Eventually, he said,

'I'd like to meet Brian.'

'He'd like to meet you too, Thomas. I'm sure Gary and Yvonne would love to have you over again. I could take you to the club. We'd have a great time.'

He said he'd like that, and we left it there – there was a lot for him to think about.

On Stephen's Day the family went up to the bungalow in Clondalkin for lunch with Madge and Larry. I say lunch but, as usual, Madge did things in her own time and it was nearly three o'clock when we eventually sat down. There was some finger tapping from Joe, but he managed, just, to remain in festive mode. As we were leaving Larry slipped a ten-pound note into my hand, putting his finger to his lips to tell me to keep quiet. This was a week's wages for me – they were so generous, and I loved them for it.

The next day it was Peter and Maria's turn to play host at their flat in Tallaght. It was a little cramped, but we all managed to squeeze around the dining room table. There was jelly and ice-cream for the kids and Whiskey cake for the adults – Maria didn't tell Joe and Ace that they were consuming alcohol but they both had a second helping and were very merry for the rest of the day.

My short break passed very quickly and then it was back down to the North Wall to board the ferry back to Liverpool. Saying 'good-bye' again was as hard as it had been the first time, but I now knew that I had made the right decision. I had a plan for my future. I had a job and the opportunity of a college course down the line. I had also begun to consider the possibility, in the not too distant future, of renting my own little flat. It was all good. It was all positive.

As I waved them 'Good-bye' from the deck, there was a lump in my chest but no tears. I was already looking forward to my next visit to The Bears Paw and the excitement I knew that would bring.

Chapter 38 – Confirmation.

Despite my resolution, I did feel low on my return to Claughton Village – the family and Thomas were such an important part of my life, and it was hard being so far apart. The Coles did their best to keep me cheerful as I settled back into my Birkenhead routine.

On the first Sunday in the New Year, 1974, Gary took me out to a club he belonged to in Moreton on the Wirral. We left Yvonne at home to cook the Sunday lunch. He said it was a cabaret club, and the show would be good fun. We arrived in plenty of time and Gary insisted we sat at a table right up the front, almost touching the small stage.

He went up to the bar and bought the first round. As in Benidorm, there was no question of drinking orange juice and a Bacardi and Coke was placed in front of me. As I looked around, there were no posters or anything else to show who would be in the cabaret, but it did strike me that there were a lot of men jostling for places near the stage.

Eventually the lights dimmed, and a man appeared on the stage with a microphone. After a few introductory remarks he said,

'Please welcome to the stage Miss Crystal Corolla.'

The music started and between the strands of a silver strip curtain, Miss Crystal appeared. She was dressed in a bright red cowboy outfit – hat, neckerchief, waistcoat and chaps. It soon became apparent that she didn't intend to stay dressed as a cowboy for very long. As she danced round to the music, first one piece and then another of her ensemble were seductively removed and flung to the side – each time this happened there was a great cheer from the male members in the audience. She kept a fixed smile on her face throughout the performance, but I was watching her eyes. I had a nasty suspicion that she was scanning the audience, looking for a victim. By the time she was down to two tassels and some very skimpy knickers, I was pretty certain that the victim was going to be me. She now danced to the side of the stage, down three steps and back across the front. Her large boobs with their spinning appendages came nearer and nearer to our table. I could see that her panties were held in place by two buttons on the left-hand side. She came right up to me and, with great dexterity, released first one and then the other button. As the music reached a final crescendo, she flung the panties aside and thrust her gee into my face.

I felt quite nauseous. Gary was cheering loudly with the rest of the audience, so I did my best to smile. It was a great relief as I watched her naked buttocks retreat back onto the stage and off behind the silver curtain.

'Wasn't she great?' said the compere.

Well yes, I suppose she was if you were a hot-blooded heterosexual male. But I now knew that wasn't me. Brian had told me and having had time to think about it, I believed it to be true. I was a homosexual. If I hadn't been sure, Miss Crystal Corolla had rid my mind of any lingering doubts.

'And now, would you put your hands together and welcome Miss Fantasia.'

Miss Fantasia was some kind of dominatrix. She was wearing a skin-tight black leather body suit with her ample breasts spilling out over the top. Her high black stiletto-heeled boots came up over her knees but left plenty of naked flesh at the top of her thighs for the men to ogle. She carried a riding crop and, attached to her belt, I noticed three lengths of rope. As she went into her act, it became apparent what the ropes were for. One by one she selected three men from the audience. After looping one end of a rope round each of their necks, she led them up onto the stage and tied the free ends to rings on a pillar that had appeared through the back curtain. Then, having her victims in place and in time to the music, she proceeded to unbutton and remove their shirts. After a bit more dancing round, she started to whip the semi-naked men on their bared chests with her riding crop. The audience started chanting,

'Harder, harder.'

I don't think it could have been too painful as the victims certainly looked as though they were enjoying themselves. Their pleadings for her to stop were very half-hearted, especially when she started planting kisses onto their punished flesh with her snake-like tongue.

This had been a very enlightening afternoon for me. It was the first time I had ever seen a naked woman and I wasn't keen on repeating that experience. The whipping scene took me straight back to Thomas McCarthy's house and the afternoon he'd whipped Thomas and me. I didn't understand the reason then why he'd wanted to do that and was none the wiser now. What was becoming clear to me was that sex involved a lot more than kissing and cuddling, and that The Bears Paw was obviously going to be the best place for me to explore the subject further.

From then on, I went across to Liverpool every Saturday night and stayed till the early hours of the morning. The last train back to Birkenhead left at ten to twelve. To get home after that meant walking down to the road tunnel and getting the night bus that ran through to Hamilton Square. I then had a thirty-minute walk back to Claughton but after a good night out, that didn't bother me.

I was becoming much more confident in myself. I'd become a member at The Bears Paw and was quite happy to turn up on my own, knock on the door and say, 'Hiya Allen'. Each week I got to know more of the many characters who frequented the club.

I met Walter, who always wore an overcoat with an astrakhan collar, summer and winter, indoors as well as outside.

'It's so cooold' he'd lisp.

I occasionally bumped into him in Birkenhead.

'Just going to get a bit of spam for me husband's tea.'

Cod and Hake were presumably fishmongers. They spent the whole evening sitting at the bar and the noise of their laughter frequently drowned out the disco. Robert definitely invented Pole Dancing. He'd stand wrapped around one of the metal pillars that supported the roof. If anyone paid him the slightest attention he'd slink round the pole, stare lasciviously and dart his tongue in and out in their direction. Nurse Plum worked at the Seaman's Dispensary – the euphemism for the clap clinic. Apple Annie was very round - I could find no other reason for his nickname. Dennis was in his sixties. He read your palm and always seemed to have a 'nephew' from Ireland with him. They were all great fun.

The younger gays tended to congregate on the upper level, around the dance floor. I became friendly with one very camp boy with a big loose afro hairstyle. His name was Billy. He was a great dancer and I got on well with him. It felt so liberating to be able to dance without having to worry about your wig slipping, or a sock falling out of your bra. I don't think I had ever felt happier than I did dancing at The Bears Paw.

There were some aspects of the gay scene that I didn't find so appealing. One Saturday evening, quite late on, Billy said,

'Would you like to go to the starlit ballroom?'

I was immediately transported back to Butlins with the glitter-ball spinning and the band playing. Were we going to a posh club that I hadn't heard about? A club where they did ballroom dancing?

I followed Billy up the stairs and out onto the street. He linked my arm and led me across the road and down a narrow alley that I hadn't noticed before. It was dark but as my eyes adjusted, I could make out another couple walking ahead of us. We followed them for a hundred yards or so but, on turning a corner, they disappeared.

We seemed to be at a dead-end, up against a high corrugated-iron fence. Billy had been here before and knew where the gap was. Pushing the loose panel back he led me through onto the other side. We were now in an open space – maybe a building site or undeveloped bombsite from the war.

As I looked round the 'starlight' appeared. Not from a glitter-ball in the sky but from the cigarette ends of fifteen to twenty men standing around the perimeter. The arrival of 'fresh meat' was their cue to take a drag. The glowing red ends of their cigarettes thus alerting the new arrivals to their whereabouts.

'It's a cruising area,' Billy said.

'A cruising area?'

'Yea, yer know – for trade.'

'Trade?' I said. 'What's trade?'

Another list of new words for my vocabulary. I didn't understand why we were there, standing in the cold and dark. We'd been having a great time dancing at the club. When Billy explained what was happening, I felt so naïve and very uncomfortable. This wasn't for me. I mumbled some excuses and made my way back out through the gap in the corrugated iron.

The following Saturday the starlit ballroom wasn't mentioned. I was again upstairs at the club dancing with Billy. My attention, however, was on a young guy standing at the side. It must have been obvious that I was staring, because Billy said,

'Do you like him?'

Before I had a chance to reply, he'd gone over to the man. A few words were exchanged, and they were both walking back towards me. Billy introduced him as Barry, and then disappeared leaving us to dance together.

Chapter 39 – Barry Prescot.

Barry was nice. Not particularly good-looking but that didn't matter. He lived in the Liverpool suburb of Prescot where his parents had a butcher's shop. He was well known in the gay community, where everyone called him either Barry Prescot or Miss Prescot. Barry, like my boss Terry Hymes, liked 'chickens' and I soon learnt that he had quite an entourage. We danced and chatted for quite some time and then, as the evening drew to a close, he offered to drive me home. I protested that it was too far, and he would have to come all the way back through the tunnel, but he insisted. As we made our way out of the club, the doorman said,

'Have yer got a new chicken, Barry?'

We had quite a kissing session in the car outside the house in Palmerston Avenue and planned to meet again the following week. Barry was my first ever boyfriend.

As arranged, we met the following Saturday night at the Bears Paw. He'd bought me a present - a bottle of Brut aftershave. I opened the box to reveal the classic green bottle with its long neck and silver cap. I didn't know what to say but he seemed pleased with my embarrassment.

I'd mentioned Barry to Gary and Yvonne and they, very generously and open-mindedly, had said that I was very welcome to bring him into the house. After another night of dancing, he again drove me home. We got to Claughton at about one o'clock in the morning. The house was in darkness apart from a small table-lamp in the hallway. We took off our shoes and crept up stairs and along the hall to my small bedroom at the front of the house. The Cole bedroom was next to mine and, as we passed their door, I could hear deep breathing – they were long asleep.

I don't know why, but I was very nervous and insisted we put the lights off as we undressed and got into bed.

All my previous sexual experiences had been as a girl and had never gone past kissing and groping. I was now in bed completely naked with a man I judged to be quite experienced in this field. I didn't know what to expect so I just followed his lead. We kissed and cuddled and then began a slow, more intimate examination of each other's bodies. He seemed impressed with what I had down below, and I was soon very excited. When he started to use his mouth, I couldn't believe it. This was totally unexpected, and the sensation was incredible. I had to push him off to prevent a sudden ending. He then gently rolled me over onto my stomach. I'd gathered from the boys at work that there was more to this 'love making business' but, at this moment in time, I wasn't prepared to go any further. I turned back to face him, and he accepted my refusal graciously. He got dressed and we both went down to his car.

He clearly hadn't been put off by my inexperience as he said he'd like to take me out to dinner the following weekend. We arranged that I would be at Liverpool Central station at eight o'clock, where he'd pick me up in the car.

I spent the whole of the next week thinking about my first real sexual experience. This wasn't something I was prepared to discuss with the other boys at work, not even Brian. I would have loved to have had a session with Thomas on the stairs at Walkinstown Parade – talking to him was different. I'd really enjoyed what had happened and the totally new experience of oral sex blew my mind away. I couldn't wait to repeat that and to return the compliment. However, as to going further, I really wasn't sure. I don't know whether it was my Catholic upbringing – there was still a lot of guilt surrounding my homosexuality and I could see Sister Equinus's candle foretelling the perils of perpetual hell. Maybe it was lack of experience – I was very much a novice. It just didn't feel right and, I somehow knew I wouldn't be able to do it with Barry.

The next Saturday seemed ages in coming around. I was so excited at the prospect of seeing Barry again. At eight o'clock on the dot his car drove down Ranelagh Street and stopped in front of the station. He had two of his chickens in the back, Berni and Sean. I'd met them both before at the Club. They were nice and I was pleased to see they were going with us. Barry drove us out to Woolton where we were meeting John the Australian at the White Elephant pub and restaurant.

Joe had taken us out as a family for fish and chips and I'd been to Bewley's for afternoon tea with Ace and Madge but dining out with friends at a restaurant was another first. It seemed one nice thing after another was happening to me. As we studied the menu Berni said,

'I'm going to have pate.'

'What's pate?' I asked.

They all thought this was very amusing – simple Irish boy up from the country. No-one explained, so I played safe and ordered the soup.

The rest of the meal passed pleasantly and uneventfully until it came to paying the bill. Barry said that he was going to treat everyone. This was very good of him, but I have always liked to contribute. I discretely slipped him a pound note under the table. Instead of quietly accepting or refusing my offer – a pound was a lot of money out of my wages, he made a big fuss. Waving the pound note in the air he said,

'Well, this won't go very far.'

Once again there was a lot of laughter at my expense and I felt very small in front of them. I let it pass – it was very generous of him to treat us all.

After the meal Barry drove us on to the Bear's Paw where we enjoyed ourselves on the dance floor. At one point I was dancing with Billy, the boy who'd introduced me to Barry.

'I hear you went to bed with Miss Prescot.'

'What! How do you know that?'

'Keep yer hair on luv, everyone knows.'

I didn't like that at all, in fact I was furious. This was a very private part of my life and I was horrified to think that others knew about it. I wasn't sure that it was right to have sex in the first place and it certainly wasn't right to talk about it to other people. There was only one person who could have told him.

This was my third weekend with Barry, which apparently meant that we were now officially an 'item', an 'affair' and I was now off-limits to anyone else. I did like him a lot but wasn't sure about my new status. He was a lovely generous guy but, in the restaurant, he'd gone for a laugh rather than supporting me – that was upsetting. I also hated the fact that he had talked about what we did in bed. I was beginning to have doubts about the permanence of my first relationship.

The following weekend was already planned. Barry and I had been invited to supper by two of his friends from the Wirral. Brian and Robert lived in Heswall and Barry picked me up en-route. They were a nice domesticated couple who'd been living together for some time. They'd obviously gone to a lot of trouble over the meal.

After the sweet, while Brian made coffee, the rest of us went through to the lounge. As Barry and I sat down, Robert knelt on the floor and from under the settee pulled out a large cardboard box. It was full of homosexual pornographic magazines. Barry didn't bat an eyelid. It looked as though this was the routine here, and what he'd expected to happen after the meal. I, on the other hand, was shocked and amazed. This was pre-internet days. I'm sure you could get pornography in Ireland, at least the heterosexual type, but I had never seen any. Young Irish boys got their thrills from women's underwear magazines. I had to ask,

'Where does it come from?'

The answer was a bit vague. Some of it was passed from friends. Most was brought into the country from holidays abroad and apparently you could buy it from a shop in Liverpool.

If there's one thing to kill conversation, it's a box of pornography. As we sipped our coffee, apart from the occasional guffaw, the room went silent. My sexual education was about to take another giant step forward and I began to wonder if this was going to lead to a post-prandial orgy. As I turned the pages of the magazine that Barry had thrust into my lap, I could only look and wonder. If Thomas had been with me, we would have been roaring with laughter at the antics portrayed on one page after another. The models were of all ages and all very handsome, you had to say that. What they got up to was staggering - sometimes on their own, more often in pairs and, on some pages, in larger groups. In some of the pictures you couldn't make out what was going on – who was doing what to whom - I wanted to ask but didn't dare. I knew they'd mock my innocence.

The final straw for me was a double page spread showing a middle-aged man with his legs in the air. Stuck into his bottom were five lighted candles. I didn't know whether to laugh or cry. Was this what they were going to get me to do?

It was a great relief that the boys were content with just looking. The evening came to an end and we thanked our hosts and said our goodbyes. As Barry drove me back to Claughton I sat in silence, thinking. When we pulled up in Palmerston Avenue it was clear he wanted to come in for another session. It was now or never.

'Barry, I'm really sorry but I don't want to go out with you anymore.'

He was genuinely shocked and started to cry. He was a lovely guy, but I knew he wasn't for me. I couldn't explain why. I just felt it deep inside.

'I was going to buy you a colour television' he said.

This was not the thing to say to me. I was not impressed by materialistic gestures, however grand. I held his hand and kept repeating how sorry I was.

We sat there for about twenty minutes, mainly in silence. I had to end it.

'I'm going in now, Barry.'

I kissed his cheek and got out of the car. He started the engine, gave me a sad little wave and drove away. My first short affair was over.

Chapter 40 – Doctor in the House.

Three or four weeks passed before I went back to the Bears Paw. But the lure was too strong – I couldn't stay away forever. I was dreading seeing Barry again, but I knew I would have to speak to him at some point. Besides, I'd used my staff discount at Temple Jensens and bought a new suit – a smart light-grey houndstooth. I'd also been shopping at George Henry Lee's where I'd acquired a black silk rose. Attached to the lapel of the new suit it looked special. I wanted to show off my new outfit.

I was anxious going down the staircase and was relieved to find that Barry wasn't anywhere in sight. The place was crowded and buzzing. June was on the organ going through her 'songs from the shows' repertoire and the choir was in good voice. Having fought my way to the bar for an orange juice, I went over to talk to Les and Frank. Les was from St. Helens, a rugged-looking builder, about fortyish. His partner, Frank, was a handsome lad - smartly dressed in a dark blue blazer with a spotted red hankie in the breast pocket. He was about thirty. We'd met several weeks earlier, and I'd immediately liked them. They were friendly and open with no edge about them. What's more, they were a real 'affair'. They'd been together for about eight years - a long-term loving relationship. That's what I wanted for myself. I knew that now.

They commented on my absence from the club but didn't press me on the reason why. I felt at ease in their company. It was nice to be missed and it was good to be back on the scene – I was really happy.

As we talked, someone else joined the circle. He knew Les and Frank and I was introduced. His name was Mike. He was a good-looking guy, aged between twenty-five and thirty I thought. He was friendly and had a lovely smile - not at all camp. We chatted for a while and then I excused myself. I wanted to go upstairs and dance.

The dance floor was packed. I made my way round to the far side and stood watching all the activity. A short while later I noticed that Mike had come up and was standing at the top of the stairs. Our eyes met and he came over.

'Would you like to dance?' he asked.

We pushed our way into the melee of people on the floor and began to move in time to the beat of the music. The room was too crowded to do much more and far too noisy to carry on a conversation. After a few minutes the thumping beat gave way to a much gentler sound. The familiar notes of one of my favourites, Mamma Cass singing Dream a Little Dream, reached our ears. We quite easily moved into each other's arms and continued dancing to the gently swaying rhythm. We were both singing along to the well-known melody. It all felt very natural. When the music finally stopped Mike, with one finger, lifted my chin and placed a very gentle kiss on my lips. We were both smiling.

Back downstairs we found somewhere to sit and talk. He had recently qualified as a doctor at Liverpool University and was now going into General Practice. I told him about my dreams of going to art school. The conversation flowed very easily. When it came to where we both lived, it turned out that he had a house in Birkenhead, just five minutes up the road from Yvonne and Gary – it had to be a good omen. He had a car and, naturally, offered me a lift home.

As we drove into the Mersey Tunnel, past the queue waiting for the night bus, I felt very relaxed. When he asked,

'Would you like to come back for a coffee and see the house?'

I replied,

'Yes please. That would be good.'

At the other end of the tunnel he paid the one and sixpence and, instead of turning right, drove straight on up Borough Road, in the direction of Oxton. I was now on new territory. We passed a very grand building fronted with columns, which was the Birkenhead Library. A bit further on, I saw a sign for Gary's famous Tranmere Rovers Football Club. Then, turning right up Balls Road, we went past the Williamson Art Gallery. I didn't even know the town had an art gallery. It hadn't been mentioned on Yvonne's list of 'Things to do in Birkenhead'.

This area seemed a little grander than Claughton. The road was lined with Victorian semi-detached houses with large front gardens. We passed an old church with a tower and then a very posh hotel, The Bowler Hat Club. Mike then turned down into an estate of recently built townhouses, called Ringwood. It looked pleasant with open-plan front gardens. We did a left and then a right past two enormous old Beech trees, one a Copper Beech and the other green. The car slowed and came to a halt in front of

Number 40. The security light came on and I could see that the front garden was neatly laid out with heather plants and conifers – Mike was a gardener.

We went in and up to the first floor where the living room and kitchen were. While Mike made the coffee, I had a look round. I was in a large room that stretched from the front of the house to the back, with a picture window at each end. At the front I could see the road we had just driven down with its two Beech trees shining in the light of the streetlamps. The houses were only on one side, the other being bounded by an old stone wall and neatly kept lawns.

At the back of the house there appeared to be a small garden and then, beyond a Hawthorne hedge, a field.

'That's the Old Parkonian's Rugby Club' said Mike from the kitchen. 'Great on a Saturday afternoon if you like beefy men.' We both laughed.

He'd only recently qualified and the house was quite frugally furnished. The large pink rug that covered part of the boarded floor had obviously seen better days. Mike brought the coffee through on a tray and we sat on an old green sofa that he admitted had come from his sister, along with the rug. The small dining table had been donated by a good friend, Jean Ruscoe, and the four chairs around it borrowed from the local Scout hut. The only new furniture was a large G-Plan wall unit which housed the television, a record player and a lighted cocktail cabinet – he was obviously very proud of this. The wallpaper was covered with bright orange, brown and cream circles and swirls of various sizes – we both agreed that this had been a mistake and needed replacing.

We chatted quite easily over coffee and laughed a lot too. I told him how I'd met Gary and Yvonne in Benidorm and how I came to be living in Claughton. He told me he was in Birkenhead because Liverpool University was the only place that would have him.

Up to now there had been no mention of seeing the top floor of the house but as we finished our coffee, Mike said,

'Would you come up to the bedroom?'

He immediately picked up my hesitation. This was our first meeting and I really was very shy.

'We could just lie together for a few minutes before I take you home.'

I really felt I could trust him and allowed myself to be led upstairs.

Mike's bedroom was at the back of the house overlooking the rugby field. He had purchased a new single bed and some white bedroom furniture. The wallpaper here was much more subtle and the room looked nice in the dim light coming from the modern glass-domed bedside lamp.

We lay on the bed, fully clothed and kissed and cuddled and smiled. He was true to his word and didn't once try to progress the encounter. He was quite content, as indeed I was, just to lie there in each other's company. After a while he said,

'I'll take you home now.'

As he'd said in the club, it was only five minutes down Shrewsbury Road, and we were back in Claughton Village. We didn't say much in the car, but we did hold hands. I directed him to Palmerston Avenue, and we pulled up in front of Gary and Yvonne's. He then said the words that I really wanted to hear.

'Can I see you again?'

The answer, of course, was 'Yes' and we arranged to meet the following Saturday – he would pick me up at 7.30. We had one more kiss and I got out of the car.

I watched as Mike turned the car round and drove off up the avenue. I just stood there in a trance. That evening I had met someone who knew nothing of my troubled past. Someone I didn't have to dress up for and pretend to be someone else - someone who wanted me exactly as I was. It was May 5th, 1974, I was eighteen and I don't think I'd ever felt so happy in my whole life.

During a very long week I thought of Mike constantly and couldn't wait for Saturday to come round. When at last it did, I was waiting outside on the step when his red Fiat came around the corner at 7.30. sharp. As it pulled up, I could see there was a big smile on his face.

As I got in beside him, he took my hand and said he'd missed me.

'I'm going to cook dinner for us at home. I hope that's alright?'

'Sure,' I said. 'That's very good of you.'

Mike would be the first to admit that he was not a cook. The meal started with Findus Savoury Pancakes and this was followed by Findus Fruit Pancakes. He later denied this and said I was thinking of two separate occasions. There were some frozen vegetables with the first course and ice-cream with the pudding. We also had a bottle of Liebfraumilch. It was the first time I had drunk wine. Mike poured it out of the green bottle into his large crystal glasses. It had a sweet taste and I quite liked it.

At least he'd made an effort. We had a lovely evening and I suggested that the following week, if he wanted to, I could bring some food with me and prepare a meal for the two of us. He thought this was a great idea and said he would get the wine and chocolates.

And that's what happened. I'd had some experience cooking at home with Ace and Mike seemed very impressed with the results. Almost without realizing this became our Saturday routine. Mike would pick me up after I'd shopped and then I would cook a meal for both of us. We were very happy and relaxed in each other's company. Occasionally, after eating, we would go over to The Bear's Paw, but its role in both our lives was much reduced.

We had started a relationship. We didn't rush things. It wasn't till the fourth weekend after we'd met, that I actually stayed the night at Ringwood. Mike's friend Jean was keen to meet me. She had invited us both to Sunday dinner at home with her husband Ron and their three children. So, I stayed the night, and on the Sunday we spent our first full day together.

Chapter 41 – Changes and a Brick.

I had been living at Palmerston Avenue with Yvonne and Gary for eight months and it was becoming clear that it was time to move on. They had both been very good to me, but Yvonne was now pregnant and was dropping not so subtle hints that my room would make a lovely nursery. I was ready for a change and ready for more independence.

It was Jean's mother, May Richmond, who found my new accommodation through a friend of hers, Nan Kinlock. Nan, despite being in her upper eighties, ran a nursing home where most of the residents were younger than she was. She lived-in at the nursing home but also owned a house nearby, ready for her retirement.

26, Alfred Road was a semi-detached Victorian building, just around the corner from the Williamson Art Gallery. It had a small front garden and a back yard. One half of the house was for Nan. The other half was split into two bed-sits – one upstairs and one down. It was the upstairs one that was vacant and at a very reasonable rent which I was sure I could afford.

The flat came furnished. Under the window that overlooked the front garden was a small dining table and two chairs. I had two armchairs placed in front of an electric fire and, on the wall opposite, a divan bed. Also, in the far corner was a small bamboo table with a Pampas grass on it.

Along the wall to the left of the entrance was a fitted wardrobe. When I slid back the two doors, I was amazed to find that it contained, not shelves and hanging space, but a kitchen. There was a sink with hot and cold running water, a Belling Electric Hob with four hot plates and, under the work-surface, a small refrigerator.

The bathroom was situated just outside my door and this was shared with the downstairs tenant, an elderly gentleman called Mr. Fitzpatrick – he went everywhere on a bike, which blocked the downstairs hall. I soon discovered that he had bad catarrh which shook the house every time he tried to clear his tubes.

The flat had everything I needed, and I moved in. Mike picked me up from Palmerston Avenue with my cases and gave me a glass vase with a single red rose in it as a house-warming present.

I now had a place of my own where I could entertain. Some Saturdays we would eat in Alfred Road rather than Ringwood, though it was quite difficult cooking a three-course meal in the wardrobe.

The next big event in my life was a new job and again it was Jean who was instrumental in the change. I'd discussed moving on with both Mike and Jean. I still enjoyed being one of Terry's chickens and working with the boys, but my design course was still four years away. I kept thinking there must be something more artistic that I could do in the meantime. You can only get so much satisfaction arranging shirts and trousers. A friend of Jean's had told her that the hairdresser in Claughton Village was looking for a new apprentice and she wondered if I might be interested. I'd had no previous experience, which is perhaps surprising considering I grew up in a household with four females. I had become quite proficient at dressing wigs and also, I had occasionally trimmed the hair on Phil's dolls – that had been fun, but not worthy of being added to my C.V.

After much thought and discussion, I decided to apply. On the appointed day I made my way to Hair by Norman to be interviewed. I took along my portfolio, which was slowly growing, and my reference from Mr. Curtis at Blackwood Hodge.

I was greeted by the receptionist, Pam. She had a lovely welcoming smile which put me at ease.

'Mr. Norman's with a client at the moment, but if you sit there, he'll be with you shortly.'

Sitting in the waiting area I was able to take in my surroundings. Everywhere looked pristine and efficient. All the staff were wearing black trousers and black V-necked jumpers that had a white Fair Isle pattern on them. At the far end of the salon I could see an older man whom I took to be Norman. I watched while he worked on a woman whose hair was bright red. He'd moulded a large onion shape around her head and was now completing a smaller one on top of this – it looked amazing and quite unlike any hairstyle I'd ever seen.

The interview took place by the front desk and was quite informal. He looked through my portfolio, read my reference and listened to my plans for the future. He told me what my duties would be. There would be in-house training and, one day a week, I would be required to attend the City and Guild's Hairdressing course at Colquitt Street

College in Liverpool. We also discussed my wage. This would be about the same as I was getting at Temple Jensens but, with the salon only being a twenty-minute walk from Alfred Road, I would have no travelling expenses. Also, there would be tips!

I worked a week's notice at the shop and started my new career on the following Tuesday morning – the salon was closed on Mondays. Joe would be very proud when he got my letter with the news. I was now an apprentice and, if I stuck at it, would have a trade – an artistic one at that.

There wasn't much artistry involved in the first morning, which I spent in the back room picking hair out of rollers with a pin, but I was used to mundane tasks. I put the wet towels in the washing machine and folded the dry ones as they came out of the spin dryer. I also spent some time familiarising myself with the various products stacked on the shelves in the stockroom.

In the afternoon I was allowed front of house and instructed it the art of shampooing at the backwash. I was also responsible for sweeping up the cut hair from around the stylists' chairs – everywhere had to be kept spotless.

It was a large busy salon. As well as Pam, the receptionist, there were three other stylists working alongside Norman, four apprentices and a trainee beautician. Over the coming weeks I got to know a bit about them.

John was the senior stylist. He was a good-looking man. I overheard one of his clients say to her friend,

'He looks like Warren Beatty. He's got a bum like two peaches in a handkerchief.'

Carol, one of the two female stylists, told me her husband was related to Anwar Sadat, the President of Egypt. When I eventually met him, he had blond hair and snow-white skin – he must have been a very distant relative.

The other apprentices were Keith, Leslie and Graham. They were all friendly and helpful to me. None of them was gay and it was quite a nice change not to be bombarded with 'camp palare' all day.

Mike and I had now been together for nearly six months. In fact, he informed me that our six-month anniversary was coming up on November 5th. It seemed very significant to him. We had discussed our past lives as part of the getting to know you process. I'd told him about my short fling with Barry and he said that, since coming to Liverpool eight years previously, he had been in five significant relationships, of varying lengths. Two of these he had ended – the rest had been ended for him. Both his and my parents had had long, loving relationships and we both agreed that this was what we wanted for ourselves. The longest time Mike had been with someone in the past was six months, hence the significance of November 5th.

The other significant date fast approaching was December 25th. I desperately wanted to spend our first Christmas together. In fact, Jean had already invited us both to have Christmas dinner with her family. On the other hand, Christmas was a family time and I had never spent one away from mine. Ace's weekly letters had been full of hints. The cake had been made, the turkey ordered and then finally, did I know when I would be home? This was a dilemma.

There was also the question of money. Because of the busy pre-Christmas period, I wouldn't be able to get away from the salon till late Christmas Eve and flights then would be expensive. After paying my rent, most of my spare cash seemed to go on buying food. Mike kept saying that he was quite happy to pay but it was important to me that I played my part and made a financial contribution, however small, to our growing relationship.

We had become very close and I was spending several evenings a week at Ringwood, though I only stayed over at the weekends. Neither of us had raised the possibility of me moving in on a permanent basis. Though the words had not been spoken, I knew in my heart that we were falling in love, but six months wasn't long enough to make a total commitment. Whatever my feelings for Mike, I wasn't yet ready to give up my recently gained independence.

In the end I made a decision about going home. Mam and Dad knew that I had a new friend called Mike, though I hadn't elaborated. I'd also mentioned Jean in my letters. I wrote and said Mike and I had been invited to have Christmas Dinner with Jean (which was true) and that I would get home, hopefully for a week's holiday, in the New Year – Easter at the latest. I stamped the letter and posted it.

The second it disappeared through the red slot in the pillar-box I began to have doubts that I'd made the right choice. I knew how disappointed they'd be, Mam in particular. I could see her sitting in the kitchen reading the letter, and hear her saying,

'Ah, Joe. Leo's not coming home.'

I tried not to think about it, but the nearer Christmas came the more it was on my mind – for the first time ever I wouldn't be at home with the family.

In the build up to the holiday Normans was frenetic, and all the staff were expected to do a lot of overtime. The Christmas tips were very generous, which made me think I could have afforded the flight home after all, but it was too late now.

Mike was very excited that I was going to be with him and that helped me a great deal. We decorated Ringwood together and put up the Christmas tree.

The next time I was at Ringwood, I noticed that a present with my name on it had appeared under the tree. It was the shape and size of a house-brick, beautifully wrapped in gold paper and tied with a ribbon. On the top, the label was held in place with one of those stick-on decorations. Mike insisted I didn't go poking around.

When Christmas morning finally arrived, he presented me with the mystery present. Now that I held it in my hands, what had looked like a wrapped house-brick under the tree, actually felt like one – it was heavy and hard and had sharp corners. Mike had gone to town on the wrapping. There were several layers to remove - it was like pass-the-parcel without the music. Eventually I came to the final layer of red tissue paper. I carefully removed this and found myself holding – a house brick.

Mike had sat silently watching all the unwrapping and was now laughing. He could see the bewildered look on my face and said,

'Look underneath.'

I followed his instruction and, stuck on the base of the brick with several strips of Sellotape, was a folded envelope. I managed to get it free and opened the flap. Inside was a plane ticket from Liverpool Airport to Dublin. My Christmas present was a trip home, and the flight was leaving at 11 a.m. the next morning, Boxing Day.

Mam and Dad didn't have a phone at that time, but one of the neighbours did and had kindly agreed that I could ring at 12 o'clock on Christmas Day to speak to them. I was able to tell them about Mike's present. Needless to say, they were over the moon, as I was, and said they'd pick me up at the airport.

The rest of the day passed in a whirl of excitement. I had to go back to Alfred Road to pack before we went to Jean's for the meal. I stayed the night with Mike and at 8 a.m. the next morning we set off for the airport. He insisted on parking the car and coming in to see me off. After the formalities of booking-in, we walked together towards the Custom's barrier where we had to say goodbye.

I went through the gate and turned back for one last look. Mike blew me a kiss and mouthed,

'I – Love – You.'

I smiled, gave a little wave and mouthed back,

'I – Love – You – Too.'

As Mike turned to go, I stood for few seconds longer watching him walk back across the concourse. I really believed I had met the man I would spend the rest of my life with.

Afterword – From That Day to This.

Some six months after that first Christmas Leo moved into Ringwood with Mike, though he didn't give up his bedsit until they had lived together for a year. He continued as an apprentice at Hair by Norman and attended the day-release course in Liverpool. In June 1976 he passed his hairdressing exams, gaining a distinction. In 1977 he continued his studies and passed the Advanced Course.

Not content with this, his next project was a Further Education Teachers' Certificate which he gained in June 1978. He went on to teach hairdressing at the Liverpool Community College with the staff that had taught him.

Four years after Leo left Ireland for England, Thomas finished work at Burtons in Dublin. He enrolled on a seven-year training course at the seminary in Maynooth to become a priest. Having completed six years, he realised this was not for him and left.

Gay life in Ireland was still virtually non-existent and, like Leo, Thomas reached the conclusion that he was not going to find fulfilment there. He too emigrated to England

and stayed with Leo and Mike for a short while. During this time Leo took him to The Bears Paw where he got chatting to a man of about his own age. The man came back to Ringwood with them, and that night Thomas had the first real sexual experience of his life – he was 28. After a few days he moved on to London, where he was going to stay with a cousin.

In 1985 Leo finally achieved his ambition and went to art school. After a one-year foundation course at Withens Lane College in Wallasey, he gained a place at John Moore's University in Liverpool to study Textiles and Fashion. In June 1989 he was awarded a Bachelor of Arts degree with Honours. He was the first member of the Donaghy's to achieve a degree and this was to be a great family occasion. Joe and Ace came over to England for the ceremony which was held in Liverpool's Anglican Cathedral. Joe, of course, filmed the whole event from the bridge spanning the Cathedral's central aisle.

Thomas did various jobs in London, including working at Aquascutum in Regent Street. He finally settled at the London Royal Free Hospital as a receptionist, where his easy-going manner endeared him to both patients and staff.

In 1988 he met John and fell in love. They now live in Brighton and have a Civil Partnership. They have been together for thirty-two years.

Leo and Mike now live in Shropshire. Leo has his own studio where he both paints and teaches art (and cuts Mike's hair). He and Mike have a Civil Partnership. They have been together for forty-six years.

Although Leo and Thomas are no longer able to get together on the stairs at Number 30, Walkinstown Parade, they remain the best of friends and two or three times a week have long chats on the phone.

May 2020

Printed by Amazon Italia Logistica S.r.l.
Torrazza Piemonte (TO), Italy